Insuring Medical Malpractice

Insuring

Medical

Malpractice

Frank A. Sloan
Randall R. Bovbjerg
Penny B. Githens

New York   Oxford
Oxford University Press
1991

Oxford University Press

Oxford   New York   Toronto
Delhi   Bombay   Calcutta   Madras   Karachi
Petaling Jaya   Singapore   Hong Kong   Tokyo
Nairobi   Dar es Salaam   Cape Town
Melbourne   Auckland

and associated companies in
Berlin   Ibadan

Library of Congress Cataloging-in-Publication Data
Sloan, Frank A.
Insuring medical malpractice / Frank A. Sloan, Randall R.
   Bovbjerg, Penny B. Githens.
p.   cm.
Includes bibliographical references and index.
ISBN 0-19-506959-5
1. Insurance, Physicians' liability—United States.   I. Bovbjerg,
Randall R.   II. Githens, Penny B.   III. Title
[DNLM: 1. Insurance, Liability—United States—legislation.
2. Malpractice—United States—legislation.
W 33 AA1 S6i]   HG8054.S56   1991   368.5'64—dc20
DNLM/DLC for Library of Congress   90-14361

9 8 7 6 5 4 3 2 1

Printed in the United States of America
on acid-free paper

PREFACE

Why this book? The resurgence in the 1980s of an apparent crisis in medical malpractice insurance—indeed, in liability coverage generally—focused public attention anew on this important branch of the property-casualty insurance industry. In contrast to the mid-1970s, when the issue for physicians was availability, this crisis has been one mainly of affordability. But there is also the issue of its fairness in pricing and its effects on medical providers, especially physicians, the key decision makers in our health care system. In keeping with this status, physicians are held responsible for most of the damages in malpractice and hence pay more of the total premiums than hospitals or other individual practitioners.

Many policy participants see the behavior of the insurance industry as a major contributor to the crisis. Some physicians, consumer advocates, attorneys, and public officials have been known to harbor dark suspicions that the insurance market is insufficiently competitive, underregulated, and subject to considerable overpricing, at least in certain periods. At the same time, uncertainty exists as to how regulation affects premium setting and returns.

Thus, policymakers want to know whether malpractice insurers as a group price accurately, in accordance with cost, whether fair or excessive returns are earned, and to what extent insurance cycles exacerbate underlying loss trends, affecting availability and price. Insurance practices of underwriting, establishing rate categories, and pricing are of genuine public policy and research interest.

Insurance is also the mediating mechanism between the medical, social, and legal factors that create claims and the health care system that must contribute funds to pay claims and otherwise respond to the incentives created. Our tort regime must accomplish its goals of compensating wrongfully injured patients and deterring substandard medical practice through insurance mechanisms—or not at all.

In the wake of the crisis, renewed proposals have been heard for stricter regulation to control allegedly excessive profits and other aspects of the insurance business. Further "tort reforms" to rein in perceived excesses of the legal system also continue to receive major legislative attention.

However, policymakers weighing various calls for relief have found virtually no reliable objective information in the public domain (Sloan and Bovbjerg 1989). This situation persists not for lack of public attention or interest, but because no one has joined carefully analyzed data with institutional knowledge of the field. No single book has successfully addressed the policy issues. Lack of information is one reason that there is so little agreement on the causes or cures for the crisis. Much common knowledge is simply not written down. What descriptions of insurance practice do exist tend to be quite technical and inaccessible to policymakers and analysts outside the industry. Information about observed dynamics in the industry is even less accessible. More analysis is needed to enable us to assess the pricing behavior of insurers, the comparative performance of physician-sponsored versus commercial stock insurance companies, the role of insurance regulation, the institution and effects of reinsurance, and comparisons with other lines of coverage. So, policymakers have had to rely unduly on the expertise of advocates on various sides of the debate.

Hence the project that has spawned this book. Funded primarily by the Agency for Health Care Policy and Research (then the National Center for Health Services Research and Health Care Technology Assessment), our goal has been to describe the workings of physicians' professional liability insurance. Our related work has focused on the effects of past tort reform (Sloan 1985; Sloan et al. 1989a; Zuckerman et al. 1990) and possible new reforms of law and insurance (Bovbjerg et al. 1989; Sloan 1990). This book describes the physicians' malpractice sector of the industry, its practices, and its regulation, then analyzes its performance empirically and puts the results in a policy context. We have addressed this book both to policymakers and to specialists in an effort to reach the several constituencies interested in this information.

The book's organization and style reflect this need to be accessible to general readers while presenting often technical material. Hence the book begins (Chapter 1) with a nontechnical introduction and ends (Chapter 10) with a conclusion also written in accessible style. Each chapter similarly begins and ends in nontechnical fashion. Quantitative presentations have been kept as clear and concise as possible. Often, particular material is boxed for a separate mini-presentation to avoid breaking up the main text; and, where possible, we have used figures instead of large numerical tables. Heavily technical material appears in separate subsections, sometimes accompanied by a nontechnical summary box. Notes are presented at the end of each chapter; references are at the end of the book. Primary sources of information are explained at their first use in the book; many are covered in the Appendix to Chapter 1.

Nashville	F.A.S.
Washington, D.C.	R.R.B.
Nashville	P.B.G.
January 1991	

ACKNOWLEDGMENTS

The authors are most grateful to many who made this book possible. Our research support came from the Agency for Health Care Policy Research, Grant Number 1 R01 HS05693, with additional assistance for Chapter 8 on risk and rating from the Robert Wood Johnson Foundation, Grant Number 12412. We also want to thank the insurance companies that responded to our Survey of Malpractice Insurers (see Chapter 1), as well as the numerous individuals within the industry and its regulatory agencies who have contributed to our understanding on a less formal basis. Special appreciation goes to the Physician Insurers Association of America, whose annual convention we attended, and to Tillinghast, a Towers-Perrin company, whose seminar for malpractice executives we have also drawn on.

We regret that reasons of space as well as confidentiality preclude listing everyone by name. Circumstances dictate one exception. Peter Sweetland, Secretary-Treasurer of the Physician Insurers Association of America and President of The New Jersey State Medical Underwriter, who died at age 54 in April 1990, was very helpful to this project. We greatly appreciate his sharing institutional knowledge and persuading others to cooperate with our surveys. Peter was a large man in every sense of the word. He was trained in commercial insurance but instrumental in the growth of the physician insurers. He was devoted to his industry, yet public-spirited and appreciative of the value of independent appraisal. He believed in advancing knowledge of malpractice risks and insurance. And he was confident enough to run the risk of assisting outside researchers. He is greatly missed by all who knew him.

Several colleagues not named as authors have contributed to parts of this book. Mahmud Hassan, Chee Ruey Hsieh, and Paula Mergenhagen, all previously at Vanderbilt University, worked on the empirical analyses in many chapters. Joseph Valvona, Athena Lee, and Jay Caldwell contributed to the early stages of data base construction and preliminary analyses. Thomas Hoerger, of the Department of Economics and Health Policy Center at Vanderbilt University, took the lead on some of the reinsurance analysis described in Chapter 5. Stephen Zuckerman and Mo Cyr of the Urban Institute ran the premium regressions for Chapter 7. John Newmann, also then with the Urban Institute, joined Penny Githens in doing the survey interviews.

Finally, Sharon T. Stanley of Vanderbilt's Health Policy Center has our greatest respect for dealing so capably with many drafts and revisions throughout production. Of course, the authors are responsible for the contents of the book.

CONTENTS

LIST OF TABLES

LIST OF FIGURES

LIST OF BOXES

Insuring Medical Malpractice

1

Introduction

BACKGROUND

If aging Doctor Kildare were to return to medical practice today, having been in suspended animation since the early 1960s (Brand 1941), he would find enormous changes in his malpractice insurance coverage. The first surprise is that the physician's malpractice coverage has become so important. No longer can he practice at his hospital without it. And much higher limits are needed to protect his practice and other assets against the financial risks of lawsuits. The annual bill takes up to 5 percent of his gross revenues from practice, compared with a fraction of 1 percent while he was building his practice. He also encounters much more variation in rates across many more risk categories than he was accustomed to, with a major distinction being whether he wants to continue delivering babies or not. And he is astonished to learn that his standard coverage no longer protects him from all lawsuits arising out of this year's practice, no matter when the claim comes in, but instead covers only claims filed this year—and then only claims arising from prior years when he was covered with the same company.

No longer can he buy a policy from any of innumerable "commercial," mainly stock, insurance companies, perhaps through his regular insurance agent, perhaps through his medical society's sponsored carrier. Instead, he finds far fewer sources of coverage operating in his state. Many of those sources are wholly unfamiliar entities. They include his state's physician-sponsored malpractice carrier, called an "interinsurance exchange," a number of national stock companies that sell liability coverage of various kinds, a "self-insured" plan from the university medical center where he has hospital privileges, a joint underwriting association (an organization connected with the state insurance department), and a "risk retention group" headquartered in a distant state and not exactly an insurance company. All together, this now multi-billion-dollar industry collects and disburses far more money than before, with far greater implications for the practice of medicine. The threat of lawsuits is now a staple of medical conversations, and he gets advice from his carrier and other sources on "risk management," a completely novel concept. In short, there has been a virtual revolution in the organization, operation, and influence of the malpractice insurance industry since a generation ago.

This book describes this industry as it existed in the middle and late 1980s and analyzes its performance over a number of years. The industry's rise to prominence, its changing relation to the medical profession, and its high public profile all have their roots in the perceived "malpractice crisis," to which we turn next. (We have used quotation marks here to indicate some doubts about the nature and effects of these periods of convulsion. Crises exist in the eyes of their beholders, and their extent is typically disputed. See, for example, Dunningham and Lane 1980 and Goddard 1985.

PERIODIC CRISES: THE 1950s TO THE 1980s

The story of malpractice insurance crises is relatively well known. A number of readable summaries exist, both for the 1970s (Law and Polan 1978, Chapter 1; Robinson 1986; Bovbjerg 1989, 501–11) and for the 1980s (Priest 1987; Winter 1988b; Bovbjerg 1989, 503–11). Careful assessment of the empirical evidence about the crisis is, however, rare (Sloan and Bovbjerg 1989, 1–12).

The Mid-1970s and Before

Most policymakers awoke to medical malpractice as a public issue during the first major insurance crisis in 1974–76. Interrelated sets of events compelled public attention (Danzon 1983a; American Medical Association [AMA] 1984a, 2–5): First, numerous medical malpractice insurance companies suddenly withdrew from selected state markets or announced very large price rises. Some physicians could not find coverage at virtually any price, at least in the key states of California and New York. Second, as a result, some doctors conducted "slow-downs" of medical services and even seriously discussed strikes. Medical groups lobbied heavily for remedial legislation. Both California and New York passed emergency statutes during 1975. The New York and California crises were repeated in less severe fashion across the country. The crisis or fear of incipient crisis triggered remedial or preventive legislation in most states, even those without such significant problems (Feagles et al. 1975; Warren and Merritt 1976; Bovbjerg 1989).

The events of 1974–76 are not well documented by insurance statistics, for few exist. One result of the upheaval during those years was to command more attention for this line of insurance. Only in 1976 did insurers begin to report official malpractice claims and financial data to state insurance departments separately from general liability coverage, of which malpractice coverage had previously been a very small part. These data aggregate all types of malpractice coverage, whether for physicians, hospitals, or dentists, for example. (Such data are compiled by A. M. Best. For a more general description, see the Appendix to this chapter.) Statistics for the pre-1976 era are therefore fragmentary, but it is clear that many firms stopped selling coverage, at least temporarily, and that many others got large premium increases (Danzon 1983a; Robinson 1986).

The mid-1970s' crisis had several roots. One was an unexpected surge in claims; rating bureau data show that the mild frequency growth in 1966–70 was followed by great rises in the early 1970s—12 percent a year for the whole period but 19 percent annually for 1971–73 (Danzon 1982). Severity—the mean amount paid on a claim— rose more consistently throughout this period (Danzon 1982). These rises in insurance costs coincided with the post-oil-shock recession, which reduced earnings on insurers' investments. Insurers may have been too slow to react, and regulatory lag did not improve their financial posture.

By some counts, the 1970s' crisis was not the first but the third in modern medical malpractice insurance. In the 1950s, malpractice insurance was an exceedingly stable line of coverage. Agents typically sold policies to individual physicians as a sideline to coverage for automobile and premises liability. The chance of a claim's ever being made for professional negligence was very small. One American Medical Association study found that only one physician in seven had ever faced a claim in his professional lifetime (AMA 1957). Very large recoveries were exceedingly rare, and policies were priced accordingly. Insurance rating had only two classes of insureds—physicians and surgeons—and rate-making was extremely simple.

In the late 1950s and early 1960s, however, tort doctrines became more liberal, claimants more assertive, and physicians more willing to give expert testimony. Claims frequency and costs rose, and the old order vanished. Under new cost pressure, the market became more sophisticated and specialized. Quasi-group sales came to dominate the market, with state medical societies choosing a "sponsored" plan to make coverage available to their membership. All this occurred without public attention, much less intervention.

The late 1960s saw further rises, with claims frequency again playing a leading role. Also rising steadily was claims severity. Malpractice concerns claimed national attention for the first time, and Congress held hearings (U.S. Senate 1969). Overall, the malpractice premium volume (physicians and hospitals) increased fivefold in nominal dollars during the 1960s—from about $65 million in 1960 to $330 million in 1970 (Kendall and Haldi 1973, 494; Posner 1986, Chart 1, p. 49). In 1971, President Richard Nixon directed the Secretary of Health, Education and Welfare to create a study commission, which in turn commissioned the first collection of empirical information about many facets of malpractice (U.S. DHEW 1973a, 1973b). The Secretary's Commission concluded that no crisis existed in the early 1970s, as insurance was readily available from numerous insurers. Of course, no sooner had the report appeared than the much more serious crisis reclaimed attention in 1974.

Industry and Legislative Response

The 1970s' crisis generally abated within two years, however, as indicated by the renewed availability of insurance. Several factors contributed to the increase: New provider-run insurers entered the market, underwriting the higher levels of coverage that were needed and committing their companies to stay for the long term. The first such physician company was founded in mid-1975; by the end of 1977, more than 15 were in operation. Ten years later, 41 companies were based in 33 states, many beginning to offer coverage beyond their home states (AMA 1984a, 5–6; Physician Insurers Association of America [PIAA] 1987). (The hospital market is separate; there, too, provider companies have developed, but hospital self-insurance or insurance through a "captive" insurer is common [Posner 1986].)

In addition, many states mandated that other private insurers "backstop" malpractice coverage through "joint underwriting associations (JUAs)." Where they exist, JUAs underwrite physicians otherwise unable to get private coverage, with a lead carrier collecting premiums, paying claims, and the like. However, other insurers in the state must contribute pro rata to cover any net losses above premiums (and often retroactive assessments on policyholders as well), hence the joint underwriting aspect of JUAs (Posner 1986). Often created on a standby basis, a number of JUAs were never even activated (Bovbjerg 1989). "Patient compensation funds (PCFs)" were also mandated in a number of states (Posner 1986; Bovbjerg 1989). PCFs operate somewhat like an "excess" insurer, covering losses for physicians and other providers above the maximum limits (typically $100,000 per occurrence) of their primary private coverage. Run by a state or under state contract, PCFs are funded by a surcharge on primary insurance premiums. Like many JUAs, PCFs often also have the authority to assess insured physicians for shortfalls retroactively.

Stability in the insurance market also benefited from a shift from "occurrence" to "claims-made" policies. Claims-made policies cover only claims actually filed in the policy year, rather than covering incidents occurring during the year, so long as they arose at an earlier time when a policy from the same company was also in force (Posner 1986). The approach was traditional for Lloyds of London (Kendall and Haldi 1973, 508), which has long been a major reinsurer of primary insurers of malpractice liability. But its "retail" use in malpractice was pioneered by The St. Paul in 1975 and over time was approved for use in almost all states. The new policy basis greatly simplified adjustment of rates in response to changes in frequency and expected future payouts on claims. That insurers and regulators agreed on the need to increase premiums naturally also helped stabilize the market. Total premiums passed the billion dollar mark in 1976.

A final, poorly understood contributor to stability was the unexpected decline in the upward trend in claims frequency. One analysis showed a rise for 1971–75, then a decrease for 1975–78, such that the average annual growth was a negative 0.3 percent for 1971–78 (Danzon 1982, 5). The mid-decade "spike" in claims was considerably less severe for product liability and manufacturers' and contractors' bodily injury claims, and rates of automobile liability claims were stable throughout the 1970s. Claims severity continued to rise throughout this period, as for comparable lines of insurance. Physicians' coverage experienced 12.4 percent annual rises during 1971–78, hospitals 18.9 percent, product liability bodily injury 19.4 percent, and automobile bodily injury 14.1 percent (Danzon 1982, 6–7). By the end of the 1970s and the beginning of the 1980s, however, there was, if anything, a surplus of capacity to provide malpractice coverage. Real prices even declined in some instances, although experience varied by state (Posner 1986). Claims frequency was down; claims severity, although up, seemed predictable; and insurers could earn high real rates of return on their investment of reserves.

Renewed Crisis in the 1980s

By the early 1980s, the situation had once again deteriorated, with rising claims and falling net revenues for insurers. Large premium hikes again appeared, this time building on a far higher base. Total malpractice insurance premiums approached $3 billion by 1983 as the next crisis gathered. Even this large number understates the price rises because it does not count the growing coverage through self-insurance or many captive insurers (Posner 1986). It somewhat overcounts rises in rates because it ignores the growth in insureds during this period and in policy limits purchased. The American Medical Association declared a new crisis in 1984 (AMA 1984a, 1984b, 1985).

This time, however, the malpractice crisis was more general, affecting many other insureds (Harrington and Litan 1988; Huber 1988). Frequency of claims again rose markedly for physicians' malpractice coverage in the early 1980s. Premiums rose swiftly as costs rose and insurance capacity shrank, particularly in reinsurance (where, by some accounts, many reinsurers lost confidence that the results of the tort system were predictable over time). Investment earnings were also squeezed by a decline in interest rates (Law and Polan 1978, Chapter 1; Danzon 1983a). The rises in premiums and the increasingly unequal burden across specialty rating groups caused particular concern. Noteworthy in their problems were obstetricians, who were on the cutting edge of difficulties, a position relinquished since the 1970s by the anesthesiologists.

Availability was much less of an issue for physicians in the 1980s, however. The presence of physician-sponsored insurers in most states seems to have helped prevent the major upheavals in the marketplace that had occurred in some states in the 1970s. Nonetheless, there are reliable reports of limits on insurance capacity. The St. Paul, the nation's leading malpractice carrier, took the unusual step of announcing in 1986 that it would no longer underwrite new applicants for coverage. Existing insureds were covered, the company noted, but the legal-regulatory climate was too uncertain to justify committing new capital. The same company and others also withdrew altogether from several states. Anecdotally, it is said that reinsurance also contracted during this period, but data are unavailable to quantify this effect. To judge from informal reports, the situation was far more critical for many other liability insureds, public and private, including small businesses, municipal officers, and nurse midwives (*Wall St. Journal* 1985; Huber 1988).

Results from our own Survey of Medical Malpractice Insurers and Survey of Former Medical Malpractice Insurers, which we conducted during the course of this study, confirm that a number of insurers have left particular markets or have otherwise cut back in this period. This is discussed further in Chapter 4.

Trends in Premiums and Claims

The conventional wisdom is that the 1980s was marked by a crisis of affordability rather than of availability. Premiums have certainly soared anew. In real terms, however, prices did not rise enormously from the prior peaks of 1976 and 1977. Figure 1.1 shows the constant-dollar price of a constant unit of physicians' malpractice insurance for five specialties during 1975–86, as compiled by the authors.

Premiums shown in Figure 1.1 for most states for most years are for mature claims-made policies with limits of $100,000/$300,000 ($100,000 per occurrence, $300,000 in total for all claims attributable to the policy year; hereafter referred to as a "100/300 policy"). The data charted come from a 51-state regression that controls for type of coverage and policy limits; it can be roughly interpreted as the price for a mature claims-made 100/300 policy. However, this chart fails to reflect that 100/300 coverage buys much less protection today than it did a dozen or so years ago. In fact, physicians buy considerably more coverage today than during the last crisis. In the mid-1970s, 100/300 coverage was considered fully adequate; as of mid-1985, the most

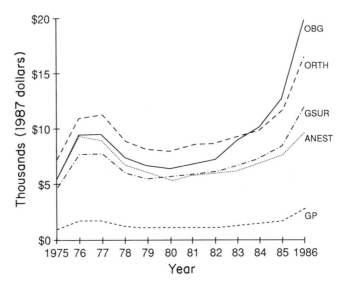

Figure 1.1 National trends in medical malpractice insurance premiums, 1975–86. Note: Mean annual premiums for $100,000/$300,000 policy limits. (Source: Unpublished data from the U.S. Health Care Financing Administration analyzed by the authors)

common coverage limits purchased even for low-rated general practitioners ranged by state from $0.5 million/$1.5 million to $3.2/$6.6 million (U.S. GAO 1986a, 60). It is very hard to present a long, consistent time series of representative prices because the companies writing coverage have changed over time and because of the shift from occurrence (coverage of claims against a policyholder resulting from incidents occurring in a year) to claims-made coverage (coverage of claims against a policyholder filed in a year).

The 1980s also witnessed striking rises in the rates of claims frequency and severity that underlie premiums. Figures 1.2 and 1.3 summarize recent nationwide claims information collected by this project (see the description in the Appendix).

During much of the 1980s, the frequency of claims rose rapidly. The figures cannot illustrate earlier trends because the data before then are immature. These data come from claims-made policies, by the end of the period virtually the only form of coverage bought in almost all states. The switch to claims-made policies began in the mid-1970s; for the first few years, few claims can occur, because occurrences in a prior year are covered only if the policyholder had purchased coverage with the same insurer. Claims-made experience is therefore not considered to reach a mature level for 5 years, and hence the figures exclude the late 1970s.

A large majority of claims are settled by insurers rather than tried in court. But a particular concern is the rising trend of jury verdicts because jury awards set the benchmark against which all settlements are made, both before the verdict and on appeal. Here, no reliable national data are available. For California superior courts, the Insurance Information Institute reported that the total annual census of malpractice jury verdicts began at 137 for 1972, peaked at 226 in 1976, and stood at 152 in 1983 (cited in

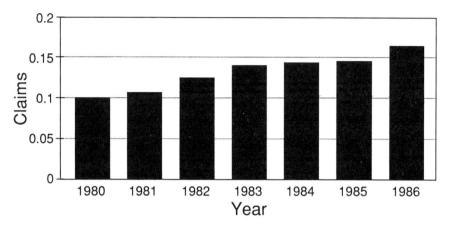

Figure 1.2 New claims opened per exposure year, 1980–86. Note: Based on claims-made coverage. (Source: Urban Institute–Vanderbilt University Survey of Claims Frequency and Severity)

AMA 1984a, 21). The average (nonzero) award, however, rose from $200,000 to almost $650,000.

Researchers at the Rand Corporation analyzed jury verdicts over 20 years in Chicago, San Francisco, and other parts of California, jurisdictions that have reasonably complete private reporters (e.g., Shanley and Peterson 1983). They reported that the annual number of trials in San Francisco peaked in the mid-1970s (just over 20 per year), whereas it has climbed steadily and rapidly in Cook County—from 10 per year in 1960 to over 30 in 1980 (Shanley and Peterson 1983, 51). Malpractice awards reportedly rose considerably faster than those for other high-stakes cases, like product liability and worker injuries; mean and median awards were also higher for each period (e.g., a mean of $457,000 for malpractice plaintiff awards in 1975–79, a median of

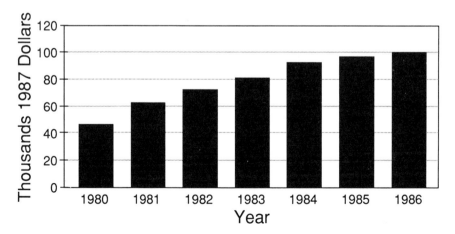

Figure 1.3 Paid claims severity, 1980–86. Note: Based on claims-made coverage. (Source: Urban Institute–Vanderbilt University Survey of Claims Frequency and Severity)

$70,000 vs. $219,000 and $57,000 for products liability [Shanley and Peterson 1983, 31]). Controlling for factors such as severity of injury that distinguish malpractice plaintiffs from others, medical malpractice awards were considerably higher than for other types of cases, according to a Rand report (Hensler et al. 1987), a finding strongly reaffirmed by our own research (Bovbjerg et al. 1990). It is unclear, however, from our research that the differences are due in large measure to case selection by plaintiffs and their attorneys as opposed to unusual generosity by juries.

1980s Responses

The 1980s saw a resurgence of reform efforts. California's Proposition 103, approved in the election of November 1988, demanded a rollback in casualty insurance rates and more regulation (e.g., Stevenson 1988; *The Economist* 1988). Its success sparked similar efforts elsewhere.

Tort reforms also remain popular. At the state level, most enactments resemble the 1970s' versions in attempting to curb the numbers and size of awards. Three major differences are discernible between the decades, however (Bovbjerg 1989): First, the 1980s saw far more generic tort reform, aimed at all personal injury lawsuits, rather than purely malpractice reform. Second, the federal government directly intervened for the first time—to promote insurance availability through the Risk Retention Act and to document instances of malpractice and physician discipline through the Health Care Quality Improvement Act.[1] Third, lawmakers in the 1980s were ready to consider more sweeping reforms of today's system of tort law and liability insurance, such as the Neurologically Impaired Infants Acts of Virginia and Florida. These acts created a new compensation system for this category of severe birth injuries to replace the system of tort law and liability insurance that traditionally covers malpractice (Bovbjerg 1989).

In the late 1980s and early 1990s, even more broadly sweeping changes in traditional tort law and insurance practice were receiving serious attention. At the same time, the crisis, measured in terms of both premium increases and claims frequency, was subsiding, probably again only temporarily (Schiffman 1989; Wish 1990). The American Medical Association proposed a fault-based administrative alternative to conventional litigation and claims settlement (AMA 1988). So did the Physician Insurers Association of America (PIAA 1989) and others.[2]

REASONS FOR PUBLIC CONCERN

Malpractice insurance is a public issue for three main reasons: First, its availability and price affect physicians' well-being. Second, these factors may indirectly affect patients' access to care and the prices that patients and other health care payers have to pay. Third, insurance developments may affect the quality of care available.

Insurance Availability and Price

Access to malpractice coverage at a reasonable price is the traditional focus of public concern. Insurance crises as perceived by premium payers have been the driving force of tort reform and stronger public intervention in the insurance industry—whether through renewed application of the antitrust laws or enhanced regulation. It is difficult to document the extent of availability problems, although anecdotal evidence is extensive (Sloan and Bovbjerg 1989; Institute of Medicine 1989a). Premiums are more readily charted than availability, as noted in Figure 1.1.

Higher Prices for Medical Care and Reduced Access to Care

Public access to medical care at a reasonable price is the second major public interest. There is good evidence that higher malpractice premiums cause higher prices for physicians' services (Sloan 1982). Indeed, physicians seem not merely to pass through the full cost of insurance increases to patients but also to raise prices even further. A given rise in premiums seems to raise fees by about twice that amount (Sloan and Bovbjerg 1989, 29–32). However, since premiums remain a very small component of physician expenses on average, even with a double effect of fees, the contribution of premium increases to physician fee inflation has been minor.[3] The most plausible explanation for the double pass-through is that physicians provide more care per service—better record keeping, more time talking with patients, and the like—which raises their costs of service. Whether presumably higher levels of service are worth their price is not obvious in the heavily subsidized medical services market; the issue has not been analyzed in systematic fashion.

Frequent statements by physicians suggest that the extra care is not worthwhile. Extra tests and procedures are said to be done more for potential legal defense than for value in health care. Very high estimates exist of this cost—up to $15 billion annually in 1985 dollars (AMA 1987; Reynolds et al. 1987). This defensive padding of services is widely believed to occur, but its extent is very hard to document, for factors other than malpractice fears also promote service-intensive care—including patient demand and physician profit seeking (Tancredi and Barondess 1978; Sloan and Bovbjerg 1989).

Effects on access to medical services are potentially even more troubling than those on the cost of care, and some physicians may have withdrawn certain medical services in response to malpractice fears. One of the defining features of the mid-1970s was the threat and occasional reality of a near strike by concerned physicians, especially in hospital-based and emergency practice. There are also many reports of physicians who have left practice early, have reduced their practices by eliminating riskier procedures, or have practiced "negative" defensive medicine by refusing to treat certain patients or certain conditions deemed at too great a risk of malpractice claim. ("Positive" defensive medicine, described above, consists of providing too many services—more than medically indicated.) Here again, the evidence is largely anecdotal (Sloan and Bovbjerg 1989) and occurs against a backdrop of rapidly rising numbers of physicians seeking to practice.

Obstetricians are often said to be most affected (Institute of Medicine 1989a; Klerman and Scholle 1988). The American College of Obstetricians and Gynecologists (ACOG) has published results from national surveys of its membership in 1983, 1985, and 1987, indicating that many physicians have indeed reportedly made changes (Opinion Research Corporation 1988). Among respondents, 27 percent had decreased their volume of high-risk obstetrical care and 12 percent no longer practiced obstetrics. One should recall that the ACOG data were self-reported in an atmosphere of crisis and political mobilization. Moreover, although a physician who curtails his or her practice clearly loses access to certain patients, it is less clear that his or her former patients lose access to care. Virtually nothing reliable is known about impacts on patient access to care. It seems improbable, for example, that the birth rate has declined in many areas where obstetricians report cutbacks or that many babies have been delivered at home other than by the choice of the parents involved. There are stories, however, of patients having to travel long distances for care or being dumped in public facilities.

Another physician response is to "go bare," or refuse to buy formal liability coverage, thus withdrawing on the demand side, just as insurance companies withdrew on the supply side. A small percentage seem to go bare, but documentation of this phenomenon is not good.[4]

Quality of Medical Care

Medical quality is the third reason for public concern about malpractice coverage. Maintaining good incentives for quality is a major rationale for tort law (generally called its "deterrent" function), and there is concern that defendants' purchase of liability coverage may overinsulate them from quality incentives. There is no evidence that any surge in low-quality care or unexpectedly poor outcomes caused the rapid rises in claims frequency seen during the crises (Brook et al. 1975; Mills and Lindgren 1987). Nonetheless, both 1970s and 1980s crisis-induced legislation aimed to upgrade quality protections (Bovbjerg 1989, 519–20, 535–38), partly as a quid pro quo for tort reform favoring physician defendants. Insurance indeed protects defendants from the major financial consequences of their professional mistakes, requiring a premium in return. "Experience rating" of some form is needed to maintain the direct financial incentive to avoid malpractice; of course, incentives are also maintained by the prospect of time lost in litigation and damage to reputation even where liability coverage pays the direct costs of litigation and any settlement.

CHAPTER PLAN

The balance of this book proceeds as follows:

Chapter 2 describes the malpractice insurers that make up this industry. The chapter describes notable characteristics of liability insurance generally and idiosyncracies of malpractice coverage that distinguish it from many other lines of liability coverage—such as the recent dominance of physician-sponsored companies. It then considers explanations. It discusses the nature of the risks that insurers take. Insurers really engage in two interrelated businesses: First, they assume risk when they sell policies. Second, they manage and invest cash flow. Various types of risk facing policyholders and insurers' owners are considered as well. The chapter sets out formal analytic models of firms' decision making under varying assumptions, as well as for quantifying insurers' risk and analyzing what return on premium is fair. This chapter sets the stage for subsequent chapters' analysis of different facets of the business, from state regulation of insurance to the profitability of its firms.

Insurance is a traditionally regulated industry, and this regulation serves as the focus of Chapter 3. States have long regulated insurance, a custom legitimized by the federal McCarran-Ferguson Act of 1945. That act also exempted companies from the procompetitive regulation of federal antitrust law to the extent that states regulate them directly. Above all, state regulation attempts to assure insurers' solvency. It also addresses rate making and sets other requirements. This chapter is largely descriptive. It covers the nature and extent of regulation; the forms of regulation that states impose on malpractice insurers (especially of entry and premium rates); and how this can vary by type of insurer (e.g., stock, physician mutual), as well as the premium taxes applied.

Then, using results from our Survey of Medical Malpractice Insurers, a detailed survey of 14 medical malpractice insurers we conducted as part of this study during late 1987 and early 1988, as well as information from other sources, we consider several relevant questions. How much do specific solvency and other regulations affect insurers' entry into each state market? What specific regulations of rate filing or solvency affect insurers' premiums in each state? Their rate of return? How much do insurers report relying on actuarial analysis and premium regulation versus competitive forces in an open marketplace? This has been a constant tension in regulatory theory and approaches. Other aspects of the business are also influenced by regulatory policy, as subsequent chapters show.

Chapter 4 turns to the overall structure of the industry. It describes and analyzes how firms enter and leave state markets and how competitive those markets are. Included are such issues as these: What are the impediments to entry, regulatory and otherwise? Is a malpractice insurer a natural monopoly? Are there substantial economies of scale or scope? Are there other barriers to competition in the malpractice insurance industry? Are there differences between physician-sponsored companies, JUAs, and commercial stock insurers? To what extent have firms entered or left particular states over time? What are the differences in market concentration across states? Why are some states dominated by physician-sponsored mutuals, others by stock companies?

The market as it is today could not exist without reinsurance, the focus of Chapter 5. Just as ordinary individuals (or firms) seek insurance to protect themselves against unanticipated losses, so do primary insurers seek reinsurance. Reinsurance protects primary carriers against the shock losses of very large claims, diversifying the risk of loss and spreading the costs across multiple years. It also allows firms to write higher limits of coverage than they otherwise could by expanding their capacity, which is particularly important to a new company just starting up.

The chapter describes the forms of reinsurance, their functions, and their practices in reinsuring. What types of reinsurance policies are written? How frequent are the various types of reinsurance? What particular cost-sharing arrangements are observed? Who are the reinsurers? Its empirical analyses cover such issues as these: What amounts of premium income are ceded to reinsurers (percentage retained versus reinsured)? What factors explain the demand for reinsurance?

Chapter 6 examines how insurers manage claims and hold dollar reserves against future claims. Good reserving is extremely important to a company. If it underreserves, it increases the risk of bankruptcy as future claims come in, but overreserving requires uncompetitively high premiums. The pattern of past reserves is the major input into actuarial calculation of the premiums needed for future policies. And investment returns on reserves are, of course, a major source of future earnings. We describe the life cycle of a claim, from opening of a claims file to its closing, together with the practice of claims valuation and management. We also address whether insurers have systematically over- or underreserved over time, whether these patterns of valuation show any manipulation of reserves, and what discounting of future obligations to present value, if any, is appropriate.

Chapter 7 addresses insurance rate making and premiums. High rates or rapid growth in premiums are the main reason the average person and legislators pay attention to insurance issues. Public concern over the fairness of rate making has spilled over even into election results, as shown by California's Proposition 103, noted above. Of course, if premiums are inadequate, the two-edged rate-making sword cuts in the other direction; insurers may fail, leave the market, or precipitously raise future premiums. Whether rates should be highly regulated or more competitively determined is the major policy issue. This chapter describes the rate-making process, from actuarial projections, through regulatory oversight (if any), to market-driven adjustments. It addresses such issues as these: How are premiums computed to reflect a company's actual or projected loss experience? Do developments in investments (notably, available interest rates) influence the premiums charged to physicians? Do insurance regulators constrain rates relative to a more competitive approach?

Chapter 8 discusses various approaches for classifying physicians into risk categories and experience rating. We address such issues as these: What risk classes are used by insurers and how are they developed? What is experience rating and how is it done? We describe in depth the experience-rating plans implemented by several insurers. These case studies show considerable variation in design and implementation of experience rating. The chapter concludes with some recommendations.

No insurance topic draws public ire quite like reports of excess profits squeezed out of rate payers by liability or other insurers. Chapter 9 examines this important issue. Firms must earn a net return in order to stay in business, as well as to expand. How much retained surplus a company has built up determines not only the number of customers they can insure but also their ability to offer higher limits of coverage to those customers. Here we examine such issues as these: How profitable has malpractice insurance been (computed retrospectively), compared with fair rates, using alternative approaches? Does profitability of malpractice insurance vary by type of ownership? Has profitability changed over time?

Finally, Chapter 10 presents our summary and conclusions. The chapter revisits the major issues and highlights our major empirical findings. We also discuss here the policy implications of our findings, notably on how medical malpractice does or could serve as a link to quality assurance in medical care, the policy choices between competition and regulation, the continuing dominance of physician-run insurers, redistributional aspects of legislative change, and the respective performance of the various actors in the insurance system.

CONCLUSION

Malpractice insurance has been a major public issue for about two decades. Unfortunately, public policy has been mainly crisis driven. Interest waned after the 1970s' malpractice crisis but was rekindled by the broader 1980s' problems with liability insurance. However, the fading of the immediate 1980s' crisis in the late 1980s and early 1990s leaves many important issues unresolved.

This book adds considerable new information about medical malpractice insurers for policy consideration. The following nine chapters address the issues raised above, drawing on a variety of sources, many newly created or analyzed for this book. Our goal is to help make the reaction to the next crisis or to interim reforms better informed than in the past.

NOTES

1. The Risk Retention Act was first passed in 1981 to assist insureds seeking product liability coverage (P.L. 97–45). It responded to specific concerns about manufacturers' ability to purchase coverage even prior to the full-blown crisis of the 1980s. In 1986 the statute was expanded to include liability coverage generally, including medical malpractice (P.L. 99–563). The Health Care Quality Improvement Act of 1986 called for the creation of a federal data bank to maintain records on physicians, containing reports on all malpractice settlements with payment and all significant hospital disciplinary actions, as well as those by state licensure authorities (P.L. 99–660, T. IV).
2. The Physician Insurers Association of America (1989) report reviews numerous proposals.
3. According to one major survey of physician revenues and expenses, 1987 malpractice premiums were 4.5 percent of the median physician's gross revenues, having risen during the preceding 5 years more than three times faster than all physicians' expenses, themselves growing at double the general rate of inflation (CPI) (Holoweiko 1988, 162, 178). In 1982, median malpractice premiums accounted for about the same percentage burden as professional-car upkeep, about 40 percent that of office space; in 1987, premiums were over double car expenses, about 80 percent that of office space (Holoweiko 1988, 177).
4. AMA data from a 1983 national survey are said to show that about 2.5 percent of physicians nationally had discontinued their liability insurance completely (Zuckerman 1984). According to a survey by the California Medical Society (Purdy 1982), some 6 percent of California physicians were not covered by liability insurance in January 1982—up from only 2 percent in December 1974.

This study used numerous sources of data, including surveys we conducted for the purpose of this research, as well as several sources of published and unpublished data.

SURVEY OF MEDICAL MALPRACTICE INSURERS

A substantial amount of pertinent information on insurers' practices and procedures is not available from various published and unpublished sources. For this reason, we conducted a survey of 14 medical malpractice insurers during late 1987 and early 1988. The survey instrument included sections on general management, claims management, loss reserving, premium development, underwriting and rating insureds, regulation and its effects, reinsurance, and competitive environment. Companies were sent a copy of the questionnaire in advance. The survey itself was conducted either by telephone or in person. Typically, several different respondents answered different parts of the survey. Occasionally, the chief executive officer answered all questions. A copy of the survey instrument is available from the authors.

We selected a sample of 14 insurers that are representative of medical malpractice insurers, both with respect to sponsorship and to ownership and geography.

The 14 respondents were:

CNA Insurance Companies
The Doctors' Inter-Insurance Exchange
Illinois State Medical Inter-Insurance Exchange
Medical Inter-Insurance Exchange (New Jersey)
Medical Liability Mutual Insurance Company (New York)
Medical Mutual Liability Insurance Society of Maryland
Medical Protective Company
Michigan Physicians Mutual Liability Company
Minnesota Medical Insurance Exchange
Mutual Assurance Society of Alabama
Mutual Insurance Company of Arizona
St. Paul Property and Liability Insurance Company
State Volunteer Mutual Insurance Company (Tennessee)
Utah Medical Insurance Association

The 11 physician-sponsored insurers were selected in this way. First, all nine companies supplying data on claims frequency and severity for a study by Danzon (1986), which we updated, were contacted. Only one of these companies declined to participate. We selected another physician-sponsored company in the same state as a replacement. Second, we added two other companies to broaden our perspective: State Volunteer Mutual Insurance Company (Tennessee) was added to increase the sample size from the South and the Michigan Physicians Mutual Liability Company was selected to represent a company selling occurrence policies. Of the three commercial stock companies in our sample, one (Medical Protective) is privately held.

In addition to the one insurer that refused to participate, another declined to answer major portions of the survey. Thus, we obtained 13 responses to most of the questions.

SURVEY OF FORMER MEDICAL MALPRACTICE INSURERS

As noted in the text, several national insurance companies withdrew from the medical malpractice line during the mid-1970s and a few did so later. We originally intended to conduct a structured interview parallel to our Survey of Medical Malpractice Insurers, with the primary emphasis on why the companies withdrew from the medical malpractice line. However, most of the companies contacted indicated that they preferred to provide information in a narrative form. The companies that provided us with information were Aetna Life and Casualty, Chubb Group of Insurance Companies, Hartford Insurance Group, and Travelers Indemnity. Some of these companies wrote malpractice insurance for hospitals, clinics, health maintenance organizations (HMOs), and non-physician health care providers at the time of the survey. We were interested in their withdrawal from the physician portion of the market.

REGULATORY SURVEY OF INSURANCE DEPARTMENTS

During 1988, we surveyed all state insurance departments to request information on denials of medical malpractice rate filings—frequency and years and insurers for which rates were denied. There were very few denials of rate increases in the recent past, and often the respondent's institutional memory was not sufficient to recall whether there had been rate denials in the more distant past (over one or two years prior to the survey). For this reason, we do not rely on results from this survey in our analysis of insurer regulation (Chapter 3).

We obtained information of state premium tax statutes from the National Association of Insurance Commissioners (NAIC 1987), lists of state filing requirements for the mid-1970s (Samprone 1975), and more recent filings (NAIC 1987).

PREMIUM AND CLAIMS DATA

Premium data are used in Chapter 1 and in our analysis of premium determinants in Chapter 7.

Premium Data

We tabulated insurance premiums from a national data file maintained by the Health Care Financing Administration (HCFA). Once a year, HCFA obtains insurance company rate sheets for malpractice coverage from one or more insurers for each state and the District of Columbia. The companies included are always the leading writer or one of the leading writers for the state. HCFA's purpose is to develop a liability insurance component of the Medicare Economic Index, the cost of practice index by which Medicare updates prevailing charges each year. With few exceptions, the premiums are for policies providing \$100,000/\$300,000 coverage. HCFA maintains the hard copy of these filed rates, and this project automated data for mature claims-made (and occurrence, if available) policies for five specialties (general practitioners, anesthesiologists, general surgeons, orthopedic surgeons, and obstetricians/gynecologists) for 1974–87. These data were also used in previous research on medical malpractice premiums (e.g., Sloan 1985).

Our premium analyses used data from 49 states (including the District of Columbia but not Hawaii and Alaska), although there were some missing values for certain states in selected years. In approximately 12 states, multiple areas were used to establish insurance rates. To obtain one statewide premium, we computed a weighted average premium across rating areas, where the weight is the proportion of the state's physicians in a specialty in each rating area. Finally, we conducted a small survey in California in order to be certain that we had comparable data from the two main insurers in the state, the only one that did not have statewide carriers. We computed an average of the rates from both companies to obtain statewide premiums in a manner similar to our approach with multiple rating areas.

Claims Data

We obtained data on claims frequency and severity by state from a national sample of malpractice insurers. With the collaboration of Patricia Danzon, we began with the national data file for 1975–84 that she had previously constructed (Danzon 1986). In addition to the companies in her study, we added others (Mutual Assurance, Inc. [Alabama], Minnesota Medical Insurance Exchange, and Utah Medical Insurance Association) in the interests of completeness and balance. Then each company gave us additional data for 1985 and 1986 and, in at least one case, also corrected the prior years' database.

Many of the companies reported information for very few insured physicians or for very few closed claims. To reduce randomness in our underlying data, we treated the number of claims per insured physician as missing when a value for a company was based on fewer than 30 physicians; in addition, when an insurer covered fewer than 5 physicians, we excluded the observation from the severity analysis. However, as a result, there were a number of states for which fewer than five years of data were available, making state effects difficult to estimate. Therefore, the entire state was excluded from the regressions when we had fewer than five nonmissing values of the dependent variables.

For some states, we had only frequency data from insurers selling occurrence insurance. It is inappropriate to compare frequency under occurrence coverage to frequency from the early years of claims-made coverage, because the exposure to suits is much lower for the latter coverage. Therefore, we dropped occurrence frequency data from our analysis.

These comparability problems between claims-made and occurrence data are not critical for the analysis of severity. Danzon computed severity using both occurrence and claims-made data. We followed this same approach here. However, in order to present a severity model that can be directly related to our frequency model, we also estimated a severity model based only on claims-made data. Our frequency regressions were based on 36 states, and our severity regressions were based on 40 states (both types of data) and 37 states (only claims-made data). Our severity analysis, based on 40 states, excluded Alaska, Connecticut, Delaware, the District of Columbia, Hawaii, Michigan, Nevada, New Mexico, Oklahoma, Pennsylvania, and Rhode Island. The severity analysis of claims-made date also excluded Massachusetts, New York, and Utah. The frequency analysis excluded all of the above states and New Hampshire.

DATA FROM A.M. BEST COMPANY

Best's Insurance Reports—Property/Casualty

The A.M. Best Company publishes reports annually on individual property/casualty insurance companies. We used data from these reports in our analyses of market structure (Chapter 4), reinsurance (Chapter 5), loss-reserving practices (Chapter 6), and profitability (Chapter 9). In some analyses, we combined data from several editions, 1978–87 (1977–86 data). In others, we used a single cross section (1986). The latter time period corresponds to information available to respondents to our Survey of Medical Malpractice Insurers (the first section of this appendix).

We selected companies selling medical malpractice insurance from these reports on the basis of these criteria: (1) membership in the Physician Insurers Association of America (PIAA) or (2) being identified by A.M. Best (in *Best's Review*) as one of the top three insurers in any state between 1978 and 1986, and with data on losses and loss reserves published in *Casualty Loss Reserve Development*. The companies included are listed in some of the tables in the text (see Chapters 6 and 9). The multivariate analysis of reinsurance included some companies in addition to those listed in the tables.

Best's Casualty Loss Reserve Development

A.M. Best publishes *Best's Casualty Loss Reserve Development* on an annual basis. For purposes of our analysis of loss-reserving practices (Chapter 6) and profitability (Chapter 9), we assembled medical malpractice loss data from 1978 through 1986 (reported in 1979–87). Later years reported information covering a 10-year loss development period; earlier reports gave individual year runoffs beginning with 1975. The sample for our analysis of loss-reserving practices and profitability included 49 companies—24 physician-owned companies that were members of the PIAA that had loss development information reported in 1985; all commercial companies identified as being one of the top three insurers in any state between 1978 and 1986, and for which information was available from the 1985 loss development reports; Continental Casualty and Argonaut Insurance, two companies that were included in other analyses because of their former activity in the medical malpractice market; and the Group Council Mutual Insurance Company, the Health Care Group, and the PHICO Insurance Group.

Best's Reproduction of Convention Statements

Each year A.M. Best publishes *Best's Reproduction of Convention Statements* of a number of property/casualty insurers. We selected 24 companies that wrote medical malpractice insurance. There are a few physician-owned companies in this group (e.g., Medical Liability Mutual Insurance Company [New York]), but the majority of companies included by Best's were commercial companies. In addition, we obtained convention statements directly from a few companies: COPIC Insurance Company, State Volunteer Mutual Insurance Company, Mutual Assurance Society of Alabama, Utah Medical Insurance Association, Physicians Liability Insurance Company, New Mexico Physicians Mutual, and the Mutual Insurance Company of Arizona.

To analyze the relationship in loss reserve errors across lines, we took information from Schedule P of the annual convention statements, 1978–86, for 12 multiple-line insurers, all from *Best's Reproduction of Convention Statements*. These were Aetna Life and Casualty, American International Group, Continental Insurance Companies, Crum & Forster Insurance Companies, Farmers' Insurance Group, Fireman's Fund Insurance Companies, Fremont Insurance Group, Hartford Insurance Group, Insurance Company of North America, St. Paul Group, Travelers Indemnity, and U.S. Fidelity and Guaranty Group. The five lines chosen for comparison were automobile liability, Workers' Compensation, multiple peril, other liability (farm; home; commercial; boiler and machinery; and ocean, marine, and aircraft), and medical malpractice.

Market Share Data

Market share data were obtained from two sources. For 1978 to 1987, we obtained the top three malpractice insurers in each state from *Best's Insurance Reports— Property/Casualty* (1979–1987 editions). In a few instances (e.g., New Mexico), market share data was supplemented with information on total premiums from the insurer. The market share information for 1986 was replicated for all insurers in a given state using information from the *Market Share Report—Medical Malpractice, 1986* published by the NAIC. The NAIC reported direct premiums by company. In order to compare the NAIC's and Best's data, the NAIC data were aggregated to the company group level.

OTHER DATA SOURCES

Several additional data sources were used in our analysis of insurer profitability (Chapter 9). Data on stock market returns came from a file compiled by the University of Chicago's Center for Research in Security Prices (CRSP). A copy of the file was available to us at Vanderbilt University. Balance sheet information on selected commercial stock insurance companies was taken from Industrial Compustat, a copy of which was also available to us at Vanderbilt.

2

Conceptual Framework and Institutional Context

A PORTRAIT OF INSURANCE PRACTICE

What makes medical malpractice insurance tick? How can we explain the behavior of malpractice insurers? This chapter discusses the nature of the product of malpractice insurance, the nature and behavior of insurance firms, and the structure and behavior of the market. We start by describing some relevant characteristics of the malpractice product, firms, and market. Some of these are common to the property-liability insurance industry, of which malpractice insurers are a part. Other features are more specific to the malpractice insurance line.

Such a descriptive base of information is important as a background to the rest of this chapter and the rest of the book. We cannot paint a detailed portrait of malpractice insurance in part of a chapter (for general insurance practice, especially in property-casualty, see Webb et al. 1984a, 1984b and Troxel and Breslin 1983; for a rather extensive, if dated, description of the malpractice line, see Kendall and Haldi 1973). What we can do is to sketch out key characteristics of the business. The rest of the analysis seeks to understand just why and how these "stylized facts" of insurance (as economists would call them) are as they are. Later in this chapter, we begin to set out an analytic approach for the rest of the book. Compared to other forms of liability insurance, such as automobile liability, general liability, multiple peril, and Workers' Compensation insurance, the malpractice insurance industry is small (Table 2.1).

THE NATURE OF THE INSURANCE PRODUCT

Salient features of malpractice insurance include the following.

The Risk of Insurance

All businesses are risky. But risk is the essence of insurance. Investors and managers must decide in advance what goods or services to produce, and how, in light of expected sales even further in the future. Insurers, however, have to make such projections not only on production and sales, but also about developments even beyond the point of sale. Any insurance product is unusual in that, even at the point of sale, the

Table 2.1. Comparison of Selected Liability
Insurance Premiums, 1989 (Billion $)

Line	Premiums Written
Automobile liability	$55.7
General liability	$17.9
Medical malpractice	$ 4.0
Multiple peril	$35.6
Workers' Compensation	$26.9

Source: Wish (1990), pp. 21–24, 107, 109.

cost of production is not known. Product development, sales, and certain administrative expenses are incurred up front. However, the major expense is not such "loading," but rather future payments to policyholders on claims plus the associated cost of resolving those claims.

Moreover, unlike most goods and services, production costs depend in great measure on who the customer is, in ways that can be hard to predict. Any business's costs may vary by customer where some customers demand in advance that product enhancements must be made or better after-sale service guaranteed. Beyond this, for an insurer, the key production cost of future claims settlements can vary enormously according to who buys a standardized insurance policy. Predicting claims for a specific class of insureds or for specific insureds, under a given insurance policy, is thus central to production decisions.

In short, the business of insurance is risk bearing and management. This fact helps explain the importance to insurers of their underwriters (who assess the riskiness of prospective insureds), their claims managers (who actually settle claims and largely determine the dollar reserves needed to pay for pending claims), and their actuaries (who predict the course of future claims based on patterns of past and pending claims). Moreover, in various facets of their operations, from writing a policy contract to lobbying for legal changes, insurers are necessarily always in search of ways to limit their exposure to risk. No matter how well they write their policies, underwrite their insureds, and predict their future claims costs, their results are uncertain. The volatility of these results has major implications for insurance prices and profits.

Legal Liability as a Risk

Most insurance risks involve natural phenomena, as mediated by human behavior. Thus, life and health insurers cover losses from death and sickness, thought to be in most ways objective occurrences beyond the control of insureds and hence insurable. Similarly, much property-casualty insurance covers damages from accident, fire, or natural disasters. However, all malpractice insurance (and much other insurance) covers only the naturally occurring damage deemed legally the responsibility of the insured policyholder. The extent of damages, too, is ultimately determined by legal rules, not by policy provisions. The law of "tort" (civil cases for damages wrongfully caused) varies by state and can change markedly over time. (Keeton et al. 1984 is the most thorough and basic legal reference book.) Moreover, legal claims are brought by lawsuits against alleged wrongdoers, a more expensive and unpleasant process than an insurance claim, and injured parties' willingness to sue can vary. Further, lawsuits are ultimately resolved by juries (or settled in expectation of what juries would do), and juries' attitudes may also change. These legal uncertainties are in addition to the basic variability of medical injuries (or any other liability risk).

Third-Party Insurance

Malpractice insurance finances payments to injured parties on behalf of policyholders who may have responsibility for those injuries. In contrast to such "third-party" coverage, in "first-party" insurance, like automobile collision or fire protection under a homeowner's insurance policy, the injured party and the policyholder are the same. The first-party insurer's customer is a potentially injured party. By contrast, in third-party insurance, the customer is a potential defendant facing a claim or lawsuit from an injured party. The insurer has no contractual relationship with the injured party. Hence the injurer cannot monitor the moral hazard (the propensity of individuals to engage in less loss prevention when covered by insurance) of parties subject to injury through policy provisions. For example, there is a normal tendency to spend more on an injury if someone else is paying. Nor can the insurer motivate the use of safety precautions by potentially injured people (for instance, by giving premium discounts for smoke alarms). Instead, the third-party insurer can select good risks only by assessing the characteristics of insureds who are not likely to have claims filed against them rather than the characteristics of persons likely to be injured (although malpractice injuries involve known classes of patients, unlike, say, automobile injuries to unpredictable strangers).

The insurer can also oversee actions of the potential defendant in an effort to prevent injury or mitigate its consequences. One action of insured defendants that can greatly affect the cost of paying claims is how well they conduct their legal defense (including the competence of the lawyer and the litigation strategy). For this reason, liability policies commonly provide that the insurer can select the attorney and control the litigation, including whether to settle out of court and for what amount. Otherwise, insured defendants, facing no pecuniary cost of defense, may want to defend their reputations to the last, quite expensively, even where liability is clear. Such an insured can afford to hold out in the final hope of vindication, whereas a calculating insurer facing the high expense of an all-out defense through a jury trial would prefer to settle voluntarily—though the individual defendant holding out for a trial does face higher costs in lost time to prepare for and attend the proceedings, and the costs of adverse publicity are presumably higher after a public trial than after a private settlement. Alternatively, a publicity-shy defendant may want to settle even a defensible case quickly (and quietly) for a relatively high amount, whereas the insurer may prefer to try it.

This highlights another difference in perspective between the individual defendant and the liability insurer. Past payments on claims affect the size of future claims and awards, especially if they result from a jury verdict and most especially if they are upheld on judicial appeal, which becomes a formal legal precedent. One defendant cares openly about his or her own case, say, of how much to pay for a wrongfully broken arm, whereas the insurer faces a higher cost of a high award—the prospect that similar pending cases and future claims will also rise as a result, even before premiums can be raised to accommodate higher awards. Nonetheless, malpractice insurance policies typically include a "consent to settlement" clause that allows a physician to veto a settlement. Both defendant and insurer share an interest not to publicize a settlement amount, especially a high one, which explains why an insurer sometimes will settle at a higher amount if successful plaintiffs and their attorneys agree not to disclose the amount; court records may even be sealed to the same end.

Low-Frequency, High-Severity Risk

Unlike most insurance, malpractice insurance has traditionally featured low claims frequency yet high severity. That is, claims are relatively rare phenomena, although they have increased greatly in recent decades, as noted in Chapter 1. Still, depending on the medical specialty, only 5 to 20 percent of physicians face any claim during a given policy year. Many insured events are far more frequent (like health care claims), although some are much less frequent (like earthquakes or claims on life insurance). But malpractice is also unusually high in severity for property-casualty insurance, that is, dollars per claim or especially per paid claim.

Automobile accidents, the largest field for property-casualty insurers, generate many low-dollar claims, especially for property damage, as well as infrequent cases of very severe personal injury. Malpractice claims, on the other hand, are very high in average payment and greatly skewed to very severe injuries. This combination makes actuarial prediction more difficult (Chapter 6) and increases the importance of reinsurance (Chapter 5).

Lag Between Premium Inflows and Cash Outflows

For all insurance, premiums are received before claims payments have to be made. This lag varies by the type of coverage involved. Claims on health insurance, for instance, tend to come in quickly during a policy year and then to be settled quickly. Life insurance generally features a long time to claim, but again, prompt settlement when the insured risk of death finally occurs. In first-party insurance generally, payment is made with very few exceptions (such as death by suicide), whereas liability coverage pays only after a demonstration that the hurt suffered by an injured party was the insured's fault. Proving fault can be a lengthy process, so settlement lags are longer for liability coverage.

Lags from premium to claim can also vary. Certain obvious injuries, like automobile accidents, tend to become legal claims quickly, if at all. Others, like environmental damage, may take many years to become manifest. The total lag from premium to claims payment is much longer for malpractice than for most other lines of third-party insurance, as both claims lag and settlement lag are long. In a recently publicized case, a physician was sued in 1982 for a childbirth in 1961, and the case was not settled until 1988 (Drimmer 1989). Better data come from the GAO survey of claims closed in 1984. Typically, a claim takes a year or a year and a half to file, another year and a half or two to settle once filed, with paid claims taking longer to settle (GAO 1987a, 32 and 33; see also Table 6.1).

One tort reform enacted in most states in the mid-1970s was a reduction in the statute of limitations—the maximum length of time following an injury one has to file a lawsuit. Except for cases involving minors, fraud, or an injury that is not discovered immediately, the claim lag in malpractice is thereby limited. The statute of limitations for malpractice runs from two to four years in most states (Bovbjerg 1989).

Earnings from Underwriting and Investment

The core of the insurance business is assuming (or "underwriting") the risk of uncertain future events in exchange for a premium. Insurers' profits consist, first, of underwriting profits, the difference between premiums and what is paid out in claims plus other costs incurred in this process. Insurers are also in the investment business, however, for they invest cash flow from the sale of insurance, from which they also derive a return in the lag between collecting premiums and paying claims. Investment income is the second source of an insurer's profits.

Insurers in this way resemble a bank or other company that continuously sells travelers' checks for cash (at face value plus a service fee), holds the money on behalf of customers, then pays it out when "claimed" by the cashing of checks—and that earns considerable income by investing the "float" that results from the lag between collecting the cash and returning it. Although premiums may be less than undiscounted future losses, insurers have use of the funds for the period between the time revenue is collected and disbursements are made to make investments.

Ex ante, that is, at the time the premium is set and the policy sold, how much is earned from underwriting depends on the risk premium charged, the lag to claims payment, and the expected returns to be earned on investments with the premiums funds in the interim. Ex post, actual underwriting returns depend on these factors and on how well the insurer predicted and managed the cost of claims. Valuation of risk to the insurer using various financial theories is a complex matter, one not yet resolved by experts.

There has been considerable confusion in the rate-making arena about the appropriate role, if any, of investment income in approving premiums that adequately compensate insurers for the risks they assume. (We discuss the role of investment income later in this chapter. Chapter 7 on premiums considers this issue in more detail, as does Chapter 9 on fair profits.)

Diversity of Organizational Forms

Firms providing malpractice insurance have a multiplicity of organizational forms. Some diversity is notable for property-casualty insurers more generally, but not typically to the extent of malpractice insurers. As with other lines of insurance, some firms are organized as stock companies, mutuals, and direct underwriters (e.g., Lloyd's Associations). But mutual ownership (by physician policyholders) and similar arrangements not technically in the form of mutuals (physician reciprocals and trusts) is more common in malpractice. Moreover, other, state-mandated organizations that also supply insurance have been prominent, namely, PCFs and JUAs.

Almost all physician-sponsored insurers, whether organized as mutuals or otherwise, have appeared since the malpractice crisis of the mid-1970s. They have since been organized in most states and have increased their market share to almost one-half (Table 2.2). The extent and rapidity of this change in the insurance field are striking.

These different ownership forms create different incentives for the parties directly

Table 2.2.   Net Malpractice Premiums
Written[1] (Percent Distribution)

Year	Stock	Mutual	Reciprocal/ Exchange	Total
1977	71	14	15	100
1980	56	22	22	100
1983	57	23	20	100
1986	60	20	20	100
1989	51	24	25	100

Source: *Best's Aggregates and Averages*, 1987 edition, pp. 88–
9, 97, 101; Wish (1990), p. 24.

[1]Net premiums = gross premiums + premiums assumed from
other companies (reinsurance assumed) − premiums ceded to
other companies (reinsurance ceded to other companies). The
data shown in this table include medical malpractice insurance
sold to nonphysician health care providers as well as to physicians. Self-insured plans and some of the rarer organizational
forms (e.g., patient compensation funds) are also excluded from
the information in this table. This book's focus is on medical
malpractice insurance sold to physicians. There is no comparable series on premiums paid by nonphysicians to insurers by
major ownership form.

involved—policyholders, managers, and owners. They also operate under distinct
competitive advantages and disadvantages, some of which are state conferred. There
are also contractual arrangements between firms at different stages of production, as
occurs when a primary insurer cedes premiums to a reinsurer.

State-Specific Operations

Almost all insurance is organized on a state-by-state basis, for insurance regulation is
traditionally a function of state government, and firms must generally be state licensed
to do business. Typically, however, insurers operate on a regional or larger scale. Here,
too, malpractice is unusually state specific, especially the physician companies, almost
all of which operate only in their home states (PIAA 1987). Several explanations
beyond state licensure exist.

Liability insurance, unlike other forms of property-casualty coverage, is fundamentally affected by the jurisdiction of coverage because legal liability is determined
under state law by state courts (and occasionally by federal courts applying state law).
Thus insurance exposure to risk can vary on different sides of a boundary even within
one metropolitan area straddling different states. The practice of medicine is also tied
to the state. Not only are doctors state licensed, along with other medical professionals
and institutions, but their practice is also nearly as immobile as the hospitals in which
they do most of their work and in which most malpractice claims arise.[1] An insurer
selling a malpractice policy in a state can confidently expect almost all future claims to
arise there and to be settled under that state's law. Workers' Compensation is similar,
though many companies operate in multiple states. In contrast, automobile liability
covers drivers who can have accidents across state lines, and in products liability, both
the manufacturing process and the sale of finished goods can be national or even global
in scope. Although automobile underwriting and rate making are state specific, nation-

al insurers apply similar techniques across states. Products liability, however, is written on a national basis.

Further, for malpractice insurance, most physician companies have active or historical ties to medical societies, which themselves are organized by state.[2] Only in recent years have a few physician companies begun to sell across state lines, and then often mainly in states where no "sister" physician plan already exists.[3] Finally, some "insurers" are not private companies but creatures of the state—namely, PCFs and JUAs.

Individual Coverage

Most medical malpractice coverage is sold on an individual basis, not to groups or larger business entities. In this, it resembles automobile or life insurance rather than health insurance. Group coverage gives economies of scale in sales, and adverse selection is less of a problem when insurance is purchased by groups.

In fact, this presumably reflects the individual nature of most medical practice, for solo practitioners and small group practices predominate (AMA 1984c, 15–18). This is not true of other professional practices, such as law or accounting. The natural unit of operation is the individual practitioner, loosely affiliated with others for care in a way that varies by episode of care—not a constant medical team. Certain HMOs and multispecialty group practices are exceptions and are likely to obtain group or institutional coverage. The low-frequency, high-severity nature of medical liability, along with the great variation in risk by medical specialty, may also play a role. Where individual insureds are heterogeneous in risk, a larger pool is needed to make rates on a group basis. An insurer cannot underwrite a small group of physicians without considering them individually for risk. Nonetheless, it remains notable that so little physician coverage is provided through hospitals, the one type of entity that naturally groups individual practicing physicians together (Sloan 1990). Sale of coverage through medical society plans does, however, help achieve marketing economies, just as association or franchise policies market identical individual policies to members of professional groups, automobile clubs, and the like.

Insurance Cycles

To a greater extent than in other sectors, malpractice in particular and property-casualty insurance in general have been subject to sudden jolts in both availability of coverage and cost. The causes of these "insurance cycles" are not well understood.

CHAPTER OVERVIEW

In the remainder of this chapter, we describe the institutional forms and anomalies of the malpractice insurance industry in greater depth, why these characteristics exist, and their implications for industry performance. More specifically, we address these issues.

- What products does the medical malpractice insurer produce? How does this affect the way such firms operate? How does an insurer combine its investment and underwriting activities?

- What are the competitive advantages and disadvantages of each form of insurer ownership? In what ways does ownership form affect firms' likely decision making and performance?
- What links exist among insurers, between insurers and medical organizations, and between insurers and individual physicians? What are the advantages of maintaining separate organizations rather than integrating vertically?
- What are the interrelationships among the topics of later chapters—pricing, reinsurance, loss reserving, and profitability?

THEORY OF THE INSURANCE FIRM: THE FOR-PROFIT FIRM

This section and the following one discuss why insurers behave as they do and what motivates their decisions. It models the insurance firm using economic theory as a foundation for analysis in subsequent chapters. The for-profit firm is in many ways the least complex and the most familiar. Therefore, it is useful to begin a discussion of insurer decision making in this section with the for-profit firm, first in a competitive market, then under different assumptions. The next section considers alternatives to the for-profit organization for firms.

Assumptions

For preliminary discussion, we adopt conventional, simplifying assumptions about the firm, its product, and its market (see Box 2.1). Simplification allows us to focus clearly on the two key aspects—the insurer's underwriting and investment choices.

Competition is a useful analytic paradigm. Moreover, even in regulated industries, the task of the rate regulator is to ensure that insurers do not set premiums in excess of those that would prevail in a competitive market. Solvency regulation may be needed, however, even in competitive insurance markets, since the amount of insurer turnover consistent with competition may impose socially unacceptably high bankruptcy risks on policyholders[5] (see Chapter 3).

Insurer Price and Output Decisions in Pure Competition

"Price" often means the premium charged. Policyholders certainly take that view and, because of political pressures, so do policymakers. From a societal perspective, there is merit in focusing on the premium. However, in analyzing the basics of insurer decision making, it is useful for now to take expected losses as given—that is, as a cost of doing business—and to focus more narrowly on the price of insuring claims, beyond the direct cost of paying those claims. The foregoing assumptions and further theory allow us to develop predictions and tools for later analysis.

In this narrow sense, a second price of insurance is the total insurance "loading," the difference between the premium charged and paid loss, indemnity plus associated loss expense (for investigating and defending claims). The loading, in turn, may be subdivided into (1) expenses for marketing, claims processing, and other operations and (2) a residual underwriting profit. This underwriting profit is a third price of insurance.

The insurer's output is insurance policies. Under our simplifying assumptions, a

---

Box 2.1 Initial Assumptions About Insurer Behavior

We initially assume that:

1. the firm maximizes profits from its underwriting (insurance) and its investment businesses and is risk neutral;
2. the firm operates in perfectly competitive markets for its insurance product and in perfectly competitive markets for inputs (equity and debt capital, agents, legal counsel, claims management, etc.);
3. the firm has only a single insurance product and views all risks it may insure as homogeneous (equally likely to have a claim filed against them);
4. the insurer can do nothing to influence the outcome and/or time of the dispute resolution process; and
5. the firm is not subject to rate or solvency regulation.

The profit maximization assumption is equivalent to stating that the firm makes decisions that maximize the capitalized value of profits expected to accrue over all future periods.[4]

The assumption of competitive markets means that the individual insurer has no control over the price of insurance, but it can decide how many units of insurance to sell. In such markets, there are many well-informed buyers and sellers. There is freedom of entry and exit. Output is homogeneous. The competitive process weeds out inefficient sellers. In perfectly competitive capital markets, bondholders and equityholders must be paid the returns they "require" to contribute capital. The insurer requires equity to start the business and as a buffer in the event of unanticipated fluctuations in losses. If this capital is not paid its required return, it will flow to other sectors. The insurer's first obligation is to policyholders and then to bond- and equity holders in that order.

---

policy translates into a fixed dollar loss to be paid in the future. Thus, output can also be denominated in terms of the expected loss. In this sense, the insurer acts as a financial intermediary that sells policies to finance investment. It issues a kind of "security" (each policy is a contingent claim in the future) and uses the proceeds to buy others' securities (a claim on others). In contrast to the usual firm, the insurer's main fixed liabilities are to policyholders rather than to debt holders, and both stand to be paid before equityholders. Its problem is to decide how many policies to sell and how to invest the funds generated from its underwriting cash flow during the lag to payment of claims and various other expenses.

The usual profit-maximizing firm sets output at the level where marginal cost equals marginal revenue. In this context, marginal revenue is the marginal investment income from policyholder-provided funds that may be generated by selling an insurance policy. Marginal cost is the cost of acquiring investable funds by selling policies in the insurance market. In competitive markets, insurers may be willing to sell insurance for a less than expected loss (negative underwriting profit). The reason that underwriting profit may be negative is the offsetting effect of investment income.

Because premiums are paid first, whereas losses and many expenses are paid later, often much later, insurers may issue policies with a dollar's worth of expected loss (including adjustment expense) for less than a dollar.

In competitive insurance markets, the value of underwriting profit is fixed at a negative value (u^*). It is convenient to think of such negative prices as "costs." The profit-maximizing insurer sets output where u^* equals the expected return on investment. (Total return is thus zero—or the market-dictated, competitive rate of return, given the risk to investors, a topic to which we turn in the next subsection.) Of course, at the market level (but not for the individual insurer), u^* is variable. During periods in which investment returns are high, u^* will be high in absolute value, i.e., the underwriting profit will be more negative; the converse is also true.

Thus, this competitive model predicts that premium discounts will be high when interest rates are high, and that the converse will also hold. In every time period, however, the underwriting profit must be sufficiently high to grant equityholders the returns they require from equity contributions to firms with risks comparable to those of insurance companies.

Underwriting, Investing, and Treatment of Risk

Underwriting Risk

We turn now to the risks assumed by malpractice insurers when they underwrite policyholders' liability and by investors who contribute capital to the insurance firm—classically, the stockholders in a for-profit firm. A distinction is often made on whether a risk is *diversifiable* or *nondiversifiable*. Diversifiable risks occur largely independently of one another, like successive flips of a coin. Thus, pooling individual risks reduces the risk. When enough risks are pooled, variation in outcome is diversified away and aggregate experience becomes highly predictable, like the percentage of heads in many tosses of a coin.

Premiums can then be set and loss reserves established to cover expected losses with a low risk of error. As an insurance example, the risk of a household fire in neighborhood A is typically unrelated to that in neighborhood B; insuring houses in both areas is less risky than insuring only in one.

Nondiversifiable risks (sometimes called *systematic risks*) are causally interrelated or statistically correlated with one another. Pooling them does not reduce the variation in outcome, or the variation is not reduced as much as when risk is diversifiable. To return to the fire example, the risk of fire to adjoining structures may be interrelated, as a conflagration can wipe out an entire area. Hence early fire insurers soon learned to limit their exposure in any one neighborhood and to diversify risk by writing coverage in multiple places.

Insurers, by definition, underwrite risks. The eventual payment an insurer must make on behalf of any single policyholder cannot be known in advance. We have assumed in this subsection that expected loss (probable payment times probability of occurrence) is the same across policyholders, so the insurer, for rate-making purposes, properly focuses on predicting the expected payments to policyholders on average, as well as the variance of expected payments around the average. For relatively diversifiable risks, variance is affected by the number of policies sold. In general, if expected losses per policyholder are less than perfectly correlated, the variance of expected payments falls as the number of policyholders increases. For a given number of policyholders, the lower the correlations of loss among policyholders, the lower the variance of expected loss. If there is zero correlation among the losses, the risk is perfectly diversifiable, and insurers can virtually eliminate all underwriting risk by pooling a large number of policyholders.

Now consider malpractice claims. Correlations of losses among malpractice policyholders may plausibly be positive and may be substantial. State judicial decisions and some legislation affecting plaintiffs' ability to obtain payments may readily influence the losses to be paid on behalf of many or most insured physicians in the state. Judicial precedent can also cross state lines. Moreover, publicity about one claim may engender other claims in like cases across a broad area. Even a private settlement in one case can quickly become a precedent for other cases.

Hence, the underwriting risk in malpractice appears to be greater than for lines for which the correlations are likely to be lower. Even natural disasters have more limited scope for affecting policyholders in disparate areas. Further, it has been asserted that the correlations have increased for malpractice, so that risks are less diversifiable (Danzon 1985). To the extent that this is so, the underwriting risk associated with malpractice insurance has risen. Trebilcock (1987) argued that increased instability of U.S. and Canadian tort law has increased uncertainty for liability insurers more generally.

Investment Portfolio Risk

Insurers also face risk in their investments. They may earn more or less than expected on any particular asset and even on their entire portfolio. Insurers with relatively risky insurance portfolios tend to earn higher returns in compensation, but by definition are subject to greater interperiod fluctuations in losses. If investment earnings fall too far below the expectations used to set premiums, the insurer may go bankrupt. One way to decrease the probability of bankruptcy is to hold more equity (or retained surplus) that can be used to cover an unanticipated increase in underwriting loss (or fall in investment return).

As discussed more fully below, insurance portfolio risk does not directly affect the cost of equity capital to insurers as a whole. The cost of capital is dictated by the market; what investors require is risk-adjusted returns to equalize earnings at the margin from alternative investments. Nor, in the competitive model, can an insurer charge a higher premium if it adopts a riskier investment strategy (to earn higher returns, but with a higher risk of losses). What policyholders have to pay is also market determined. If anything, policyholders may insist on lower premiums from an insurer that is more likely to be unable to pay future claims. However, unless precautions are taken, such as increasing the surplus relative to premium income, the value of the insurer's fixed obligations, mainly to policyholders, will be adversely affected by increased portfolio risk. A higher risk of bankruptcy means that the insurer may not be able to pay claims when they fall due. This is the primary rationale for regulation, as detailed in Chapter 3.

Risk to Owners of the Insurance Company

The next step in the analysis is to consider how risk affects the return that the owners of the firm, the equityholders, require as a condition for supplying capital to the firm.

Modern corporate finance theory has developed various approaches to quantifying risks, including the Capital Asset Pricing Model (CAPM) (Copeland and Weston 1983). CAPM has some deficiencies, both in general and as applied to insurance, but it offers important conceptual insights about insurers' costs of capital.[6]

Our competitive model assumes perfect information, so investors can predict the expected gain from any investment. But the future remains unknowable, and unforeseen developments may reduce or increase the gain. So, investing remains a risk. CAPM partitions risk into the two components already described—nondiversifiable risk and diversifiable risk. Risk-averse investors are concerned about, and must be compensated for, nondiversifiable risk, for investors can obviously eliminate diversifiable risk by adding a sufficient number of assets issued by different sources to their investment portfolios.[7]

Suppose, for example, that the investor holds stock in 50 firms. In any year, a few will suffer major losses or even go bankrupt because of unwise business decisions, but, at the same time, a few will "strike it rich" because of brilliant decisions that were not anticipated at the time the investor supplied equity to the firm. These are diversifiable risks. However, during a recession, a number of firms may experience depressed earnings, and it is not possible for investors in equities to escape the recession completely. Hence recession is a source of nondiversifiable risk. Securities issued by some firms are more "recession-proof" than others and hence offer comparative safety in a recession.

In the CAPM framework, such firms have relatively low nondiversifiable risk. The degree of nondiversifiable risk is captured by a quantity termed "beta." (See Box 2.2.) Beta captures the volatility of any risk relative to a well-diversified portfolio of stocks and other assets. If beta equals 1.0, the firm's nondiversifiable risk is average; betas above 1.0 suggest higher than average nondiversifiable risk, betas below 1.0 the converse. The beta of a government bond is about zero. Investors require higher returns ex ante from investments in higher-beta securities than in lower-beta ones.

An insurer's beta is the weighted average of two underlying betas. The first is the beta of the insurer's investment portfolio. If the insurer holds risky (nondiversifiably risky) securities in its investment portfolio, the beta of that portfolio will be relatively high; the converse is also true.

The second is the underwriting beta. This beta reflects the variability of underwriting results relative to the variability of returns on a well-diversified portfolio of securities. The sign of this beta indicates whether the underwriting return tends to rise or fall as the return on the well-diversified portfolio of securities rises or falls. If the two streams move in the same direction, the underwriting beta is positive; if they move in opposite directions, it is negative. The size of the beta indicates the magnitude of the response in underwriting profit.

Overall risk to the investor depends on how the two underlying betas are related. If the underwriting beta is negative, then selling insurance reduces the overall nondiversifiable risk of the insurer's stock because underwriting profits tend to increase (since losses fall) during periods when the overall economy is depressed (or otherwise systematically affected); the converse is equally true. A positive underwriting beta indicates, however, that selling insurance policies adds to the overall risk faced by investors in the company's stock.

Box 2.2 Investor's Risk and Rewards

Although bonds may have nearly zero betas, it is well known that yields on government bonds differ. A major factor accounting for variations in such yields is default or credit risk. If a bond has a 0.1 probability of nonrepayment, it will be priced to yield a higher ex ante return than a bond with no credit risk. After the fact, for each bond with a 0.1 risk of default, there will have been repayment or not. For a portfolio of such bonds, assuming independence of outcomes, the realized default rate will be 10 percent. With a large enough portfolio, investors should be able to diversify away the risk of high probabilities of default (assuming that the underlying default rate really was 0.1).

With a non-zero beta, yields (outcomes) on securities are not independent. Thus, the investor cannot fully achieve predictability by diversifying. Risk-averse investors (a plausible assumption for investors) must be compensated for bearing such risk. Compensation takes the form of higher ex ante returns.

Beta, a parameter from the CAPM, measures the extent to which the returns on a given security move with a well-diversified portfolio of securities. The market has a beta value of 1.0. A security that is twice as volatile as the market (e.g., when the market climbs 10 percent, it climbs 20 percent) would have a beta of 2.0. One that is half as volatile as the market would have a beta of 0.5. A bond that provides the same return regardless of where the market heads has a beta of approximately zero, implying virtually no nondiversifiable risk.

Next, consider the competitive level of underwriting profit. It depends on the following factors: the length of the tail (the difference between the years in which claims are paid and the year in which premium income is collected)—longer tails allow the cash generated from the sale of insurance to be invested for longer periods, and therefore to produce a lower underwriting profit; the underwriting beta—a higher beta (more positive or less negative) raises the required underwriting profit; the (risk-free) interest rate—a higher interest rate lowers competitive rates of underwriting profit; and the market risk premium, or the amount investors require for assuming another unit of nondiversifiable risk—the higher this premium, the higher the underwriting profit rate required.

If the underwriting beta is high, selling additional policies will add to the overall riskiness of the insurer as viewed by investors. As such riskiness increases, the firm will either have to pay a higher return on equity, using underwriting profits for this purpose, and/or make offsetting reductions in overall riskiness by adding lower-risk, lower-yield securities to its investment portfolio.

Once the underwriting return is known, the premiums are known, because losses and expenses are taken as given and return on equity is dictated by the capital market (by assumption). Increases in loss and/or other expenses, such as the cost of defending claims, should be reflected in higher premiums to maintain the competitively determined profit rate.

Role of Reinsurance

As seen thus far, the total risk of the insurance portfolio affects the probability of insurer bankruptcy. Insurers may offset an increase in bankruptcy risk by increasing the amount of surplus or equity they hold. To the extent that purchasers of insurance recognize a change in the probability of ruin, at least in the idealized world of competition, this will affect their willingness to pay for the insurance.

Once an insurer has contracted to pay a contingent claim under an insurance contract for a premium, it remains legally obligated to pay all covered claims. However, in practice, insurers may get other insurers to share the risk of claim. Specifically, the initial insurer may decide to insure all, or more likely part, of this liability with a second insurer that, on assuming the liability, receives all or part of the premium paid. The first insurer is the "primary" or "ceding" insurer, the second the "reinsurer." Typically, primary insurers seek to reinsure the high end of losses.

There are several reasons for the existence of reinsurance markets, which are discussed more fully in Chapter 5. The purchase of reinsurance improves the primary insurer's ability to withstand higher than expected losses. Therefore, it may increase the premium policyholders are willing to pay and hence increase the value of the primary insurer (Doherty and Tinic 1981). Even if premiums were unaffected by bankruptcy risk, under certain circumstances the value of the primary insurer—the sum of the value of contingent claims "owned" by policyholders and the surplus owned by equity holders—may be increased by purchasing reinsurance (Hoerger et al. 1990). Reinsurance may also provide a substitute for surplus. Rather than maintain a large surplus, the primary insurer may cede some of its liabilities to protect the company against fluctuations in frequency and severity of losses. By reinsuring, the primary insurer may be able to assume larger individual risks (higher limits of coverage, for example) than it would otherwise desire or be able to handle, thus providing more coverage. Whereas a primary insurer may not be able to diversify away highly correlated risks (like the risk of numerous high claims after a landmark legal decision), reinsurers, which pool risks of various kinds over a much larger geographic area, may be more efficient in risk bearing. Reinsurers typically reinsure many different types of primary coverage throughout the world.[8]

Relaxing Some of the Assumptions

Here we introduce variations to the original model of an insurer. The variations allow one to relax the assumptions of the pure competition model.

Competition

What happens to the model if an insurer is allowed market power? This shift from price taker toward monopoly introduces three important changes. First, output is restricted below the level obtained under competition. Premiums are no longer fixed by market forces, but rather depend on the number of policies sold. Output is a decision variable of the insurer. Second, the firm's owners are likely to receive higher returns on their investments under monopoly than under competition. Third, there is a case for rate regulation, which seeks to achieve competitive prices and output levels in an otherwise imperfectly competitive market (Finsinger and Pauly 1986). Sources of market power include imperfect information on the part of policyholders and barriers to entry, often imposed by licensure or solvency regulation.

Single Line of Coverage

Insurers may sell more than one line of coverage. Introducing multiple lines of insurance changes the calculation of variance in the insurance claims "portfolio." The variance cannot be computed by simply adding weighted estimates of the variance of each line. The covariances, which reflect the correlations of the ratio of loss and expense to premiums among the lines, also affect portfolio variance. Positive covariances add to insurance portfolio variance and conversely.[9] In short, if adding lines helps an insurer diversify its risks, this will be reflected in low covariances.

An efficient insurance portfolio is "mean-variance efficient." The mean underwriting profit and its variance can be computed for every possible insurance portfolio, that is, for different mixes of insurance lines. A portfolio is mean-variance efficient if, for any expected underwriting profit, the associated variance is lower than for any other insurance portfolio that can be constructed.[10] High variance exacts a cost on the insurer in terms of higher bankruptcy risk. Additional resources (e.g., higher initial capitalization, more retained surplus, or more reinsurance) must be expended by the insurer's owners to eliminate such added risk.

It is possible that many multiple-line insurers dropped the medical malpractice line in the 1970s because having a portfolio with medical malpractice was mean-variance inefficient. This would occur to the extent that underwriting profits were low for malpractice, the variance of the malpractice underwriting profit was high, or the covariances with the underwriting profits for other lines were positive and high.

Insurers may also achieve "economies of scope" (a term used by economists for efficiencies realized by offering two or more products) by offering several lines of insurance, thus being able to offer each at a lower price to policyholders. Efficiencies may be realized in marketing, in making actuarial projections, in dealing with regulators, and/or in managing claims. The extent to which such efficiencies exist cannot be deduced, but rather must be determined from empirical analysis.

Exogenous Losses and Homogeneous Policyholders

The competitive model assumed that all policyholders were alike (homogeneous in expected loss), and that claims costs were fixed and thus exogenous to the insurer's decision making. More realistically, losses may vary by policyholder in nonrandom ways and may be subject to some control by insurers. More specifically, risk may be endogenous in four ways.

First, insurers may try to select the better risks within each premium class. For various institutional reasons that are not well understood, malpractice insurers seem to prefer to refuse to insure the worst risks in each class rather than to charge them higher premiums through "experience" or "merit" rating, as discussed further in Chapter 8.[11]

Second, to varying extents, malpractice insurers undertake "risk management" to help control the losses. Such activities include instructing physicians on how to prevent claims and how to act to minimize loss once a claim has been filed.

Third, insurers themselves manage cases in order to minimize the loss (Schlesinger and Venezian 1986), especially through their control over defense and settlement negotiations. Better defense, however, plausibly costs some money to achieve its savings. Insurers may be expected to invest in defending cases up to the point at which a dollar's extra outlay in defense cost yields a dollar's saving in anticipated indemnity.

Fourth, it has been alleged that insurers sometimes manipulate their reported loss reserves to reduce fluctuations in the profits they report or for tax or regulatory purposes.[12] This matter is covered further in Chapter 6. Finally, insurers sometimes engage in political activity to promote tort reform to alter the legal system and hence the extent of losses. Such reform could have results that varied by insurers, even if applied across the board.

No Regulation

The bankruptcy rate of insurers resulting in the absence of government intervention may be unacceptably high. One reason for regulation is to protect policyholders from bankruptcy. In competitive markets there is no role for price regulation, but such regulation may be appropriate in markets in which sellers have market power.

Insurance regulations are discussed further in Chapter 3, but the main roles of regulation are to assure that insurers will be able to pay future claims and to assure that premiums are adequate but not excessive. Various regulations try to assure that insurers will have sufficient wealth and liquidity to meet all of their contractual obligations to their policyholders. The effect of solvency regulation (e.g., to require safe and liquid bonds for reserves) may just be to shift the mix of assets in the insurer's investment portfolio to another mix of assets that is equally mean-variance efficient. If so, such regulation has no effect on the required underwriting profit. However, certain investment constraints could make the insurer invest in securities that the insurer judges to be overpriced. In such cases, the investment portfolio may no longer be mean-variance efficient; and the required underwriting profit, and hence premiums, would have to rise as a consequence (D'Arcy and Doherty 1987).

The rationale for premium regulation is twofold. Adequate premiums help assure solvency, so regulators may set price floors. However, insurers with some monopoly power may obtain excessive premiums, so regulators may set price ceilings. The objective of price regulation is to produce prices that would be established in a well-functioning competitive insurance market.

In practice, regulation may have some unintended side effects. To the extent that prices are constrained below competitively determined prices, insurer entry may be deterred and exit encouraged. Further, there may be quality degradation (e.g., claims may be processed less expeditiously), and insurers may be less willing to insure the worse risks. On the other hand, if the regulated price is set too high, insurers may compete for business by making quality improvements that policyholders would not pay for under competition (e.g., processing claims faster, using more effort in defending claims).

THEORY OF THE INSURANCE FIRM: ALTERNATIVE ORGANIZATIONAL FORMS

A large share of medical malpractice insurance is provided by firms not organized on a for-profit basis with stockholders as the residual claimants of profits (Table 2.2).[13] Thus it is useful to go beyond the for-profit paradigm to consider other ways that insurers may organize. Malpractice insurance in fact features several organizational forms. Prior to the mid-1970s, when A.M. Best first began to publish separate data for the medical malpractice line and when physician-sponsored companies began to be organized, stock companies supplied most all such insurance (Kendall and Haldi 1973, 602–8).

Rationale for Alternative Organizational Forms

Before describing and assessing the performance of the alternative organizational forms of firms in the industry, it is instructive to examine the reasons why the standard for-profit organizational form may not best serve the malpractice insurance line. The organizational forms that survive may be those that yield greatest consumer satisfaction for the dollar while at the same time covering production costs (Fama and Jensen 1983b, 327).

Incentive Incompatibility

Alternative organizational forms involve different mechanisms for managing the company and controlling the managers. In almost any enterprise, one or more persons, the principals, engage another person or persons, the agents, to act on their behalf. In the simplest case, the principal delegates some decision-making authority to the agent by means of a contract (Jensen and Meckling 1976). Principals and agents often have conflicting incentives, and such conflicts are controlled at a cost. Agents with more latitude may be more likely to act in their own rather than in the principals' interest. Yet monitoring the agents is costly to the principal. Some organizational forms are likely to be more efficient in monitoring and controlling incentive conflicts among the parties than others. (They may have other advantages as well.)

Conflicts Among Managers, Owner-Risk Bearers, and Policyholders

In the context of insurance, there are not two but three parties of interest: managers (agents), owners-risk bearers (principals), and policyholders (principals).[14] Managers run the business; they set premiums, invest the premium income, market the product, and manage claims and litigation. The owners supply equity capital to the firm and, in turn, have a claim on residual profits, once contingent claims due to the policyholders have been paid. Policyholders pay premiums and, in return, are promised payment in the event that certain specified losses are incurred.

The self-interests of policyholders and owners of the insurance company clearly differ in several respects.[15] Once insured, policyholders may not take the precautions to avoid the loss that they would take without insurance. And once sued, policyholders may not mount a sufficiently vigorous defense, reasoning that they are not liable for amounts below the policy's liability limit. These are problems of moral hazard that arise after insurance is in place. Before insurance is bought, prospective policyholders may know more about their likely future losses than any insurer can know and have a self-interest in concealing the true probability of loss. This is a problem of adverse selection resulting from asymmetry in information between policyholder and insurer about the policyholder. The asymmetry also runs the other way. That is, prospective policyholders may be unable to distinguish among insurers of varying soundness; the insurers, in contrast, are likely to have inside information on their own risk of bankruptcy.

Once the premium has been collected, the owners have an incentive to raise dividends by selling off the firm's assets. But raising dividends lowers the value of the policyholders' contingent claims because the probability increases that the insurer will not be able to honor all of its contingent claims. At the same time, the value of the firm's stock increases, thus benefitting the current equity holders. Further, because third-party insurance policyholders may be unwilling to mount a vigorous defense on their own behalf, provision of legal defense is typically bundled in with third-party insurance. However, once this is done, the insurer will decide how much to spend on legal costs by weighing potential reductions in the indemnity payment against marginal legal expense. The insurer may not consider the costs of time, lost reputation, or psychological harm to the defendant of losing the suit and, for this reason, may underinvest in legal expense. On the other hand, if policyholders paid for defense counsel and anticipated the loss within policy limits, they would see optimal legal expense as the amount at which the marginal cost of legal counsel equaled the marginal benefit denominated in terms of changes in time, personal reputation loss, and "pain and suffering" and in indemnity paid by their insurer.

Responses to Conflicting Incentives

Control mechanisms are available to deal with each of these conflicts in incentives. Normally, cost-sharing provisions, that is, deductibles and coinsurance, are specified to help motivate policyholders to prevent or mitigate losses. Cost sharing is not common in malpractice insurance.[16] Rather, coverage tends to be complete up to the liability limits specified in the policy. This means that the insurer must try to control moral hazard by monitoring, such as by offering risk management programs.

Concerns about incentives of for-profit insurers to dilute the value of the policyholders' contingent liability claims are probably not relevant for malpractice insurance. In contrast to life insurance, professional liability insurance, like other forms of third-party insurance, is sold under relatively short-term contracts. Moreover, some physician-sponsored companies appear to have diluted the value of their own policyholders' claims by paying large dividends prematurely (Owens 1981). However, it is plausible to expect that a physician-sponsored company would be more likely to consider costs to physicians' reputations, as well as the psychological costs of losing in setting defense strategy (Schlesinger and Venezian 1986).

The standard for-profit form may provide a superior framework for overseeing the efficiency of the company's managers. Inefficiently run stock companies may be acquired by another owner who is better at managing or motivating the managers (Fama and Jensen 1983a, 1983b). The other ownership forms have less clear-cut mechanisms for weeding out inefficient owner-monitors. The empirical evidence that stock insurance companies are more efficient is weak at best.[17] Most explanations for the multiplicity of organizational forms relate the costs of structuring, administering, and enforcing contracts (Jensen and Meckling 1976).

Other Differences Among Organizational Forms

According to responses from our Survey of Medical Malpractice Insurers (see the Appendix to Chapter 1, for a description of the survey), loss prevention/risk management monitoring includes on-site audits of practices, physician and office staff seminars, providing individual legal and risk management advice, home study courses, and review of consent forms and protocols. Physician participation was most often voluntary rather than a mandatory prerequisite for coverage. Physician-sponsored companies may have a comparative advantage in monitoring physician behavior via risk management programs and other methods of monitoring. The notion that physician-sponsored companies have a comparative advantage in monitoring and modifying physician behavior has often been asserted (AMA 1985). However, our survey showed that the stock companies engaged in similar risk management as well. We could not determine whether the physician-owned companies were relatively more effective in loss prevention or risk management. Another relevant feature of physician sponsorship is that it gives the individual physician policyholder a financial stake in the company. This factor may mitigate the moral hazard problem as well, though the gain as one of innumerable owners may be small relative to the loss on settlement of a personal claim.

Underwriting is another area where physician-sponsored companies may differ from investor-owned stock companies. Information about variations in physicians' quality and attitudes toward their patients is not well disseminated in the market for physicians' services. In fact, the medical profession has often claimed that all (or virtually all) doctors are excellent. It may be difficult for a for-profit insurer to obtain data on doctor quality, except from its own records. One institutional response is the medical society-sponsored mutual or reciprocal. Physicians do not want to publicize differences in quality among their colleagues, but they themselves can gauge such differences. A second response is the statutorily mandated medical malpractice closed claims data bases, such as exist in Florida and Indiana and are mandated for the United States as a whole under the Health Care Quality Improvement Act of 1986 (P.L. 99–600).

Hansmann (1985) noted that consumer cooperatives often arise in situations in which the seller has a natural monopoly, as farmers may organize a coop to run the only farm implements store in the valley. By gaining ownership in the organization, consumers can seek to avoid monopoly prices. In smaller markets, this may be a reason for rejecting the standard for-profit form in medical malpractice insurance as well.

Having professional liability coverage is vital to modern medicine, for a physician very often cannot secure hospital privileges without it, even if such insurance is not statutorily encouraged or required (Bovbjerg 1989, 516). Physicians obtain an appreciable part of their earnings from inpatient services. Also, physicians unable to admit sick patients to any hospital might experience difficulties attracting patients to their office practices.

Profit-seeking firms will not enter markets that do not offer the owners the prospect of earning competitive returns on equity capital. In competitive markets, this may often mean that a good or service will not be supplied to a market temporarily, that is, until the product price can rise to generate the required return on equity. Physicians cannot afford such swings in availability. Considering the impact of nonavailability of coverage on their practices, physicians are likely to be willing to forgo a competitive return on the equity capital they supply a malpractice insurer in return for assurance that coverage will be continuously available. Of course, the physicians could go to the market and buy a stock insurer. (There are physician-owned stock companies. In most such cases, the state medical society is the dominant stock owner.) But the stock company would be subject to buyout by prospective owners who would not promise continuous coverage to policyholders.

Externalities in certain medical liability insurance functions may also play a role.

As Schlesinger and Venezian (1986) noted, it is difficult to think of situations in which a for-profit insurer in a competitive market would allocate funds to changing the probability of loss before soliciting an insurance purchase. Such activities, such as ferreting out incompetent physicians or identifying medical or surgical procedures likely to result in claims, have the character of a public good. That is, it would be difficult to keep any competing insurer (and its policyholders) from benefiting from such investments. By contrast, a monopolistic insurer would be able to reap the full return from such public investment. Nonprofit insurers, especially those affiliated with such broad-based organizations as medical societies, may not be as concerned about spillovers to competing insurers, since physician members stand to benefit from re-duced premiums.

Alternatively, physician-sponsored companies may instead be more willing than other owners to continue to sell insurance to physicians with bad malpractice records, even if this means forgoing some profit. After all, to the extent that the legal system is random or unfair to physicians, as the latter often allege, any physician might establish a bad record and be denied coverage on favorable terms by a profit-seeking insurer.

Alternative Ownership Forms

Stock Companies

The stock company provides the benchmark against which the other organizational forms may be compared.[18] The functions of owner-risk bearer, manager, and policy-holder are separate. Inefficient firms may be bought out by others that can make money by improving the firm's performance.

Conflicting incentives between equityholders and managers can be controlled by tying the manager's pay to the performance of the company's stock, appointing some of the managers to the company's board, promoting and increasing the salaries of the good-performing managers, and/or placing restrictions in the company charter to limit managerial discretion (Smith 1986). The main control mechanism over the incentive incompatibility problem between equityholders and policyholders is the possibility that policyholders may pay lower premiums to insurers that are likely to depress the value of the policyholders' contingent claims after the insurance purchase is made.

Two types of stock insurers sell medical malpractice insurance: commercial stock and physician owned. The former are multiple-line insurers with publicly marketed equity. The latter have been organized by medical societies and are single-line, medical malpractice insurers, typically operating in a single state.

Mutuals

In the mutual form, the roles of policyholder and owner are merged. The policyholders supply capital to the insurance company. Policyholders thus are given a say in company financial policies during the time their policies are in force. Incentive conflicts between owners and policyholders are eliminated, but perhaps the actions of managers cannot be monitored as well. One potentially important control mechanism, buyout of ineffi-cient organizations by others, present in the stock form, is eliminated: Physician-owned mutual companies do not appear to be subject to buyout. But physician mutual policyholder-owners are as well motivated as equityholders to vote a change in directors and officers of the firm, perhaps more so, for they suffer from bad management twice—once as policyholders and again as residual claimants to surplus.

Reciprocals

Reciprocal insurers resemble mutuals, with two major differences. First, a reciprocal is unincorporated, and the organization itself owns no capital. A separate account is held in the name of each subscriber. Premiums paid plus interest earned are credited to this account. The subscriber's share of losses and expenses is debited to the account. In effect, the reciprocal performs a pooling arrangement among independent subscribers who, in effect, band together to insure one another. By contrast, a mutual is incorporated with a stated capital and surplus.

Second, the policyholders of the reciprocal appoint an individual or corporation as an "attorney in fact" to manage the organization, with an advisory committee to provide some oversight over management. The board of directors has responsibility for management oversight in a mutual. In some cases, reciprocals have been organized by the attorneys in fact. In some reciprocals, policyholders can control management by their ability to withdraw their contribution to surplus, or policyholders as a group can threaten to force dissolution of the association by taking legal action.

Trusts

A trust resembles a reciprocal in that it is not incorporated. The major difference is that, technically, members are assessed after expenses, including policyholder claims, are incurred. Trusts typically do not pay taxes, but they also are not eligible to participate in a state's guaranty fund. Potential manager-policyholder conflict could be solved in the same way reciprocals handle problems.

Lloyd's Associations

A Lloyd's Association is like a reciprocal in that the organization issues no policies, but rather serves as a mechanism for members to insure themselves or others. A difference between a Lloyd's Association and a reciprocal is that, in the latter, all members insure one another. A Lloyd's Association insures outsiders. In the medical malpractice field, this form is used only for reinsurance.

Risk Retention Groups

Risk retention groups are not insurance companies, but they provide a mechanism for obtaining insurance. Groups of similar physicians (e.g., anesthesiologists), purchase coverage from an existing carrier. If there are conflicts with the managers, the group can obtain insurance through another company.

Joint Underwriting Associations

As a reaction to the malpractice insurance crisis of the mid-1970s, many states authorized joint underwriting associations (JUAs) as a standby on a mandatory basis (Bovbjerg 1989, 514–15). In 1987, 13 medical malpractice JUAs were offering coverage to health care providers. The 10 active JUA's in existence for more than a couple of years have market shares ranging from 3 to 80 percent (Kenney 1986). Where operational, JUAs require participation by at least all insurers that write medical malpractice insurance and frequently by all property-liability insurers that write insurance in the state. The purpose of these organizations is to be the insurer of last resort—that is, to cover providers who cannot obtain coverage from other sources. One carrier operates the pool on behalf of the state, collecting premiums and paying claims. JUAs operate as mandatory assigned risk pools similar to risk pools established for automobile insurance. As documented in Chapter 4, the JUAs insure a substantial proportion of physicians in a few states. As of 1988, 12 JUAs offered coverage to health care providers (Crane 1988).

If JUA premium income is insufficient to cover losses and expenses, each member company is assessed pro rata to make up the shortfall. To this extent, there is an enforced cross-subsidy that, in competitive insurance markets, must be recovered from the insurer members' customers in some way. The cross-subsidy introduces another "residual claimant," namely, the beneficiary of the cross-subsidy. This claimant is paid before the owners of member insurers. Suppliers of equity to a stock company will not want to supply capital for less than the competitive, risk-adjusted rate of return. Thus, the cross-subsidy must be reflected in higher premiums to regular customers, who in a state with a JUA have no regularly insured source of coverage that does not bear the "JUA tax." In the case of mutuals or reciprocals, the policyholder and equity holder roles are combined. Then it is the combined policyholder-equity holder that bears the tax. Since the tax is typically spread over many types of insurance, most of the burden is borne by the public at large.

The stated purpose of JUAs is to assure availability of malpractice insurance coverage to health care providers at "affordable levels" (U.S. DHHS) 1987, 148). Thus, by design, the JUA often sets premiums below what the market will bear. Premiums are monitored by a combination of "pressure from physicians" and premium regulation (Crane 1988). In states where JUAs have become major malpractice insurers, it appears that physicians have taken advantage of an enforced cross-premium subsidy. Most JUAs are not allowed to withdraw from the market even in response to rate denials by the state insurance department. As of 1986, a number of JUAs had serious deficiencies in their reserves (Kenney 1988).

Patient Compensation Funds

Several states have set limits per year and per claim on the amount of liability a health care provider can incur. Compensation in excess of the limit is provided by a state-operated patient compensation fund (PCF). Funding for the PCF typically comes from a surcharge on malpractice insurance premiums, as in Indiana, or from general state revenues, such as in Kansas (U.S. DHHS 1987, 149). In some states, the PCF's liability is limited, but in others, it is open-ended. This is another mechanism for indirectly cross-subsidizing physicians with relatively high claims costs. Several PCFs have had difficulty maintaining solvency, and states appear to be moving away from the PCF approach (U.S. DHHS 1987, 149).

CYCLES IN PREMIUMS, PROFITS, AND SUPPLY

Medical malpractice insurance crises have occurred on a fairly regular basis. By some counts, the mid-1980s' crisis was the fourth since the 1950s (see Chapter 1). At these times, insurers report financial difficulties—inadequate reserves and profits. They then raise premiums or, alternatively, withdraw or at least threaten to withdraw from the market. Health care providers react with outcries that premiums are too high or that coverage is unavailable. Regulators and reformers are mobilized. Some combination of factors thereafter returns insurance to normal—higher premiums, changes in underlying losses or better prediction of them, changes in liability law or practice or in insurer loss control, shifting competition or increased supply of coverage, and even the mere passage of time. The market then shifts from tight to loose, with coverage becoming more available at lower prices.

Similar, seemingly periodic crises occur in the property-liability insurance industry more generally (Harrington and Litan 1988). Their causes are not well understood; there is far more agreement that cycles of "soft" and "hard" insurance markets occur than there is about why they occur. Winter (1988a) identified several phenomena that coincide at the peak of a crisis in property-liability insurance premiums and availability: increase in premiums, higher industry profits, and decline in insurance transactions particularly concentrated in some lines.

Several theories seek to explain insurance cycles. These include recoupment of loss on investments, competition among oligopolistic insurers, loss forecasting errors, lags attributable to regulation, and variations in capacity caused by unanticipated underwriting losses.

Recoupment of Loss on Investments

One argument is that malpractice insurers have periodically attempted to recoup their investment losses by raising premiums. Cycles in the stock market affecting returns on many investments are thus reflected in cycles in malpractice insurance premiums.

Although superficially plausible, this argument has important weaknesses. As seen above, investment returns are systematically related to underwriting profits and hence to premiums. However, the relevant investment returns for computing premiums are anticipated or ex ante returns, not returns earned ex post. An insurer operating in a competitive market for insurance would be prevented by market pressures from raising premiums to recoup profits. An insurer desiring to recoup past losses through premium increases would probably be undercut by competitors that base premiums partly on expected investment returns. There is even a question of whether a monopolistic insurer would do this, since one would expect such an insurer to exploit its market power irrespective of the conditions in the stock market. Changes in interest rates would then affect the size of realized monopoly profits but not the premium charges to policyholders. Admittedly, a state regulator might view a requested rate increase more favorably following a stock market downturn.

Danzon (1985) came to the same conclusion: that stock market losses should not create premium increases. She presented a number of other interesting hypotheses about the potential impact of financial factors on cycles. One explanation she considered for the rise in premiums in the mid-1970s was the increase in the volatility of both underwriting and investment returns and the increased covariance between the two types of returns. An increased covariance, that is, an increase in nondiversifiable risk, could explain an increase in premiums and an insurer's exit from a market in which a state regulatory authority denied its request for higher premiums. Danzon asserted, but did not really show, that nondiversifiable risk to insurers increased in the early 1970s. Further, to the extent that covariance among policyholder losses made diversification more difficult, insurers would typically desire to maintain higher surplus and a more liquid investment portfolio. Increased risk provides a more plausible explanation of a one-time boost in premiums than for cycles.[19]

Competition Among Oligopolists

Nye and Hofflander (1987, 502) attributed the recurrent crises in medical malpractice insurance to the "inherent oligopolistic structure of the medical malpractice insurance market." They applied their argument specifically to Pennsylvania but suggested more general application.

These are the essential elements of their argument: Physician demand for malpractice insurance is highly inelastic. This means that the industry's demand curve for such insurance is highly inelastic. However, the demand curve of the individual medical malpractice insurer is likely to be highly elastic. Nye and Hofflander did not present empirical evidence that demand curves facing individual insurers are elastic, but it is plausible that they are. Physicians can and do change companies. This means that an individual firm cannot charge a higher premium than its competitors.

Firms, Nye and Hofflander alleged, with better service, such as a "we fight claims" reputation (p. 507), can charge a little more, but not that much more. They further asserted that insurers operate under constant returns to scale.[20] Insurers may be inhibited from selling more policies by lack of sufficient policyholders' surplus (such as St. Paul in the 1980s), but this is often not a constraint. Barriers to entry into the malpractice market from firms already offering other types of property-liability insurance are extremely low. And because of the long claims tail, a new firm offering low premiums could easily enter the malpractice insurance market and be financially viable (on the basis of short-term cash flow) for a few years until it reached the tail of early-year claims. Given the ease of entry and constant returns to scale, the inelastic industry demand curve, and the malpractice insurance industry's small size, any single firm could easily dominate a given market. This can set the stage for oligopolistic pricing.

Any insurer that raises premiums above the levels of its competitors will lose all of its customers. However, any insurer that lowers premiums without a price response from its competitors would attract a large number of new policyholders. To avoid losing market share, any price cut by one competitor will be met by the others. Price may be sticky and insurers realize profits in excess of competitive levels for a while, but one firm (possibly an entrant) eventually cuts its price. The net effect of a price war is no change in market shares but a reduction in premium levels. When the insurers realize they are headed for bankruptcy, they raise premiums approximately in concert. Industry demand is inelastic, and few physicians drop their coverage in the face of the dramatic price increase.

The authors presented some evidence to support the view that a premium rate cycle has existed in Pennsylvania. But while the patterns they observed are consistent with a cycle, they did not demonstrate convincingly that the above pricing scenario was the cause.

Loss Forecast Errors

Venezian (1985) attributed cycles in premiums and profitability in part to the way insurers forecast future losses. He argued that insurers use a naive trend extrapolation model in which extrapolations of trends in past claim costs are used to predict the future course of claims costs (see Chapters 6 and 7 for discussions of the "chain ladder method," which is an extrapolation method). Venezian showed theoretically that this extrapolation procedure can generate a profit cycle of the type that has been observed.

Cummins and Outreville (1987) criticized Venezian's approach on the ground that it implied a degree of irrationality on the part of insurers. In other words, they questioned Venezian's assumption that insurers predict losses based on historical trends alone and do not properly consider other pertinent, current information that they properly use for forecasting losses.

Harrington and Litan (1988) concluded that the 1980s' increase in property-liability premiums was due to growth in the discounted value of future losses. Not only did claims costs rise, but this increase was also aggravated by a fall in interest rates since the early 1980s. The premium increases were severe because insurers failed to anticipate the magnitude of these changes. This explanation may account for a one-time change, but unless patterns in loss growth and interest rates are cyclical, it does not account adequately for cycles in premiums and profitability.

Regulatory Lags

Cummins and Outreville specified a model based on the "rational expectations" assumption underlying much modern research in macroeconomics (Sargent 1987). According to this model, insurers use all pertinent information available at the time the loss prediction is made, not merely actuarial projections from a long baseline. Their model produced insurer profit cycles in the presence of "institutional and regulatory lags," such as are introduced by the lengthy process of rate making and rate regulation. The amplitude and length of such cycles must be determined empirically. Using data from property-liability insurers in 13 industrialized countries, the authors found cycles in each country, with lengths of about six to eight years. As in the Venezian study, their empirical analysis (using a "reduced form" equation) did not establish causality. Rather, the study showed that cycles do not depend on the assumption of insurer irrationality (which may be a valid assumption).

Capacity Constraints

Winter (1988a, 1988b, 1988c, 1989) has offered the most comprehensive explanation of cycles in insurance markets to date. He emphasized that a complete model of the cycle must explain a crisis both in premiums and in availability and why the crisis in availability is particularly severe in some lines. It is noteworthy that the most recent medical malpractice insurance crisis, which occurred during the mid-1980s, was in premiums but not in availability of coverage. As documented in Chapter 4, the physician-sponsored companies have exhibited a lot of staying power, and by the mid-1980s they were well established in this market. Winter focused exclusively on stock insurers and excluded reinsurance from his model.

Winter argued that the amount of insurance an insurer can write is constrained by its net worth (surplus). In a perfect capital market, insurers could issue additional equity at zero opportunity cost, but issuing new equity is not costless because of extra taxation on corporate investment earnings (double taxation of dividends) and because agency costs increase with higher net worth. Relative to issuing external equity, internally generated equity from retained earnings is a relatively low-cost source of capital (Auerbach 1983; Myers 1984).

In his model, the quantity and the price (premium) of insurance are determined at the intersection of the demand and supply curves of insurance. The insurer's short-run (when equity is fixed) supply curve is relatively elastic at low levels of output but becomes inelastic as capacity is reached. A random unanticipated increase in losses is a shock to capacity and shifts the supply curve to the left, making intersection in the inelastic region more likely and causing premiums to rise. Thus, just before the crisis hits, one should see an increase in losses, a drop in surplus, and an increase in the number of insurer insolvencies. Associated with the premium increase at the height of the crisis is an increase in profitability, including a decrease in the ratio of the expected present value of claims and associated expenses to premiums. Winter presented empirical evidence showing that this ratio for property-liability insurers reached low points in about 1960, 1966, 1976, and 1985—all years in which property-casualty insurance markets were tight.

Relatively uncertain (volatile) lines of coverage must be covered with relatively large amounts of surplus. When insurers' capacity is high, that is, when capacity is basically unconstrained, uncertain lines are allocated comparatively more capacity in relation to premium volume. When capacity is very low, the uncertain (capacity-using) lines are allocated the least capacity. At the same time, one observes withdrawal from those lines or less withdrawal coupled with steep premium increases. By contrast, premiums in relatively predictable lines, such as automobile liability, remain fairly stable. Although Winter's explanation is plausible, there is room for additional empirical verification of his conceptual argument.

The notion of capacity constraints is even more plausible in a market highly populated by nonstock and closely held stock companies that do not have access to public equity markets. Such insurers are wholly dependent on internally generated equity as a source of equity capital and, following an exogenous unanticipated increase in losses, have no alternative to premium increases as a way of replacing depleted surplus. Since medical malpractice is a relatively unpredictable line, it was particularly subject to fluctuations in price and availability. By running their own companies, medical providers could at least assure availability of coverage.

CONCLUSION

This chapter has set the stage for the more detailed empirical and other analyses presented in the following chapters. Malpractice coverage features a number of institutional reactions to the unique characteristics of medical malpractice insurance markets in particular and of the property-liability insurance industry of which malpractice insurance is a line. These features—single-line physician insurers, partly regulated entry and prices, and others—must be explained if the performance of medical malpractice insurers is to be understood.

NOTES

1. An appreciable share of physicians' earnings come from their hospital practices (Sloan 1984), and 70 percent or more of claims come from hospital incidents (NAIC 1980; U.S. GAO 1986a).
2. California's medical society-based insurers uniquely divide the state north and south along county lines.
3. For instance, the Utah Medical Insurance Association sells policies in Montana. Initially, the PIAA, the companies' trade association, accepted for membership only medical society-sponsored plans. The rule subsequently changed, but society plans still predominate. These practices have implications for market conduct (Chapter 4).
4. Profit maximization is often not recognized as the motivator of the for-profit insurer. More complex assumptions are made, such as that a risk-averse insurer seeks to maximize expected utility or minimize the probability of ruin (Borch 1974; Goovaerts et al. 1984). However, even if some of the parties, in particular the insured, are risk averse, it is not clear that an insurer should be any more risk averse than other for-profit enterprises.
5. In a perfectly competitive market, the value of the policyholder's contingent claim, the promissory note to pay in the event that a covered adverse outcome occurs, varies directly with the probability that the insurer will be able to satisfy its obligations to policyholders. But policyholders may be unable to gauge insurer bankruptcy risk accurately, and premiums may not be systematically lower when insurer bankruptcy risk is higher.
6. Among the deficiencies of the CAPM are instability in the betas and large confidence intervals around beta estimates (see, e.g., Cummins and Harrington 1985) and inability to reliably explain variations in returns of stock insurers (Cummins and Harrington 1988).

   One major criticism of the CAPM is that investors cannot fully diversify, as the CAPM assumes. Levy (1978, 1980) developed a generalized capital asset pricing model (GCAPM) to be applied to investors holding imperfectly diversified portfolios as a special case. Cox and Griepentrog (1988) used data from a sample of 21 property-liability insurers to compute GCAPM betas and fair underwriting profit rates. Results depended in part on the share of the portfolio assumed to be well diversified. Not surprisingly, imperfect diversification resulted in a higher underwriting risk.

   Aug and Lai (1987) developed another generalization of the CAPM for determining fair insurance premiums.
7. A parallel argument cannot be made for policyholders. Purchasers of insurance are by definition risk averse and incompletely diversified; otherwise, they would self-insure.
8. Kimball and Denenberg (1969, 185) listed some additional purposes of reinsurance: "Avoiding violent swings in underwriting experience which, though well within the insurer's financial capacity, might shake the confidence of investors and the public, hence stabilizing operating results and avoiding surplus fluctuations. . . . Preserving surplus by the early recovery of prepaid expenses. An insurer can write a larger volume of business than its surplus would normally permit by sharing with the reinsurer the burden of the unearned premium reserve, hence reducing surplus depletion. . . . Sharing the risk when a company enters a new or unfamiliar line of business. An inexperienced company can draw on the knowledge, as well as the surplus, of a reinsurer."
9. This point is discussed by Cooper (1974, 32–34) and Bachman (1978, 32–35).
10. See Bachman (1978, 65–74) for a further discussion of this point.
11. See Sloan (1990).
12. See, for example, Grace (1990), Troxel and Breslin (1983, 105), and Weiss (1985).
13. Physician-owned companies currently write more than half of the physician malpractice premiums in the United States. Data in Table 2.2 show that, in 1989, mutuals and recipro-

cals wrote 45 percent of medical malpractice coverage. There is no inconsistency here. First, some of the physician-owned companies are organized as stock companies. Second, malpractice insurance is sold to physicians, hospitals, dentists, pharmacists, nurse anesthetists, clinics, and so on. And many of the nonphysician purchasers of malpractice insurance obtain their insurance from stock companies.

14. More realistically, there are also debt holders, but we shall not consider this class in order to focus on the special features of insurance.

15. See Mayers and Smith (1981) for further discussion of some of these issues.

16. There are two reasons that malpractice insurance is complete. First, small cases that would not otherwise be reported may unexpectedly (from the policyholder's perspective) turn into big cases if the proper actions are not taken at the outset. Hence, the insurer has an incentive in having each potential claim reported. Second, information on the probability that a claim will be filed against a physician may be costly for the insurer to obtain. Even a small claim may be predictive, and therefore, the insurer wants to know about it.

17. See Chapter 4 for empirical evidence.

18. See Smith (1986) and Mayers and Smith (1987) for a further description of the various ownership forms. This discussion of stock insurers, mutuals, and reciprocals is based on theirs.

19. In fact, Danzon's analysis concentrated on the malpractice insurance increases of the 1970s rather than on cycles.

20. They based this contention on results of cost studies from the larger property-liability insurance industry and the observation that very small firms appear to compete over the long term with much larger ones.

3

Regulation and Its Effects

REGULATION AND COMPETITION

Among insurers, it is an article of faith that theirs is a heavily regulated (and taxed) industry. And so it is, in many ways. Among consumer advocates, it is an article of faith that most regulations codify industry preferences and that most regulators barely scratch the surface of insurers' behavior, so that much stronger regulation is needed. And so they do, in other ways.

The practical result is an evolving mix of competition and regulation across different spheres of operations, and over time, as different influences wax and wane. An unusual feature of the malpractice marketplace is the recent rise to dominance of provider-sponsored insurers (Chapters 1, 2). Along with self-insurance, this leading role for the insureds themselves creates a kind of private regulation in the interests of dominant professionals. Primary insurers must also answer to their reinsurers (Chapter 5), who have a strong interest in many aspects of primary insurers' practices. Market competition and the duty to shareholders (especially in physician-sponsored companies) are also strong forces. To what extent regulatory versus other factors affect insurance practice is a major policy issue.

By tradition and by act of Congress, the states regulate the business of insurance, and the industry is largely exempted from procompetitive antitrust regulation. In underwriting and sales, claims settlement, and even rate making, coverage for medical malpractice is predominantly local. In financing, risk pooling, and investment management, however, the business is more national and (for reinsurance) international. So there is a coherent argument for some national oversight. Periodically in Washington, D.C., a continuing debate surfaces about whether national regulation should be imposed or the antitrust enforcers unleashed (e.g., U.S. Department of Justice 1977; Crenshaw 1990). But little has yet come of the continuing arguments, so the business of regulation remains a state enterprise, and this chapter focuses on the states.

CHAPTER OVERVIEW

The next section of this chapter describes the history of insurance regulation. How did we get where we are? What roles are played by different levels of government? We next discuss the goals, methods, and structures of regulation in the third section. In implementing its goals, what forms does regulation take? What developments are of particular importance to the malpractice line? Thereafter, the fourth section considers different perspectives on regulatory performance and effects. In the fifth section, we discuss relevant past analyses of regulation and the evidence on malpractice insurance developed by this project. What explains regulatory behavior? What effects do various types of regulation have on industry practice and outcomes relative to other influences? Our Survey of Medical Malpractice Insurers was particularly helpful here. The sixth section discusses where the locus of responsibility for dealing with regulatory agencies lies within the companies. The conclusion is given in the seventh section. The two largest issues discussed in the chapter are how much difference regulation may make to the operation of the malpractice insurance market and to what extent regulation treats different forms of insurers differently.

A BRIEF HISTORY OF INSURANCE REGULATION

The Early Development of Regulatory Authority

Insurance regulation first arose almost simultaneously with insurance itself. Both can be traced back to the Renaissance, where policies were first written in the 1300s in the city-states of Genoa, Florence, and Pisa; the earliest extant policy was written in 1347 (Patterson 1927, 574ff). By the end of the century, regulation had also appeared as Genoa banned insurance of the safe arrival of foreign ships on the ground that the mechanism was frequently used for gambling—an early "anchor pool." Florence was the first to create a specialized agency to oversee insurance transactions based on a 1523 statute. Two centuries later, in the New World, fire insurance was first tried in North America in 1721, but failed. Philadelphia saw the first success in 1752; its fire insurance associations not only covered fire damage but also fought fires, as admirers of Benjamin Franklin will recall. The Insurance Company of North America (INA), still a leading property-casualty writer, was founded in Philadelphia in 1794.

Initially, insurance regulation occurred through legislation. Statutes granted original charters to companies, also setting some requirements, such as financial periodic reports. Its goals are said to have been (1) to protect the public, (2) to protect American companies from formerly dominant British insurers, and (3) to raise revenue—through the sale of licenses and taxes on premiums (U.S. GAO 1979, 5–6). But there was no ongoing oversight of insurers' operations.

Continuing exercise of regulatory authority seems to date from 1851. In that year, New Hampshire created the first regulatory body, a full-time board of insurance commissioners. More commonly, however, states used part-time boards composed of other state officials serving ex officio, following the example of Massachusetts' board, established in 1852. In 1859, New York created the first permanent, separate administrative agency with broad administrative powers. The National Association of Insurance Commissioners (NAIC) was founded in 1871, with the goals of promoting uniformity in state practice, disseminating information among regulators, protecting policyholders, and preserving regulation as a state activity. By 1919, 36 states had permanent administrative agencies. But truly extensive state involvement came only after the next world war, marked by more specific delineation of state authority, in the wake of the federal McCarran-Ferguson Act (see Dobbyn 1981, 253–65, for a good brief history).

Early Legal Developments

In early America, state power over insurance was simply accepted as part of basic state sovereignty. State regulation of insurance was upheld by the U.S. Supreme Court in *Paul v. Virginia* (1868), holding that issuing a policy of insurance is not a "transaction of commerce," (p. 183), so that state authority is not federally preempted under the Commerce Clause of the U.S. Constitution.[1] Early regulation, however, was not very extensive, as already noted.

In the key area of rate setting, property-casualty regulation responded to developments in fire insurance, the line where insurers first learned to underwrite casualty risk. Early fire insurers were wholly dependent on independent agents to market their product, and rates were often virtually dictated to companies by agents (Wandel 1935, 11). No broad-based pool of information was available to assist in underwriting, classification of risks, or setting of rates. This lack left companies vulnerable to arbitrarily set rate structures, to rate wars, and to insolvency in the event of a conflagration (NAIC 1974). Some insurers entered compacts to fix prices and agents' commissions, but these generally failed, as competition undercut the fixed schedules, and some states legislated against such concerted activity. Areawide rating bureaus also grew up in the late 1800s, especially after disastrous fires in Chicago in 1871 and in Philadelphia the following year. State regulatory authority was presumed (given the *Paul* decision), but actual oversight was slow to emerge. The main regulatory consequence was that the rating bureaus were thought to be exempt from federal authority, including antitrust laws against anticompetitive collusion enacted in the 1890s. Some states became concerned about inadequate rates in open competition, which they saw as threatening insurer solvency. In 1911 a New York legislative committee recommended state-overseen joint rate making, and the U.S. Supreme Court soon recognized state commissioners' power to regulate rates (*German Alliance Insurance Co.* 1914).

State Authority in the Current Era

The current era of regulatory authority dates from the *Southeast Underwriters* decision (1944). In this landmark case, the U.S. Supreme Court overturned the *Paul* precedent, holding that insurance is commerce. Then, on antitrust grounds, the Court invalidated joint price setting by 198 member companies of a private rating bureau for six southeastern states, which had 90 percent of the fire and allied lines insurance. The decision also called into question the power of states to tax and regulate insurance more generally. Congress responded promptly by enacting the McCarran-Ferguson Act (1945). McCarran-Ferguson reinstituted state authority to regulate insurance and continued to insulate the business of insurance from antitrust law, but only to the extent that it is state regulated.[2] States quickly moved to some form of regulatory authority over rate making, typically following the NAIC model for statute and accompanying regulation.

There has been some narrowing of the federal antitrust exemption,[3] and federal lawmakers have acted to ease risk pooling outside the conventional scope of state regulation (P.L. 97–45 1981). Further federal action always remains possible,[4] but by and large, insurance remains regulated by state administrative agencies, outside the procompetitive ambit of federal antitrust law, and subject to federal regulation only through tax provisions.

GOALS, METHODS, AND STRUCTURE OF REGULATION

Goals of Regulation

The rationales for regulation have often been discussed, with commentators giving various typologies of regulatory goals (e.g., Kimball 1961; Mehr and Cammack 1980; Pauly et al. 1986). Four goals dominate: (1) maintain insurers' solvency; (2) keep premiums at reasonable rates; (3) assure availability; and (4) secure information and fair play for consumers. (Such descriptions of goals implicitly assume that regulators are interested in the public.) This subsection discusses each of these four goals in turn. The following subsection discusses the methods of regulation, using the same fourfold typology.

Solvency

Historically, the first and still the overriding goal of regulation is to assure the solvency of insurers. Policyholders pay premiums up front in the expectation that any future claims they may bring will be covered, and states have taken a number of steps to help ensure that funds will be available to pay claims as needed. If insurers become insolvent for whatever reason, they will fail in their obligations not only to stockholders (like any other unsuccessful firm) but also to policyholders, whose very purpose in purchasing a policy was to avoid risk. In general, regulation aims to protect consumers rather than investors, but safeguards affect the risks faced by both types of claimants on insurers' funds.

In policy terms, the main justification for regulatory intervention is consumer ignorance. Private monitors of insurers' financial status exist, for Moodys and Bests both rate insurance companies' creditworthiness. But such services mainly serve investors, who want assessments of a company's prospects in insurance, just as in any other investment that carries a risk. Consumer-policyholders can, of course, also check an insurer's rating before buying a policy; indeed, insurance advertising sometimes mentions a high rating, and so does *Consumer Reports*.

Yet such information is considered insufficient protection for policyholders, who buy insurance not to take a risk in exchange for a return on investment, but rather to reduce their risk of financial loss. Policyholders are seen as being unable to understand insurance risks. Moreover, insurance is an unusual consumption good; not only do the insurance services occur long after purchase, but policyholders generally hope never to have recourse to them. Under such circumstances, policyholders can find it difficult to judge the merits of insurance policies and likely future claims service. In short, the cost of obtaining adequate information about the probability of default is high for most individual consumers. Unregulated private markets could address such issues by providing this information in understandable and convenient forms, but the traditional social consensus has been that consumers should be able to act with confidence in the financial soundness of insurers, much as with banks, with a public guarantee that future claims will be met (e.g., Fischer 1968).

Concerns about solvency underlie regulatory strictures at many stages of companies' operations. Regulators want insurers to start with enough money, to charge high enough rates for the risks underwritten, to have enough capital to back up their coverage written, to maintain adequate reserves for future claims payments, and to contribute to a state backup fund to protect policyholders should all of the above prove inadequate. The steps taken to achieve solvency goals are discussed in the next subsection. Of course, regulators may have standards that are too high as well as too low, which could inhibit entry of other carriers.

Reasonable Rates
Although concern about solvency remains the bedrock of regulation, foremost among other goals is fair premiums for policyholders (Chapter 9). Whereas for solvency purposes both companies and regulators are concerned that rates be adequate to meet future claims, the converse is also a problem—assuring that insurers do not take advantage of policyholders by charging excessive rates. As already noted, concerns about overcharging underlay turn-of-the-century expansions of regulatory authority. Concerns that private rating bureaus setting premiums in concert could hurt consumers underlay the Southeast Underwriters' holding that antitrust law could examine price setting, and Congress in McCarran-Ferguson reestablished the antitrust exemption only to the extent that a state regulates its insurers.[5]

Again here, consumer ignorance is a key rationale for regulatory intervention. It is often thought that insurance policies are too technical for consumers to understand and that the multiplicity of policies available, sometimes with confusing minor variations among them, makes price comparisons very difficult. Many agents work exclusively for one company (although independent agents do not), which further increases search costs for physicians. On the other hand, "direct marketers" that do not use agents at all have also found a market niche, in malpractice coverage and other lines, which indicates that some consumers feel able to shop on their own, understanding insurance choices without an agent (NAIC 1974, vol. 1, 68). To what extent public oversight should rely on market competition to determine prices, for example, rather than on active or threatened regulatory review remains an active debate today (see Chapter 7).

Availability
Other regulations seek to assure that insurance is readily available to consumers. There is said to be a social interest in a healthy insurance market, which can help people feel more secure in taking certain risks in their business or personal life. Some types of insurance are seen as essential to socially valued undertakings—including the delivery of medical services. In particular, physicians' malpractice insurance is frequently required or strongly encouraged by law (Bovbjerg 1989) or by hospitals as a condition of physicians' admitting privileges (Chapter 1). For these reasons, legislators and regulators have sometimes intervened to try to keep insurance available. The tendency of competitive markets to exclude some potential policyholders as bad risks has drawn particular attention, especially in automobile insurance but in malpractice as well.

Information and Fair Play
Actual or potential discrimination in risk classification and other insurance matters is another policy concern first raised in the last century but addressed most vigorously in more recent years. In rate review, for instance, commissioners are enjoined not to allow premiums that are "unfairly discriminatory" (NAIC 1985). Many other forms of consumer protection have also become common (NAIC 1985). Departments are particularly concerned about avoiding misinformation and fraud by companies or agents. Some-

times particular groups of consumers are singled out for special concern—including, for instance, family farmers, small business, and physicians (U.S. GAO 1979).

Other Goals

Finally, other purposes can also be cited for insurance regulation. One is raising revenue for the state. Most notably, states almost universally place a tax on gross insurance premiums—in addition to whatever corporate income or franchise tax may apply (Commerce Clearing House 1987). Taxes may be held necessary to finance regulation, but are seldom earmarked for regulatory purposes, and collections far exceed insurance department spending (U.S. GAO 1979, 22–23).[6]

Methods of Insurance Regulation

Regulators take many steps to meet the four goals discussed above. Again here, many different typologies of insurance functions exist (see Box 3.1), but the fourfold division serves well.

Solvency

Various regulatory provisions address solvency, accentuating the normal, prudent business practice of insurance companies. Licensure is typically required before an insurer can sell policies in a state. Agents are also licensed, so entry to the insurance business is controlled, although in practice just what activities bring an insurer within a state's regulatory reach is a major legal issue. To be licensed, insurers must conform to various formal requirements, most notably that they meet standards of minimum capi-

---

Box 3.1. Typologies of Insurance Regulatory Functions

As is often the case with typologies, many competing versions of this one exist. A simple-minded one is to note the standard administrative or operating divisions of insurance departments. These include company licensing and taxation, financial regulation, agency licensing, policy form review, rate regulation, market conduct regulation, and general administration. Any number of temporary or permanent specialized units may, of course, be formed—to handle complaints, to create licensure standards for a new form of insurer (such as HMOs in the 1970s on the life-health side), or to rewrite regulations deemed outmoded.

Another approach is to consider the goals for which these functions are undertaken. Finsinger and Pauly (1986) developed a categorization that successfully applies across lines of insurance and across countries:

(1) regulations which specify the character of the insurance contract; (2) regulations which put lower limits on the amount or composition of reserves against losses; (3) regulations which set maximum and minimum prices; (4) regulations covering the treatment of applicants for insurance whom insurers may be unwilling to cover at their current prices; (5) regulations covering entry of new firms (other than solvency regulation); [and] (6) regulations associated with the presence of public enterprises in the market.

talization. Thus, insurers have a financial cushion available to pay claims beyond those expected in setting premium rates.

Also to maintain adequate funding of future claims, regulation often requires that insurers set "adequate" premiums, that is, ones deemed capable of paying projected future claims. Various forms of oversight of premiums exist, as is considered at greater length below. Regulators also often require that an insurer's premium-to-surplus ratio not exceed a certain maximum level, say, annual premiums not more than two or three times surplus. Thus, if claims' payments ultimately do exceed funds set aside from premiums to pay them, shareholders' (or policyholders') surplus can be drawn down to avoid insolvency. To similar effect is the common rule that the maximum policy limits sold annually in a state may not exceed a certain share of total premium income, often 10 percent. No one claim can then decimate the insurer's resources.

Once received, premiums must be carefully husbanded for future claims. Special reserving requirements mandate that insurers maintain separate accounts or financial reserves against future contingencies. Because premiums are paid in advance of the period during which a risk is covered, premiums are not fully earned until the period ends—before which time an insurer must maintain at least part of the funds in "premium reserves." Once earned, an appropriate share of premiums must be put in "loss reserves" against the anticipated level of future claims (Troxel and Breslin 1983).

Regulations on the investment of reserves call for conservative investment (for example, in low-risk bonds rather than common stocks), and regulators monitor the value of assets maintained in reserve.[7] Moreover, the industry's traditional practice of valuing reserves, sometimes codified in regulation, called for claims to be reserved at their full anticipated amounts, regardless of how far into the future they were expected to be paid. That is, claims reserves were most often not discounted to present value. Again, this is extremely conservative practice, one supported by the industry (NAIC 1983). Since passage of the federal Tax Reform Act of 1986, discounting has been required for federal tax purposes. How to discount reserves or, alternatively, how to recognize investment earnings on reserves has been a major regulatory issue in recent years (see Chapters 7 and 9). Traditional rules on the valuation of assets have also been quite conservative.

Many solvency requirements are enforced in the first instance by reporting requirements. Companies must file regular financial reports with insurance departments. These "annual statement" data are published by the A.M. Best Company and form a major source of information for this study (Chapter 1). A commissioner can also require special information from an insurer. Insurance departments also undertake ongoing financial surveillance through fiscal examinations or audits of companies, both routinely and on a targeted basis. Where a threat to solvency is detected, closer monitoring may be implemented or other corrective action taken. An insurer found to be insolvent may be put into receivership and operated by the receiver or liquidated in an orderly fashion, with assets used to pay policyholders' claims. Debt holders and shareholders are paid only after primary obligations to policyholders are discharged.

Beyond such strictures applicable to individual company operations, insurance regulation also protects policyholders' ability to collect on future claims by mandating statewide guaranty funds. Almost all states guarantee that all valid property-casualty claims will be paid, if necessary, by this state-overseen fund; funds are less common for life and health insurance (U.S. GAO 1979, 40). To ensure adequate resources, every insurer of a certain type (commonly all property-casualty companies, for example) must make available a specified share of premiums to maintain emergency funds.[8] Guaranty funds "backstop" liability insurers. Where an insurer is in receivership and the changed management still cannot meet its obligations to policyholders, the receiver can draw against the state's guaranty fund as a last resort.

Reasonable Rates

State statutes typically require that insurance premiums be "reasonable in relation to benefits" and "neither inadequate, excessive, nor unfairly discriminatory" (NAIC 1985). More detailed standards for making such assessments are left to regulation and may or may not exist in a given state. The process of rate review, if any, varies considerably by state. Considerable nuances exist (see the section "Perspectives on Insurance Regulation," below), but, in general, rate review authority can be categorized as either competitive or regulated. Depending both on the formal legal authority of the commissioner and on how the authority is exercised in practice, insurers' premiums may be closely regulated by insurance regulators or left entirely to the market.

Availability

Historically, the first task of insurance regulation (actually, statutes) was to charter companies so that they could legally write coverage (and states could collect fees). Insurance codes still regulate the forms that insurance companies can take (mutual, stock, etc.).

Moreover, insurance commissioners and commentators alike have long been concerned that insurance be available to state residents (Kimball 1961). Regulators commonly address complaints about availability, as where insurers allegedly "redline" certain neighborhoods and allegedly refuse to write fire and other coverages there, or where coverage is allegedly denied on the basis of occupation, sex, or some other disfavored characteristic. For liability insurance, availability problems became especially critical during the recent crises in malpractice and other liability coverage in the 1970s and 1980s (Chapter 1).

In a positive vein, insurance regulation may seek to help fund coverage—often not with state funds but rather by imposing regulatory cross-subsidies among private coverages. For example, high-risk pools for automobile insurance are nearly universal. Such arrangements issue policies to insureds unable to obtain conventional coverage, charging higher premiums but also subsidizing rates by assessing insurers pro rata for annual shortfalls in revenues compared with claims. For malpractice coverage, many states have created either JUAs that operate much like high-risk pools or PCFs that cover levels of liability beyond those purchased under primary insurance (Chapter 1).

States may also facilitate new insurance entities. This approach was particularly important for the formation of new, physician-sponsored malpractice insurers after the mid-1970s' crisis. Some states passed legislation giving specific authorization to physician mutuals (as distinct from other mutuals) or other forms of organization.[9] Similarly, the federal Risk Retention Act, passed in the 1980s, allowed new entities to enter the liability insurance market, free of most state regulation (Box 3.2). At first, only product liability was covered, but the statute was later amended to include malpractice and other liability coverages. Various state hurdles may still confront new plans, however (Crane 1989a). How different regulation is for different forms of insuring entity is a significant policy issue.

Box 3.2. The Risk Retention Act

The Risk Retention Act is a kind of federal "end run" around much state insurance regulation. The act was initially passed as the Product Liability Risk Retention Act of 1981 (P.L. 97–45, codified at 15 U.S. Code sects. 3901–3904). During the broader liability crisis that soon followed, it was amended to apply to all other liability coverage, including medical malpractice (the Risk Retention Amendments of 1986, P.L. 99–563, codified at 15 U.S. Code sects. 3901–3906).

The congressional drafters found a multi-billion-dollar shortage of capacity in liability insurance during the 1980s. The act's response is deregulatory. The act's thesis is that loosening state-imposed strictures would increase capacity, making insurance more available and curbing upswings in prices. In particular, the act authorized "risk retention groups" to pool similar risks for self-insurance and risk "purchasing groups" to be formed to buy coverage on a group basis. These groupings of similarly situated persons or firms could operate in any state so long as they are chartered in at least one state. (Prior to 1985, they could also be located in Bermuda or the Cayman Islands.) In other states, such entities are freed of most insurance regulation (and do not get the protection of state guaranty funds). The rationale is that groups do not sell coverage to the public at large, only to their own members, so that oversight in a single chartering state is sufficient. However, other states may levy nondiscriminatory premium taxes, control certain trade practices, investigate and act on threats to solvency, and regulate certain other matters.

The act imposes few requirements of its own. Members in risk groups must be related to one another by "related, similar, or common business, trade, product, services, premises, or operation." Groups may not exclude anyone from membership solely to gain competitive advantage.

Negatively, some statutes have sought to ban cancellation or nonrenewal of coverage, notably for medical malpractice (Bovbjerg 1989). Such efforts can backfire, for insurers may respond to what they see as an incursion into their underwriting prerogatives by refusing to write new coverage. This happened in the mid-1980s in West Virginia. Our Survey of Medical Malpractice Insurers suggested that many insurers are quite concerned about freedom to underwrite—understandably so in a high-severity line like medical malpractice, where a single insured can account for a very high share of total annual loss. On a less formal level, insurance commissioners may take other steps as well, notably by "jawboning" insurers about availability, perhaps loosening or threatening to tighten other regulations to encourage a desired market response by insurers.

Information and Fair Play
Some insurance department efforts are not interventionist. They seek to provide information to consumers (about insurance choices and legal rights), for example, through brochures and other approaches. Other regulatory methods intervene more directly in insurance practice. Insurance departments have approval power over policy forms, that

is, the standardized insurance provisions that form a contract for coverage. Various requirements may be imposed—on disclosure and clarity of expression (or supposed clarity), for example. Commissioners may also withhold or delay approval for general reasons of public policy as interpreted by their departments. In practice, policies may be routinely approved or allowed to take effect without formal approval, especially if the home or domiciliary state of the insurer has already approved the form. However, this authority may be heavily used, as where a number of states refused for many years to approve the use of claims-made coverage for medical malpractice,[10] which was a major deterrent to market entry.

Regulators also generally have authority under trade practice acts to bar unfair trade practices as they define them through regulation and implement them in enforcement proceedings. Proceedings may result from a formal or informal consumer complaint-handling mechanism or from a more general market conduct examination of a company or a line of coverage. Agent disciplinary proceedings may also focus on practices deemed unfair.

Structures of Regulation

Some of these regulatory rules and powers are legislated—by an insurance department's original enabling statute or by specific legislation adding to the commissioner's powers. Others are set out in regulations promulgated by the department itself, acting pursuant to statutory authority. Still others take the form of informal rules of thumb or special orders to a particular company warranted by its circumstances. Some powers have been accumulated by custom and usual usage. Although all states have insurance commissioners and departments of some description (either may be officially called by some other name), states have varying provisions for placing commissioners in their jobs. Similarly, departments vary greatly in their organization and in staffing levels (U.S. GAO 1979, 16–35).

Most insurers operate regionally or nationally, whereas regulation is state specific. There are also far more companies and filings than any one department can hope to oversee actively. Regulators can cope with these seeming shortfalls in numerous ways. Much, in essence, may be delegated to the industry itself. For example, financial scrutiny depends heavily on the requirement that the industry report standard statistics of performance in standardized format, without much formal inquiry into the production of those figures. Rate review may rely heavily on a requirement that an actuarial memorandum accompany any request for a change in rates. Such regulatory practice is not dissimilar to securities regulators' partial reliance on the professionalism of private accountants to audit companies' annual statements.

Departments may also rely on other states' regulators to take the lead in certain areas. Again, the domiciliary state is expected to be primarily responsible for many aspects of operations nationwide. Regulators often give less scrutiny to policy forms already approved in a company's home state. The NAIC also helps structure insurance regulatory practice, producing model codes and regulations, providing some information to state regulators and a regular forum in which to exchange ideas and information with fellow regulators, and helping to organize some interstate aspects of regulation (such as the standardized valuation of insurers' investment portfolios) (U.S. GAO 1979, 173–75).

REGULATION AND ITS EFFECTS

PERSPECTIVES ON INSURANCE REGULATION

Many different types of analysis have addressed the property-casualty insurance industry generally. Much less has been written specifically about the medical malpractice line. Different perspectives yield different insights.

Formal Legal Analysis

It is relatively easy to compare the formal statutory and regulatory provisions in force in various states, sometimes also varying by line of coverage. For example, rate review powers can be detailed within numerous distinct categories, featuring gradations of technical authority. These go well beyond the simple, practical dichotomy of competitive versus regulatory approach noted above (Box 3.3).

Specific legal provisions can be very important. For example, premium tax rates can differ for insurers domiciled within a state (lower) and outside (higher) (Commerce Clearing House 1987). The difference may be as much as 3 percent, a not insignificant cost disadvantage to "foreign" companies where it applies (see also the discussion below). Another example involves exceptions to regulatory authority. Reinsurance in general is not regulated, nor are self-insured entities, trusts, or risk retention groups. In each case, a rationale is that these insuring entities do not sell coverage to the general public: Reinsurers sell only to primary insurers and participating insureds to themselves. Thus, consumer protection is less of an issue.

These unregulated areas have considerable influence or potential influence on malpractice coverage. Reinsurance plays a large role in the malpractice market (Chapter 5); physicians' trusts (see Chapters 2 and 4 for discussions of trusts) are not large but have grown very recently (Crane 1988). Similarly, federal preemption of most state regulatory authority over risk retention groups was premised precisely on the expectation that substantial deregulation would make a considerable difference in the operations of such insuring entities. However, states have asserted regulatory powers over risk groups, according to 6 of 12 respondents to our Survey of Medical Malpractice Insurers, with one state even claiming the right to approve premium rates, a claim being challenged in court.

There is another important legal aspect to a state's regulatory regime. Courts make insurance law just as insurance departments do. Thus, insurers consider the judicial climate in a state as well as the regulatory one in making business decisions about operating there. For one, under standard principles of administrative law, many decisions by a commissioner are subject to judicial review (Davis 1951; Keeton 1971). Not only do courts interpret a commissioner's authority, but they also develop insurance law on their own, especially by interpreting insurance contracts and ruling on their validity. Courts have developed a common law of insurance contracts for other areas within their jurisdiction. Judicial decisions can have as much or more impact on how the provisions of an insurance policy actually apply as do regulators that approve them on review.[11] Another particular area of concern for insurers is the increasing willingness of courts to investigate whether there was "bad faith" by an insurer in meeting its obligations under an insurance policy. An insured physician, for example, can sue his or her insurer for refusing to pay a claim or for its choice of litigation strategy. By definition, courts determine the rules of liability, so any unexpected changes can

---

Box 3.3 Forms of Rate Regulatory Authority

One source (NAIC 1974) lists nine types of regulatory authority over property-casualty insurance rates (in the context of auto coverage), which can also apply to malpractice coverage. They are reproduced below, in descending order of invasiveness.

1. State-made rates
2. Mandatory bureau rate systems
3. Prior approval laws
4. Modified approval laws
5. File and use—adherence to bureau rates required
6. File and use—bureau rates advisory only
7. Use and file—bureau rates advisory only
8. No file—bureau rates advisory only
9. No file, no rating standards, and no rates in concert

For practical purposes, a simpler, tripartite taxonomy suffices:

- Prior approval and other regulatory formats. These provisions are the most interventionist; commissioners can virtually dictate rates, and companies cannot operate without approval beforehand.
- File and use or use and file. Under these regimes, commissioners can disapprove filed rates but must take definite action to do so. Absent disapproval, companies can operate under filed rates, with the obligation to file coming either just before or just after the rates are used. How interventionist either of these regimes is depends on how the commissioner chooses to exercise disapproval authority. One hybrid of these first two categories has appeared of late, sometimes called "flex rating," under which annual rate increases above a certain percentage amount require prior approval, but lower ones can take effect automatically, though they must be filed.
- "Open competition" provisions. Here insurers can charge whatever the market allows, with no necessity to file or justify their rates.

---

quickly affect insurers' bottom line. Here, too, the judicial climate is as important to insurers as the regulatory one. Clearly, a commissioner's formal authority and the common law of a jurisdiction can make a considerable difference to the impact of regulation.

With regard to practical enforcement, it is often noted that insurance departments seem inadequately staffed and funded, given the huge number of insurers (potentially) regulated and the formal extent of regulation. The U.S. General Accounting Office presented data, for example, on workload, funding, and staffing (U.S. GAO 1979, 19–20, 26). The median insurance department in 1978 received 2,500 rate filings, 13,000 applications for agent licenses, and 15,000 policy form filings—but had only $1.2 million in annual funding and a staff of 64 people, very few with technical training, especially in actuarial science.[12] Thus, although the powers and resources of a department may seem large to a single insurer embroiled in a dispute with a commissioner, the number of fights a typical department can afford is severely limited.

What factors affect an insurance commissioner's stance on regulatory issues? Traditional thinking about regulation assumed that regulators are governed by their legal mandate, their neutral professional expertise, and the public interest (e.g., Bernstein 1955; Friendly 1962). One study specifically of insurance regulatory styles concluded that political factors are influential. That is, commissioners are more likely to adopt interventionist styles that have populist appeal where they are closest to the electorate, which takes populist pleasure in policies that seem harsh on insurers. Thus, elected commissioners, especially ones with short terms, are more regulatory than ones appointed by governors; those appointed but subject to legislative confirmation likewise are more regulatory than those not so confirmed (Miles and Bhambri 1983).

We found weak empirical support for this hypothesis of regulatory behavior in our analysis of this issue. We compared a time series of industry interviews on perceptions of orientation of insurance regulation with data on characteristics of insurance commissioners, also finding suggestive indications that elected, short-term commissioners are more apt to be perceived as regulatory than appointed, longer-term ones (not presented).[13]

On the other hand, consumer advocates often object that regulators are too soft on the insurance industry because they are recruited from industry personnel to begin with and take jobs in industry after their public service. This "revolving door" staffing is said to make regulators too sympathetic to the industry. Another theory about lax regulation is the "capture" hypothesis and similar analytic criticisms (Stigler 1971; Phillips 1975). Under this view, regulation may not be enacted in the public interest at all but rather in the interest of the regulated industry; alternatively, an agency soon loses its initial public spirited zeal once public-attention wanes, then is captured by the industry with which it deals on a continuing basis and which supplies most of the information needed by regulators. The public interest is seen as diffuse and political attention transitory, whereas industry interests are concentrated and enduring. Such critics, many of them political economists, see regulation as a way for industry to operate a more effective cartel, using legal sanctions, than would be possible by private action alone.

Empirical Research

Finally, the empirical perspective asks what has actually occurred. Rather than focusing on the law, politics, or political economy of regulation, empirical researchers investigate practical questions: For example, despite regulation, is the insurance industry more like pure competition or more like a monopoly or cartel? What have been the differing effects of different forms of regulation? We turn next to such evidence.

EVIDENCE ON INSURANCE REGULATION

What practical effect does insurance regulation have on insurers' operations and policyholders? This section discusses the three regulatory factors that seem most pertinent to market organization: (1) rules that affect entry into a malpractice insurance market (especially initial capitalization and other solvency requirements); (2) regulations about pricing; and (3) differential treatment of different types of insurers. We conclude with an overall assessment of the impact of regulation. Discussion is based on findings of this project, including our Survey of Medical Malpractice Insurers, as well as the few relevant earlier studies.

Solvency Regulation and Effects on Entry of Insurers

Evidence from Other Studies

The most detailed analysis of effects of solvency regulation on the property-liability insurance industry to date is by Munch and Smallwood (1980). First, they tested the hypothesis that solvency regulation reduces the number of firms and increases the minimally efficient firm size. Since, for a given price of capital, the optimal level of surplus that an unregulated insurer would desire to hold depends in part on the number of policyholders, specifying an absolute amount of required surplus may work to the disadvantage of small insurers. Second, they tested the hypothesis that solvency regulation reduces the number of insolvencies. If so, they sought to determine whether the reduction in insolvencies results from preventing insurers who would accept a higher risk of bankruptcy from entering the market or, alternatively, whether there is an additional deterrent effect on firms that do enter.

They found that minimum capital requirements (maximum premium-to-surplus ratio) reduced the number of insurer insolvencies. This result was achieved solely by deterring the entry of small, relatively risky insurers. Elimination of such small firms may impose two types of costs on consumers. First, it may limit the range of quality of the products available for purchase. Second, the price may be higher because of elimination of competition from such small firms. Further, administering such regulation involves costs. However, to the extent that such regulation reduces consumer search cost and risk, it may be beneficial to consumers. Based on existing evidence, it is not possible to say whether the net benefit of such regulation is positive or negative.

As noted in Chapter 2, in Winter's (1988a, 1988b, 1988c, 1989) model of the insurance cycle, negative shocks to capacity (unanticipated losses) cause premiums to rise. As a source of income, such premium increases, following unanticipated losses, are a safety valve (stem insolvencies). Winter cautioned that insurance regulators who judge solvency risk in terms of a premium-to-surplus ratio may view an increase in the ratio as a negative development. To the extent that regulators do not adapt the solvency standard to cyclical changes in premiums, such regulation may magnify the amplitude of the insurance cycle, in particular by reducing availability of insurance coverage.

Winter presented little empirical evidence that solvency regulation has in fact had such a counterproductive effect. He noted that during the last two crises in the property-liability insurance industry the ratio of revenue to surplus for the aggregate domestic property-liability insurance industry did not reach the regulatory limit of three or four dollars of premium to surplus. Rather, the ratio reached about two.

Evidence from Our Survey of Medical Malpractice Insurers

Our Survey of Medical Malpractice Insurers directly addressed the importance of regulation for entry into the business, mainly in the section of the questionnaire devoted to regulation. Insurers were asked, "Do you think initial capitalization regulations significantly affect a company's decisions to sell malpractice in [respondent's home state]?" Nine of 13 companies responding to this question replied "no," and only four said "yes," all of them physician-sponsored companies. Companies giving positive responses explained: "Need $2 million to start up." "If a new company tries to start, they need many insureds or much capital to be viable. The large commercials could come in and start, as they do have the capital." "Have to raise the money to get started. Risk retention and risk pooling skew the market to alternative mechanisms, e.g., offshore operations." "If initial capitalization requirements had been much higher, it may have been impossible to achieve. It's a barrier to entry." One commercial and one physician company volunteered that they thought regulators had not given initial capitalization enough weight. In response to a different, more general question about influences on entry, several companies commented that initial capitalization is often important, but only for the new company starting up, implying that there is little lasting impact.

Responses to our most general question about entry are shown in Table 3.1. Insurers were asked to list up to five factors they considered important influences on a company's entry into the malpractice insurance market. Responses were unprompted by any listing on the survey questionnaire. Competitive factors (market demand and size) were overwhelmingly the dominant response, listed by 11 of the 12 companies responding. The 12th company was one of five listing "market stability" (or market share), again, a market rather than a regulatory factor. Second came the regulatory environment, listed by six insurers.

Both national commercial and physician insurers (mutuals and reciprocals alike) listed both competitive and regulatory factors. Policy form approval was mentioned only by commercial companies, however, perhaps an indication that the claims-made form is resisted more when seemingly imposed by an outside commercial insurer than when sold by an in-state physician company. Interestingly, five companies listed ade-

Table 3.1. Important Factors in Entering the Medical Malpractice Insurance Market

Factor	Number of Companies Listing the Factor
Competition (market demand, size)	11
Regulatory environment, including:	6
Adequacy of rate setting	6
Policy and form approval	2
Underwriting ability	2
Market stability (market share)	5
Adequate capitalization (not necessarily required or regulated)	5
Tort reform, legal climate	4
Internal ability to service new market	4
Claims climate	3
Legislative environment	1
Mission of the company	1

Source: Survey of Medical Malpractice Insurers.

Note: N = 12 respondents. Factors were named by the companies themselves, unprompted by the questionnaire.

quate capitalization, emphasizing their internal standards for adequacy rather than regulatory minimums. These five were all physician sponsored, which may not be surprising, for national stock companies have far larger capitalization, and entry into a single state in a single line would constitute a much smaller relative commitment of capital for them. Other factors mentioned included the legal climate, including tort reform, the claims climate, and the legislative environment—not regulatory factors, but part of a state's legal regime more generally. Internal ability to service a new market was also mentioned (by both national and single-state companies), as was the mission of the company (by a physician insurer).

We also asked respondents to list the factors companies consider when specifically deciding whether to enter a new state. The question was too hypothetical for many of the companies, for the physician-sponsored insurers generally are single-state operations and have a policy against competing against another physician insurer in a different state (Chapter 4). Only eight companies responded, but the responses provide a perspective on entry (Table 3.2). The factor most often volunteered was the adequacy of premiums—which could depend on either the competitive or the regulatory climate in the market under consideration. Both national stock firms and three of the physician firms listed premiums. Next in frequency of response came the claims climate, demand, and stability of competition—all nonregulatory factors. The regulatory climate per se was volunteered by only two firms, one stock company and one physician sponsored.[14]

The reverse question yielded similar answers: What (unprompted) reasons did these insurers have for not entering the market in a neighboring state? (Insurers were asked to list up to three reasons; a nearby state was postulated so as to make service easy and the question seem realistic.) Again, nonregulatory factors dominated among the 13 respondents, although there was a split between the physician companies and the commercials. Five physician companies said that the question was inapplicable; as physician insurers, they would not want to enter because their mission was limited to serving their own state's doctors (in one state limited by statute) or because of a policy

Table 3.2. Factors Considered by Companies When Analyzing the Feasibility and/or Desirability of Entering a New State

Factor	Number of Companies Listing the Factor
Rate/premium adequacy	5
Claims climate/administration	4
Demand (buyer interest)	4
Stability of competition	4
Regulatory climate	2
Sponsorship of state medical association	2
Achievable market share	2
State insurance laws, tort reform	2
Capitalization needed (not required)	1

Source: Survey of Medical Malpractice Insurers.

Note: N = 8 respondents (the question was not answered by five insurers, which said they were not interested in expanding to a new state). These factors, cited by the companies, were unprompted by the questionnaire.

against competing with another physician company. Six companies (mainly other physician insurers) cited perceived demand for coverage or general market conditions. Similar, more specific reasons cited by five companies were that the market was too small, the rates there were inadequate, the market was too different, and in one case that malpractice insurance there was in deficit, evidently meaning that all coverage was underpriced and conditions were unfavorable. Another five, including one commercial company, said that the competition was too great. Two insurers listed the tort climate or tort reform, and one named fear of spreading its personnel too thin. Only two of the commercial companies, and none of the physician companies, specifically mentioned regulation. But those two mentioned not only regulation in general but also rate and policy form approval in particular.

The firms interviewed had a quite balanced view of regulation. The final question in the regulation section asked them to rate the regulatory climate in their home state. Most states' departments were clearly seen as neutral (five states) or nearly so (three tending to favor insurers, three tending to oppose). Only two states were seen as definitely anti-insurance company; none was considered definitely proinsurer. The two commercial companies saw more of an anti-insurer tendency than the physician companies, even in their home states. Responses to different questions showed that these foreign companies felt disfavored in premium review relative to domestic insurers. In contrast, insurers clearly saw the judicial climate as antidefendant: Six of the 13 responding firms ranked their home state's judiciary as definitely plaintiff oriented, two as leaning that way, only four as neutral, one as defendant oriented, and none as fully defendant oriented. (One company commented, however, that its rural areas were completely prodefense, although urban areas were completely proplaintiff.) On this question the commercial companies did not agree, and the physician firms likewise varied.

We included questions about investments and investment portfolio regulation. At the time of the survey, all respondents had conservative investment portfolios. A small share of their investments was in risky or illiquid assets. A few "horror" stories were mentioned—physician-owned mutuals that lost a substantial part of their surplus during a stock market downturn, and investments in condominiums and franchises that got one mutual into major financial trouble. The respondents indicated that the firms tend to have a more conservative investment philosophy than the state insurance departments that regulate them. In no case did regulatory investment policy appear to be binding on the insurance companies surveyed.

Respondents were also asked to assess the relative importance of various listed forms of regulation. Table 3.3 summarizes: Eleven companies responded, and most of the listed types of regulation were deemed "very" or "somewhat" important by at least eight respondents. The leading response for "very important" was initial capitalization, but written comments noted that this was so, of course, only for new companies. Fewer insurers saw ongoing solvency requirements as very important. Least important were marketing practice rules and premium taxes. The prompted listing unfortunately did not list rate regulation. Three companies, including both national stock companies, used the blank "other" line to add rate regulation, all ranking it "very important" (one marking it with four X's and an exclamation point). Three different physician companies added revealing comments: "Regulation very rarely impinges on our operations." "We are stricter on ourselves than the requirements of the Insurance Depart-

Table 3.3. Classes of Regulation Considered Important Influences on the Operation of a Malpractice Insurance Company

Factors Listed	Very Important	Somewhat Important	Not Important	Does Not Exist in State
Initial capitalization	6	2	3	0
Underwriting standards	5	4	1	1
Ratio of premiums to surplus	4	6	0	1
Policy forms	4	6	1	0
Amount of revenues needed	4	5	2	0
Nature of investment or reserves	2	8	0	1
Reporting requirements	1	8	2	0
Marketing procedures	1	6	4	0
Premium tax	1	5	4	1
Other, Unprompted Listings				
Rate regulation/review	3	—	—	—

Source: Survey of Medical Malpractice Insurers.

Note: $N = 11$ respondents. Answers were prompted by the questionnaire.

ment." "None of this affects us. Rate filing not an obstacle. They check our rates, but we've never had a problem."

Also with regard to entry, the survey revealed that a number of states were attempting seemingly significant regulation of new risk retention groups at the time the survey was conducted (late 1987-early 1988; see above). Of the 13 insurers responding, however, only 1 indicated that it was using the Risk Retention Act to expand operations into other states. That firm, a physician company that had been in several states, said that it was beginning to write coverage in all states. Finally, we asked about exit as distinct from nonentry. Only one of the 13 respondents had ever ceased writing in any state because of inability to get adequate rates for heavy, troublesome claims experience—evidently at least partly due to regulatory resistance.

In sum, the evidence from our Survey of Medical Malpractice Insurers suggests that solvency regulation may sometimes be a barrier to entry to new firms that may want to sell medical malpractice insurance, a result consistent with Munch and Smallwood's (1980) evidence for property-liability insurers more generally. But for established insurers, such regulation typically has little or no effect. The concern that solvency regulation may exacerbate the effects of the insurance cycle, a possibility noted by Professor Ralph Winter, appears in fact to be only a conceptual possibility in the medical malpractice line. While such regulation could in principle cause such adverse effects, at present it seems to be a distant prospect.

REGULATION OF PRICES

Evidence from Other Studies

There is an extensive empirical literature on the effects of rate regulation on prices and underwriting results in the property-liability insurance industry. Although now over a half-decade old, a comprehensive review of these studies by Harrington (1984) still provides an excellent overview of empirical evidence on this topic. Harrington's review includes studies relying on data from single states, as well as multistate studies. None of the studies deal specifically with medical malpractice insurance.

These are Harrington's principal conclusions with which, on the basis of our cross-checks of some of the major studies he reviewed, we agree. First, there is some empirical evidence that price regulation by states has led to greater temporal variability in loss ratios (incurred losses to earned premiums for direct business) than would otherwise occur, but this evidence overall is not strong. Second, empirical findings are largely inconsistent with the hypothesis that rate regulation by insurance departments causes higher prices and thus benefits insurers. We shall revisit this issue when we present results of our own empirical analysis on medical malpractice premiums in Chapter 7.

An unpublished study of the malpractice market in Florida (in Manne 1985) similarly concluded that the industry in Florida is fundamentally competitive, for numerous insurers competed for business there, including several physician-organized ones; and most companies' market shares fluctuated considerably from year to year, with the JUA garnering only a small market share, indicating that most physicians were comparison shopping for the best deal. In neither state study was regulation seen as playing a major role in industry pricing. However, it is known that subsequent to the time of the Florida study, the St. Paul left the state because it could not get regulatory approval for its rates.

The formal rules of rate review have changed over time, in general becoming more competitive and less regulatory, at least through 1986. Table 3.4 summarizes the review standards applied in 51 jurisdictions (including the District of Columbia) in 1973 and 1988. In the late 1970s, the U.S. Department of Justice discerned a procompetitive trend in rate review—in favor of leaving most premium levels to market competition rather than approval by the insurance commissioner (U.S. Department of Justice 1977). The NAIC had endorsed market-based rate making (1974), and three states, beginning with California, had completely open rating, with no obligation even to file rates. As the table shows, however, subsequent developments have not expanded the class of no-file states. Rather, there was a more modest trend toward less regulatory review—fewer prior-approval states and more use-and-file ones.

However, Proposition 103, passed in 1988 in California, called for far more stringent regulation, and other states have taken note (Chapter 1). As a result, this

Table 3.4. Rate Regulation for Property-Casualty Insurance

Type of Authority	1973	1988
No file	3	3
File and use	14	14
Use and file	4	10
Prior approval	30	23
Flex rating	0	1

Source: Samprone (1975); Regulatory Survey of Insurance Departments.

Note: Commissioner-set rates coded as prior approval.

modest trend away from the most stringent form of regulation may well reverse itself in the future.

Evidence from Our Survey of Medical Malpractice Insurers

Our Survey of Medical Malpractice Insurers asked about the influence of rate review on premium setting. The broadest question was "In the past five years, has the regulation process been a major, minor, or no obstacle in establishing premium rates?" Notably, that five-year period included the 1980s' crisis, during which requests for large premium increases were common. Two firms responded "major," six "minor," and five "no obstacle." Notably, the five responding "no obstacle" were all physician-sponsored, single-state companies. National or regional insurers, of course, had experience with more states from which to find an obstacle.

Other questions sought out the mechanisms for regulatory influence. One asked whether the company had revised its proposed premiums because of a regulatory decision within the past five years. Seven firms said no (again, all single-state, physician companies), six yes. Of those saying that rates had been revised, most cited political reasons. One complained that its overly powerful regulators always changed rates, allowing only inadequate premiums, possibly in reliance on tort reforms being implemented. One described negotiating a 100 percent increase in obstetrics rates over two years rather than taking the full amount in one year. Another, multistate company noted that revisions were "common" for three reasons: (1) the company asked for less than the full, indicated rate in order to get rapid approval (and thus perhaps avoiding being able to charge the rate for less than a year), (2) the company asked less than a rate increase ceiling to avoid a mandatory hearing, and (3) the rate was approved below the filed amount. A follow-up question asked whether rates were established in anticipation of regulatory decisions. Only the company whose response was just cited and one other admitted such a practice; one explained that they must accept regulatory decisions, and the other noted that the regulatory obstacle was not major, for the company did not do business in such states. The 11 others all said no; one of them explained that it takes a wait-and-see posture, rather than adjustment of rates in anticipation of a regulatory decision.

The regulatory inclusion of an explicit factor in rate making for interest earned on claims reserves has sometimes been controversial. So we asked what states required an interest factor in reviewing rate filings in the last five years and what the difference was between the regulators' and the companies' proposed factors. Of 13 respondents to the question, 8 did not include such a factor in their calculations. Of the five that did, four saw no difference between the company's request and the regulator's proposals. Only one experienced a difference with the regulators—resulting in a 30 percent difference in the premium in one year.

Much of the empirical analysis of the effects of rate regulation (e.g., Joskow 1973, Ippolito 1979) has focused on the notion that such regulation raises the price, with, as already noted, the "bottom line" of the evidence being that such regulation has no effect either way. By contrast, what one hears from some medical malpractice insurers is that such regulation reduces the price, among other things. Although the opinions of insurers may be dismissed as self-serving, the proof is in the empirical evidence. And up to now, such empirical evidence has been lacking for the medical malpractice line. We present our results in Chapter 7.

Differences in Rules for Different Types of Insurer

There seem to be fewer formal differences in regulation by type of insurer than one might expect. An initial distinction should be drawn: Some forms of insurance virtually escape regulation altogether, as already noted (see Box 3.4). Beyond the obvious difference for nonregulated forms of insurance, what differences exist in regulatory treatment among those coverages that are state regulated? One clear-cut difference in some 10 states is that insurers chartered within the state (or, in more sophisticated fashion, those investing in approved ways within the state) are taxed less than insurers merely licensed to do business in the state (Commerce Clearing House 1987). Domestic insurers may pay up to a 3 percent lower premium tax than foreign companies (e.g., 1 percent of premiums rather than 4 percent), a factor that encourages foreign insurers to form domestic subsidiaries; this is one reason that insurance groups often consist of numerous interrelated companies. Several states have responded by treating foreign-owned domestic companies as foreign. Most states, however, treat alike all insurers within categories (life, casualty), or only penalize foreign insurers whose home states penalize the first state's companies.[15] Indeed, taxes as a percentage of expenses are lower for the single-line, largely single-state, physician-sponsored insurance companies than for the multiple-line, national commercial companies (Chapter 9).[16] According to our Survey of Medical Malpractice Insurers, however, few respondents, either commercial or physician companies, saw premium taxes as a significant factor in market competition or entry.

Occasionally, there are other formal differences in requirements between mutual and stock companies, mainly owing to their different organization. Mutuals, for example, are allowed to treat dividends as a return of premium, whereas stocks must count them as a return on investment. But there seem to be no differences in capitalization requirements, for example. On the whole, regulatory differences seem inconsequential.

Given the rapid rise of physician-sponsored insurers, a major question is whether differential regulatory treatment has favored them as against their commercial competitors, whether organized as stock or mutual companies. Some states have enacted special legislation allowing the formation of physician mutual companies; in one unique instance, the state of Maryland actually chartered the physician-owned company. For the most part, however, physicians organizing companies simply took advantage of existing insurance mechanisms—mutual companies or reciprocals. According to respondents to our Survey of Medical Malpractice Insurers, most physician companies face the same rules on capitalization, claims reserving, premium taxation, and price regulation as their competitors.

Our Survey of Medical Malpractice Insurers did not reveal strong evidence of differential treatment of companies, whether formal or informal. One physician company noted that it is exempt from premium taxation. The multistate companies did report more problems in winning rate approvals than all but one physician company. And one multistate insurer felt that the physician companies did have too much influence with regulators about the amount of surplus needed to write coverage; it felt that the physician companies may have too little surplus to provide insurance responsibly. One physician company forcefully asserted that it was treated exactly like any other insurer.

Box 3.4 Nonregulated Insurance

Some forms of coverage are unregulated. For example, self-insurance (retaining funds to cover one's own losses over time) is often not legally considered "insurance" subject to licensure requirements and other regulation. Physicians seldom self-insure by setting aside such funds, although a certain percentage may go bare, choosing not to carry any coverage.[17] Self-insurance is rather common among hospitals, on the other hand,[18] to the point where hospital premiums are a far smaller share of malpractice insurers' revenues than they once were (Posner 1986).

A close relative of self-insurance is insurance by a "captive" insurer—a company owned by the insured or a group of insureds, often chartered offshore in the Cayman Islands or Bermuda, where insurance regulation is minimal (Bawcutt 1982). Again, physicians have used such arrangements far less often than have hospitals, although large teaching hospitals may include their staff physicians under a captive policy of this sort.

Another form of insurance that is not regulated is the self-insurance trust, which is occasionally used by physicians. A trust resembles a reciprocal in that there is no outside insurer as such;[19] instead, each physician (or other insured) agrees to be personally liable for a pro rata share of the liability costs of all fellow members of the trust. But whereas reciprocals are state chartered and regulated, trusts are not; thus, for instance, no reserves must be built up against future losses, and members get no assistance from state guaranty funds in case of insolvency. Moreover, there are differences between trusts and reciprocals in the treatment of assessments of members who leave the trust with respect to losses or gains from prior years, as well as differences in state taxation. Trusts seem to be common forms of physician coverage only in Florida and California, and they were not included in our survey or our analysis, as they report no data to standard insurance sources. Journalistic reports indicate that their policies are considerably less expensive, at least in the current era; whether they are truly lower-priced because of good risk selection or other factors, or whether they have been inaccurately priced for the longer term, remains to be seen.

Two other forms of unregulated insurance have already been mentioned. Liability risk retention groups also sell only to their own members and are exempt from most state regulation by virtue of federal preemption (see Box 3.2). Reinsurance (Chapter 5) is virtually unregulated as well, again under the rationale that sales are not made to the general public but only to other insurers, who are capable of looking after their own interests.

REGULATORY RESPONSIBILITIES WITHIN COMPANIES

Regulation of malpractice insurers is pervasive, and many departments of insurers must deal with regulatory affairs. When asked to name their top three departments with some regulatory responsibilities, the 13 firms responding to the question on our Survey of Medical Malpractice Insurers all listed multiple departments (30 of the 39 possible responses were listed). In all, eight different types of department were named, though only six by more than one company. The departments were actuarial, claims management, finance and accounting, government affairs, legal, marketing, and underwriting. Only the largest company had a formal office of government affairs, and only the physician company with an in-house actuary named the actuarial department, but in each case, that was the first in importance.

Most of our companies clearly give regulatory matters a high priority; 6 of the 13 responding companies listed senior management (often a named individual) as first in importance for regulatory affairs. Underwriting was a distant second in importance, with three mentions as most important (two of them ties for first with senior management). All of the six companies relying so heavily on senior management, however, were physician-sponsored, single-state companies. Neither national, commercial company listed senior management even second or third in importance. This pattern may also reflect that, whereas regulation has a high profile for the single-state firms, they may also simply lack the scope to have specialty departments for different types of regulation; this observation is consistent with six physician companies' also listing senior management as dealing with "most issues" on regulation. The national companies organize to handle similar regulations across different states by a specialized department (with government affairs and legal departments taking the lead for them). It may also be that the physician companies are newer, for which the memory of initial capitalization requirements and "learning the ropes" of regulation loom larger, whereas matters are more routinized in the larger, older companies. According to a follow-up question on what departments handle what regulatory issues, senior management and government affairs are most often involved in most regulatory issues, regulatory compliance and rate filing are emphasized in the underwriting and legal departments, finance/accounting handles reporting, and actuarial does rate setting.

CONCLUSION

Insurance regulation is justified mainly by consumer ignorance and by the need to protect insureds from insurer insolvency and unfair practices. The main goals are to prevent insurer bankruptcy, to promote availability and fair pricing, and to police fair play. Insurance commissioners' regulatory powers are extensive—over licensure, solvency monitoring, policy forms and rates, and other matters. And insurance departments' discretion about how to implement them is considerable, although some types of coverage are not regulated. But few commissioners are ever as interventionist as their scope of authority would allow, for reasons of policy, politics, and want of administrative resources. In all these matters, regulation of medical malpractice insurance does not differ appreciably from regulation of any other type of insurance.

Regulators in some cases have had major impacts on the structure and conduct of state markets for physicians' malpractice coverage. The state-overseen JUA in Massachusetts dominates that market, for example, and many industry sources report that New York rate regulation has greatly constrained insurers. At least two states long excluded certain malpractice insurers from their markets through their departments' refusal to approve any claims-made policy form. In the 1970s and to a greatly diminished extent in the 1980s, some companies ceased writing in states because they found approved premium rates too low. Regulation may also create a longer lag between actuarial development of rates and their actual implementation—which could contribute to cycles in insurance pricing (Chapter 2). However, empirical evidence on this issue is mixed.

According to our study's Survey of Medical Malpractice Insurers, however, for most companies for most years, regulation has not been a major influence on entry or, with some important exceptions, pricing (competitive factors loomed much larger). Nor did enactment of the recent deregulatory federal legislation, the Risk Retention Amendments of 1986, although it occurred less than two years before our survey. Still, the national commercial companies in our survey expressed far more concern about the regulatory climate than did physician insurers. The single recent instance reported on the survey of an insurer's leaving a state (while still remaining in the malpractice business) involved a national insurer. We also found some indications of differences in regulatory enforcement between commercial and local physician insurers.

The responses reviewed in our discussion on entry and pricing above indicated that regulation seems less important than competition and other factors, although there are exceptions to this generalization. The broadest question (Table 3.3) found that competitive factors were seen as more important influences on firms' operations than were regulatory ones, a pattern repeated in numerous more specific questions about entry and pricing. Regulation was never listed most often as a reason for entering (or not entering) a state, nor was regulation often seen as a major factor in pricing decisions.

With regard to industry performance, prior research had found that solvency regulation affects the number of insolvencies among property-casualty companies generally. Our Survey of Medical Malpractice Insurers casts doubt on how much difference state standards might have in the malpractice line, for the consensus of our respondents was that most companies adhered to tougher standards on their own initiative. However, our own analysis of premiums to surplus ratios does not entirely support the insurers' statements (Chapter 6). Results of an empirical assessment of the effects of rate regulation on premiums are presented in Chapter 7.

NOTES

1. Article I, section 8, clause 3 gives the federal government power over interstate and foreign commerce. Some jurisdiction is considered exclusively federal, never subject to state exercise. Other areas are considered within federal power to preempt through federal action that overrides inconsistent state provisions.
2. McCarran-Ferguson cannot be seen as entirely proregulation; it merely leaves the option to state decision. A congressional report in fact opined that "competitive rates on a sound financial basis are in the public interest" (House Report 143, 79th Congress, 1st Session).
3. The McCarran-Ferguson Act expressly subjects anticompetitive boycotts, coercion, or intimidation to antitrust scrutiny. Court decisions have also affected the scope of the exemption, such as *FTC* v. *National Casualty Co.*, 357 U.S. at 564 (1973) (no exemption where regulation is a mere pretense or sham). Other limiting cases are *St. Paul Fire & Marine Insurance Co. et al.* v. *Barr*, 98 S.Ct. 2923 (1978), and *Group Life and Health Insurance Co.* v. *Royal Drug Co.*, 47 U.S.L.W. 4203 (1977).
4. In the current Congress, a group of senators led by Howard Metzenbaum recently intro-

duced a bill that would remove the McCarran-Ferguson exemption, and on the House side, Rep. James. J. Florio has introduced an insurance industry reform that would cause a de facto repeal.

5. Courts have held, however, that regulatory oversight need not be active to effectuate the preemption of antitrust jurisdiction. A state may choose competitive rate making, without direct insurance department involvement, yet still be considered regulating for McCarran purposes. Antitrust criteria can apply where state regulation is not effectively enforced, as in *Ohio AFL-CIO* v. *Insurance Rating Board*, 451 F.2d 1178, 1184 (1971), but states are deemed to be regulating by the existence of relevant laws and departments for enforcement, as in *FTC* v. *National Casualty Co.*, 357 U.S. 563 (1973).

6. Whereas premium taxes fall in the range of 1 to 4 percent of the premium, insurance departments' budgets as a percentage of premiums ranged in 1977 from a low of 4/100ths of 1 percent to a high of 26/100ths of 1 percent (U.S. GAO 1979, 22–23).

7. Table 9.3 in Chapter 9 describes the combined investment portfolios of insurers.

8. Most "funds" do not hold assets as such but merely stand ready to assess other, solvent insurers as needed.

9. Maryland took the unusual step of actually granting a state charter to a physician company. The Medical Indemnity Corporation of Alaska was similarly created by the Alaska legislature, and initial capital was provided by a $3 million loan from the state; although the company is a quasi-public corporation, it is not a part of state government (PIAA 1987).

10. Michigan until recently barred claims-made coverage (our interviews).

11. According to one informal interviewee, at least one state court has interpreted a claims-made policy as an occurrence policy.

12. According to GAO data, half of the 46 departments replying to its 1976 survey had only a single actuary on their staff. All 46 had a total of 156 actuaries, 89 of them in the 10 biggest departments (U.S. GAO 1979, 30).

13. The results should be seen as instructive rather than definitive, for the data used were somewhat rough. The interview data came from a series of surveys conducted annually by the Connaughton Company, an insurance brokerage and research firm. The questions on ranking the states by degree of regulation were not quite consistent from year to year, nor was the same panel of insurer-respondents involved each year. Data on characteristics of insurance commissioners came from the *Directory of State Officials*.

14. Unlike the other survey questions discussed in this chapter, this question came from the portion of the questionnaire called "competitive environment," not "regulation." In a few companies, therefore, it was completed by a different interviewee. This circumstance does not seem likely to make the results of Table 3.2 incommensurate with the other evidence presented here.

15. According to the listings in Commerce Clearing House (1987), 28 jurisdictions (including the District of Columbia) treat foreign and domestic insurers the same, and 13 more the same except for retaliatory increases to the level imposed by the foreign company's home state. The remaining 10 have premium tax differentials, as discussed in the text.

16. The average physician mutual or reciprocal insurer pays about 1 percent of its premiums in taxes; the average commercial almost 4 percent (Chapter 9).

17. Some states and many hospitals require physicians to have coverage, as already noted. But although the data are sparse, a small percentage of physicians seems not to have any coverage.

18. Hospital insurance payers, among them Medicare, the largest single payer, allow self-insurance premiums as a reimbursable cost where a legitimate, funded account is kept in lieu of paying premiums to an outside carrier.

19. A Lloyd's Association is not dissimilar, except that the organization of principals risking their own assets also insures nonmembers (Chapters 2 and 4).

4

Market Structure and Conduct

This chapter addresses three fundamental questions about the market for medical malpractice insurance. First, what is the relevant market for analysis—in terms of the product bought and sold and the geographic area of sales? Are we right to analyze malpractice insurance as a market or an industry, or must the focus be property-casualty insurance more generally?

Second, in terms of its structure and conduct, is this partly regulated market competitive or is it more appropriately characterized as monopolistic? Competition is desirable because it delivers the products consumers want most efficiently, allocating society's scarce resources so as to yield the greatest benefit to society. A monopolistic or imperfectly competitive market, in contrast, features excessive premiums, a lower supply of coverage, and excessively high returns to investors in insurance companies. A major goal of insurance regulators is to avoid such monopolistic outcomes.

Third, what explains the diversity of ownership forms in the insurance industry? The most notable difference in the malpractice market of the late 1980s compared with the 1970s was the relative decline of national stock insurers and the rise of physician-sponsored, largely state-specific insurers. Is there evidence that particular physician firms conduct their business differently? Are some forms of insurer ownership relatively efficient in the provision of medical malpractice insurance? Do physician firms fill a niche not occupied by the traditional for-profit insurer? Answers are important for assessing the desirability of tax and regulatory policies that distinguish among organizational types.

CONCEPTUAL APPROACH

This chapter follows the traditional analytic method of industrial organization, which addresses an industry's *market structure*, *conduct*, and *performance*.[1] Analysis properly begins by determining what product, geographic, temporal, or other boundaries define the market. Then it examines market attributes. "Market structure" refers to many features, including the number of buyers and sellers in the market, the market shares of buyers and sellers, the extent of product differentiation, entry barriers to potential competition, economies (or diseconomies) of scale or product mix in the production and sale of the product, and the degree of vertical integration. "Conduct" includes, above all, any collusion among sellers or buyers. It also includes other

Box 4.1. The Paradigms: Competition vs. Monopoly

In a purely competitive market, six key structural features prevail:

1. *There are many independent buyers and sellers.* This means that no individual buyer or seller has the power to influence product price. All are "price takers." Furthermore, the presence of many buyers and sellers hinders collusion among parties—a major feature of competitive market conduct.
2. *There is complete freedom of entry and exit of sellers.* The threat of entry and actual entry discipline pricing; if firms in the industry over-price, new entrants will undercut them. There are no barriers to entry resulting from the way the industry is regulated.
3. *There is a free flow of information about the price and quality* of the product, and each buyer and seller can costlessly make and alter contracts when a more favorable contract can be made with another party. Thus, buyers can demand the product they want, competition gets them the best mix of price and quality, and no party can have market power for a substantial period of time, for their counterparts have ready alternatives for their business.
4. *Transaction costs are small* in relation to the product price in the market area. Low transport costs, for instance, means that no seller can charge a higher price than its competitor without losing appreciable sales.
5. *The output of all firms is identical, or any differences are easily graded.* This means that there is no product differentiation (perhaps closely linked to quality) that might create consumer attachment to a particular firm's product. Consumers thus remain flexible about switching to an identical product or one known to be different in specific ways.
6. *Firms have identical cost curves.* Inefficient firms with higher cost curves are weeded out by competitive forces, either run by new management or put out of business.

The key structural attributes of monopoly are the converse of those for competition—few sellers, entry barriers, and so on. Prime evidence of monopolistic conduct is collusion among allegedly independent firms—agreements to fix prices, to share markets, or not to compete. Other indicators include interdependent pricing even without explicit agreements among firms, pricing strategies to limit the entry of competitors, various forms of price discrimination, efforts to create unreal product differences (e.g., advertising that does not convey information about underlying quality differences and price), and overt or covert links between public regulatory agencies and individual firms or groups of firms.

Such are the marks of competitive and monopolistic market structure and conduct. In performance, the key attributes of competition are fair prices to consumers and normal competitive returns to investors, whereas monopoly yields above-competitive rates in each case.

aspects of how firms operate—such as strategies in pricing or advertising, legal or business tactics, investments in plant and research and development, and the like. "Performance" is synonymous with outcomes at the societal level—efficiency, equity, innovation, product quality, and so on. For insurance, the key outcomes are the fairness of risk classification, premium setting, and returns to investors. These topics receive more attention in the later chapters. This chapter, like other traditional analyses of industrial organization, focuses on aspects of structure and conduct deemed predictive of performance.

A useful starting point for considering market structure, conduct, and performance is "perfect competition" as opposed to monopolistic behavior. The structure and conduct of competitive markets yield socially desirable performance (see Box 4.1).

A limitation of traditional analysis of industrial organization is that the empirical links among structure, conduct, and performance often have not been adequately demonstrated, although there is a logical relationship. For example, having few sellers in a market may facilitate collusion in price-output decisions and hence inefficient performance—restriction of output below the level that would prevail under competition. This assumption, for example, underlies antitrust enforcers' concerns about mergers between competitors. But in a particular case, such market concentration may not foster collusion and hence inadequate performance. Short of direct empirical evidence on performance, it is only appropriate to conclude that the likelihood of unfortunate monopoly-type outcomes is higher where sellers are concentrated.

CHAPTER OVERVIEW

The second section describes the structure of the market for malpractice insurance. We address these specific issues: What is the relevant product and geographic market for this analysis? Are there substantial barriers to entry or exit by sellers (whether imposed by a public regulatory agency or by private organizations, such as medical societies)? How concentrated are buyers and sellers? Do insurers actually segment the market further by specializing in different underwriting risks? How readily do physicians switch carriers? Are there notable economies (or diseconomies) of scale in this industry? What is the effect of competition on the number of surviving insurers in the smaller states?

In the third section we investigate industry conduct, especially with regard to premium setting and differences in practice by ownership type. Is there evidence of collusion or at least interdependence in premium setting among insurers in an area? Are there differences in the extent to which the various types of insurers monitor the kinds of physician behavior and in defending claims against physician insureds?

The fourth section presents conclusions and policy implications.

MARKET STRUCTURE

Defining the Relevant Market

An analysis of market structure properly begins by defining the market to be analyzed. A market is the sphere in which transactions occur between buyers and sellers. A market has both product and geographic dimensions (and, sometimes, a temporal one). Each seller may make more than one product, and every buyer consumes more than one. But each market involves only one product—or, more precisely, as many goods and services as are close substitutes for one another. If only two firms provide widget services, one might fear for competition; but if many sell gidget services that consumers can readily use instead, the market is in fact much broader. A landmark antitrust case indeed turned on the product definition of a market: Because the Supreme Court in 1956 saw cellophane not as a unique product but instead as one of many wrappings, DuPont was absolved of liability for controlling cellophane production (*United States* v. *E. I. duPont deNemours and Company* 1956).

Geographically, buyers and sellers must be able to consummate their transaction. No longer must they meet physically in the town marketplace on market day. Still, distance imposes costs. This is especially so for a personal service—including forms of insurance education and sales, as well as claims adjustment and provision of legal counsel. As a practical matter, insurance and other services are not bought and sold on the same basis worldwide, even though many insurers are multinationals.

A hypothetical example illustrates the interaction of product and geographic substitution in defining a market. Consider whether all the sellers of a given product in a given area can force buyers to accept a price hike. The market is defined as the narrowest product and geographic ambit in which all sellers could profitably impose a small but significant, nontransitory increase in price without suffering an appreciable loss in sales to other firms.[2]

What would happen in this hypothetical case? It depends on the characteristics of the product, its production, and its delivery. Such a price increase would be unprofitable if buyers could easily switch to (1) other products or (2) other sellers of the same product in more distant areas. These buyer-oriented responses are the demand-side criteria for defining a market. If the buyers can switch products, then those substitutes must be considered part of the same market. If more distant sellers can successfully compete for only a small increment in price, then the market area needs broadening. Similarly on the supply side: The price hike would also be unprofitable if firms not now producing the product could easily begin to do so, either by (1) adapting an existing facility (manufacturing plant, business office) or by (2) starting a new operation (plant, office).[3] If other sellers can readily convert to producing this product, the market also needs redefinition. For example, plastic flowers may be very different from plastic toys on the demand side but very similar on the supply side, for producers can substitute one for the other on the extrusion machine. Thus, analysis should focus on the plastics fabrication industry rather than on the plastic flower industry. If entirely new entry into the market is easy, actual or potential entry will discipline existing sellers almost as though the market were more broadly defined.

Product and Geographic Market Definition:
The Case of Medical Malpractice Insurance

How do these concepts apply in our case? Consider first whether the relevant product is insurance for malpractice liability or instead for property-casualty loss. On the basis of the first demand-side criterion, the relevant product is clearly medical malpractice insurance. The service being bought and sold is protection against loss due to a claim of a health care provider's malpractice. Other forms of property-casualty insurance, such as fire insurance, cannot substitute for such malpractice coverage. The risk is simply not at all the same. Another variant of liability coverage (general liability or professional liability coverage) could be written to cover medical losses, but again, the risks remain too different to be covered at the same price. Applying the second demand-side criterion, the relevant geographic area is the state, not the nation, though many insurers operate nationally. A physician located in one state cannot purchase malpractice insurance written for another state. State insurance regulation, of course, prevents this, but there are business reasons as well. A Florida physician cannot expect to assert that his risk is typical of Georgia physicians and purchase his insurance at Georgia rates. The law of liability is by definition different across state lines, and the behavior of litigants, judges, and jurors can also differ. So, expected losses would differ across states, and insurers' rating recognizes this. Furthermore, it would be difficult to investigate claims and defend physicians from afar.[4]

The two supply-side criteria yield more ambiguous results with regard to the relevant product. How easy is it for existing sellers (i.e., insurers) or new entrants to begin selling medical malpractice coverage? Legally, any licensed property-liability insurer may normally sell malpractice coverage; and there seem to be no important barriers to entry of malpractice insurers from other states who are attracted by a price increase. Moreover, the same property-casualty actuaries, insurance salespeople, and the like can convert to a new line. Harrington and Litan (1988) argued that entry into a property-liability line is easy, but they presented no direct empirical evidence in support of their contention.

A convincing argument can be made, however, that entry into the medical malpractice insurance line is not that easy. Malpractice insurance is a service industry, and it is important to know the customers—what they want and how to assess their risk of loss. Marketing to physicians is greatly facilitated if the company has the support of the state or local medical society. Medical societies have played a key role in insurance marketing since the early 1960s (Kendall and Haldi 1973). Their support is not forthcoming merely for the asking, and in most states a dominant plan already has society backing. Of course, specialty societies, hospitals, and other means also exist for obtaining favorable access to customers.

Second, risk management and claims management, including predicting losses and managing claims and legal defenses, require considerable specialized knowledge. Medical malpractice is a low-frequency, high-severity risk, as often noted before, and prediction is more difficult for a newcomer without a database of a state's experience than for existing insurers. Our interviews with national multiple-line insurers that quit selling malpractice insurance (Survey of Former Medical Malpractice Insurers) indicated that a major reason for quitting was the difficulty they experienced in controlling losses. The large and growing market share of insurers specializing in medical malpractice insurance also suggests that the malpractice insurance business is not easily learned. A newcomer may find it hard to win new physician customers, even at a good price, because each physician may have to buy an additional tail policy when leaving one company's claims-made form for another's (see below). Thus, from the supply perspective, although less clearly than from the demand side, the product seems best defined as malpractice insurance rather than more broadly as property-liability insurance.

Consider next the geographic aspect of the market on the supply side. Insurance is regulated at the state level (Chapter 3). Thus, even though regulation alone is not an important entry barrier, any potential entrant from outside a state does have to file with the state initially and then maintain various ongoing contacts with the state insurance department. These requirements impose some cost (as may a differential premium tax for out-of-state companies). More important, as already noted, the new entrant must know the territory, that is, be able to sell efficiently to physicians, to predict claims rates, and to be acquainted with state law for the purpose of defending claims. In short, some local presence is highly desirable. The leading malpractice insurer is a national company, but it has expanded slowly over time and still considers it geographically unfeasible to operate in Alaska or Hawaii. In many cases, state-domiciled suppliers dominate their own state markets. Thus, the state seems a more accurate geographic market than the nation. Given this focus on the state market for physicians' malpractice insurance, the other attributes of market structure will be considered next.

Exit and Entry

Evidence on the Top Three Medical Malpractice Insurers per State
We have just argued that entry into the malpractice line of coverage is less easy than it might at first appear. Data on the top sellers bear this out. Since 1978, *Best's Review* has published annual data on the top three malpractice insurers by state, as measured in terms of direct premium volume. The series includes malpractice insurance sold to hospitals (and nonphysicians like dentists) as well as to physicians, although the former is of declining importance, as more institutions have self-insured or made other similar arrangements. In the vast majority of states, the top three insurers account for the majority of the medical malpractice insurance sold. Thus, although changes in the top three insurers are not precise indicators of exit and entry, this measure should be a reasonably reliable proxy.

We computed the number of changes in the top three malpractice insurers by state and year during 1979–86 (Table 4.1). A maximum of 24 possible changes could have occurred per state per year beginning with shifts in 1978–79 and ending with 1985–86. No state actually had more than 10; only 4 of 51 jurisdictions (counting Washington, D.C.) had more than 7 changes in eight years. On average, states had 4.8 changes in the top three insurers—a little more than one every other year. (Fifty-one states totaled 243 changes in eight years out of a possible 1,224 changes.) There was little change in the pattern over time; yearly changes varied from 24 to 29 in all but the crisis period of the 1980s. More changes occurred between 1983 and 1984 (41) and between 1984 and 1985 (35) than between any of the other adjacent years.

Virtually all changes involved stock companies not under physician sponsorship. Physician-sponsored companies entered the market in large numbers beginning in 1975. Once they entered, they tended to gain and hold high market shares, and they did not move off the list of the top three insurers.[5]

Barriers to Exit
There are no regulatory barriers to exit. There is, however, one major barrier: cost. In pulling out of a state, the company must maintain a claims management operation for many years until all claims are resolved. Alternatively, the company must cede all of

Table 4.1. Annual Change in the Top Three Malpractice Insurers by State

State	1979	1980	1981	1982	1983	1984	1985	1986	Total
Most Changes									
New Mexico	1	1	2	2	1	1	1	1	10
Georgia	1	1	1	1	2	2	0	1	9
District of Columbia	1	2	1	0	2	1	0	1	8
Massachusetts	1	1	1	0	2	2	1	0	8
Fewest Changes									
Illinois	0	0	1	0	0	0	1	0	2
Maryland	0	0	0	0	0	1	1	0	2
Texas	1	0	0	0	0	0	1	0	2
Iowa	0	0	0	0	0	0	1	0	1
Pennsylvania	0	0	0	0	0	0	1	0	1
Virginia	0	0	0	1	0	0	0	0	1
Arizona	0	0	0	0	0	0	0	0	0
Total, All States	29	26	29	25	29	41	35	29	243

Source: *Best's Review*, 1979–87 issues.

the business to a reinsurer, generally at a high cost. While some might not view this as a barrier in the usual sense, there are financial consequences for pulling out of a market.

Evidence from Exiting Companies

We interviewed four national property-liability companies that dropped the malpractice insurance line during 1978–86. Although we prepared a survey instrument (Survey of Former Medical Malpractice Insurers), most companies preferred to provide information in narrative form. All of these companies dropped the malpractice line in every state. One company was reentering the market in various states at the time of the survey (1988). Two dominant themes about exit emerged from the survey. Companies reported difficulties in controlling losses and in competing with firms that had medical society sponsorship. The companies reported having avoided states with regulatory environments they saw as unfavorable to begin with (thus echoing participants in our more formal survey of malpractice insurers). Therefore, adverse regulatory decisions did not appear to be a major determinant in the companies' decision to quit.

One company described a scenario of loss experience leading to premium increases, which then caused its insureds to seek coverage elsewhere or, sometimes, to form insuring groups of their own. Some of the firms had tried to market malpractice insurance from afar without establishing a local presence in a state. As a result, they had difficulties in marketing, risk management, and claims management that ultimately reduced profitability and led them to discontinue the line. Those using locally based agents to sell malpractice insurance reported somewhat more success.

To ascertain whether companies charging higher premiums than their competitors were more likely to exit, we examined unpublished premium data provided by the U.S. Health Care Financing Administration (HCFA); HCFA collects state-specific medical malpractice premium data. For the most part, data are available only from the leading writer in a given state, though occasionally state premium data exist for more than one insurer. After reviewing the data, we determined that there were several states for which at least 10 years of data existed for two or more of the commercial writers that were prominent malpractice insurers prior to the mid-1970s' crisis. (Omitted from this analysis is the comparison between St. Paul and Medical Protective in Wisconsin because the data seemed implausible; the premiums for some of Medical Protective's insureds did not change over a seven-year period.) We compared the premiums of St. Paul and Medical Protective (the current malpractice insurers) with those of Aetna and Hartford (a former malpractice insurer). As noted later, comparisons were also made between St. Paul and Medical Protective.

We obtained premiums from HCFA for five physician categories: general practitioners, general surgeons, anesthesiologists, obstetricians/gynecologists, and orthopedic surgeons. Premiums for the anesthesiologists and the obstetricians/gynecologists were not included in this analysis because of shifts in the data indicating that these groups were probably changed from one rating category to another, but these changes did not take place in the same year for the different companies. Hence, only groups for which there was consistency in the rating group were included.

Our analysis in Table 4.2 is based on the difference between the premiums charged by the two companies. If the first company's premiums were higher, on average, the difference was positive; if negative, the second company's premiums were

Table 4.2. Difference in Premiums Between Companies in the Same State,[1] 1976–85

		Differences in Premiums			
State	Companies	General Practice	General Surgery	Orthopedic Surgery	All Three Specialties
Colorado	St. Paul[2] vs. Hart-ford	164.7[a] (121.5)	69.7 (657.5)	−787.0 (2,268.5)	−184.2 (1,387.5)
Iowa	St. Paul vs. Aetna	−372.5[b] (330.8)	−2,174.7[c] (1,413.8)	−3,645.6[c] (2,316.6)	−2,064.3[c] (2,042.8)
	St. Paul vs. Medical Protective	27.2 (196.0)	−914.9[c] (592.5)	−65.7 (925.3)	−200.3 (797.1)
	Medical Protective vs. Aetna	−399.7[b] (391.0)	−1,368.4[a] (1,414.4)	−3,471.3[c] (1,659.1)	−1,746.5[a] (1,795.3)
Louisiana	St. Paul vs. Hart-ford	242.1[b] (177.5)	890.5[a] (1,006.0)	1,832.8[c] (1,196.1)	988.5[c] (1,099.6)
Nebraska	St. Paul vs. Medical Protective	186.3[b] (172.1)	41.5 (878.8)	508.4 (984.6)	245.4 (767.6)
Ohio	St. Paul vs. Medical Protective	187.1 (428.0)	5.5 (1,872.4)	1,397.2 (2,629.1)	529.9 (1,919.6)
Washington	St. Paul vs. Aetna	−229.6[b] (210.7)	−1,244.7[b] (1,057.2)	−2,884.9[a] (3,097.8)	−1,453.1[b] (2,139.4)

Source: Unpublished data, HCFA.

[a]Statistically significant at the 1 percent level (two-tailed, *t*-test).

[b]Statistically significant at the 5 percent level (two-tailed, *t*-test).

[c]Statistically significant at the 10 percent level (two-tailed, *t*-test).

[1]The difference is the premium for the company listed first minus the premium for the second company in a given year. The numbers in parentheses are standard deviations.

[2]The premiums reported for St. Paul are for mature claims-made policies; for all other companies, the premiums are for occurrence policies. To correct for this difference, St. Paul premiums were first multiplied by a factor of 1.04.

higher. A total mean difference was calculated, and difference was averaged across the three physician groups over time.

The premiums for St. Paul were for claims-made policies. In order to compare premiums for claims-made policies with those for the occurrence policies of the other three companies, the St. Paul premiums were multiplied by a factor of 1.04. (This 4 percent differential was suggested by one of the executives who participated in our survey. A separate set of calculations was performed using a factor of 1.08, which yielded virtually the same results.) The appropriateness of using this factor was further evaluated by comparing the premiums for St. Paul and Medical Protective, since these two national companies still write malpractice insurance. There were three states with sufficient data for these two companies, yielding 12 comparisons. Of these, St. Paul had higher premiums for nine of the comparisons; Medical Protective was higher for three. Only two of these comparisons were statistically different (one was higher for St. Paul, one for Medical Protective), with none of the total differences being significantly different. Hence, St. Paul and Medical Protective, both companies that continued to sell medical malpractice insurance, appear to have relatively similar premiums.

Three other company comparisons, involving a current insurer and a former insurer (Aetna and Hartford, respectively), can be made with the HCFA data: St. Paul vs. Hartford, St. Paul vs. Aetna, and Medical Protective vs. Aetna. Compared with St. Paul and Medical Protective, Aetna charged higher premiums in two states. (Of 12 comparisons, all are statistically significant.) Since Aetna withdrew from the market, this suggests that market forces are at work. This was verified by an Aetna executive who said that the company's rate increases caused its insureds to seek coverage elsewhere.

The Hartford, however, is a different story. In the eight possible comparisons with St. Paul in two different states, St. Paul generally charged higher premiums; six of the eight were higher. (Five of the six were statistically different.) Hartford had medical society sponsorship in Louisiana (1972–81) and Colorado (1971–82). After losing sponsorship they stayed in these markets, competing with newly formed physician companies for several years before withdrawing. They left feeling that the line could not be reliably priced. In this instance, it was withdrawal of sponsorship, rather than price, that led to their eventual exit.

Thus, overall, the evidence on the relationship of relative premium to exit is mixed. A larger sample of competing companies providing the same type of coverage in a common set of locations is needed to establish that the relationship exists or does not exist.

Seller Concentration

Concentration of market share among only a few firms is a major policy interest for analysts of industrial organization and for antitrust enforcers. The reason for concern is that it is presumably easier for a few firms to collude in agreeing on price, output, and quality and in monitoring the agreements than it is when there are many firms.

Measuring Concentration

The Herfindahl Index is a leading measure of concentration. This summary index is the sum of the squares of all companies' market shares (as a percentage). The maximum value possible is 10,000 (100 × 100 when there is a single monopolist); the minimum approaches 0 (when each firm has practically a zero market share). Our estimates of the Herfindahl Index by state and year were computed from premium data published by *Best's Review* for 1978 and by the NAIC for 1986 (NAIC 1987). (As before [see Chapter 2], these premium data contain some premiums paid by hospitals and non-physician health professionals, as well as by physicians.)

Best's Review publishes market shares of only the three top malpractice insurers in the state in a given year (in the same list already described), making our 1978 data on market shares incomplete. The NAIC published 1986 premium data for all malpractice insurers writing in a state. To make somewhat equivalent comparisons between industry concentration in 1978 and 1986, we assumed 20 malpractice insurers per state, imputing equal market share to 17 other hypothetical insurers assumed to share the balance of each state's market in 1978. (As a check, we did the same for 1986; these adjusted Best's data yielded Herfindahl Indexes that were very similar to those based on the more complete NAIC data.)

Concentration in Malpractice Insurance
The market for malpractice coverage is very concentrated. In the vast majority of states, the Herfindahl Index was well over 1,800 in both years (Table 4.3). A score of 1,800 is the level of concentration that the U.S. Department of Justice believes to warrant special scrutiny in merger cases (U.S. Department of Justice 1984). Only eight jurisdictions scored below 1,800 in 1986 (Table 4.3). In fact, New Hampshire represents the 1986 median, with an index of 3,014. Higher concentration is to be expected in less populous states, for a certain minimum number of insureds is needed to make physician groupings insurable. However, size does not fully explain the Herfindahls. The eight states with 1986 values below 1,800 did include some of the dozen largest states—California, Massachusetts, Ohio, Pennsylvania, and Texas. Among the notable omissions here of the most populous states were Florida (HI = 3,399), New Jersey (HI = 4,272), and New York (HI = 2,226). Judging from the responses to our Survey of Medical Malpractice Insurers, all three states are viewed as undesirable states in which to sell malpractice insurance. Massachusetts was also considered undesirable, in part because of the dominance for physician coverage of a JUA. Premiums received by JUAs and PCFs were not excluded prior to computing the Herfindahl Indexes. Excluding these premium data markedly reduced the estimated indexes in states in which such organizations were dominant—Massachusetts and Rhode Island (JUA) and Pennsylvania (PCF).

There were often very substantial changes in the Herfindahl Indexes between 1978 and 1986. We regressed per state values of the index for 1978 to 1986 (not just the values presented in Table 4.3) on year and on a measure of the size of the market. The analysis revealed that, on average, concentration decreased over time. Also, concentration was lower, on average, in more populous states.

Does this concentration call for a policy response? Antitrust enforcers have evidently not thought so. The only significant case brought concerned reinsurers accused of collusion during the 1980s' crisis.

Concentration is mainly of policy interest because it may result from anticompetitive conduct and further facilitate collusion, especially to raise prices. It also reduces consumer choice (but this is not a concern where markets are free). Our analysis of

Table 4.3. Market Concentration: Herfindahl Index by State, 1978 and 1986

1. Low Concentration (Index under 1,800 in 1986)

State	1978 HI	1986 HI	% Change	State	1978 HI	1986 HI	% Change
CA	1,537	1,027	− 33.2	MO	818	1,483	+ 81.3
IN	1,690	1,343	− 20.5	OH	1,241	1,677	+ 35.1
MD	3,301	1,670	− 49.4	PA	2,126	1,774	− 16.6
MA	1,243	1,125	− 9.5	TX	1,576	1,620	+ 2.8

II. Herfindahl Index between 1,800 and 5,000 in 1986

State	1978 HI	1986 HI	% Change	State	1978 HI	1986 HI	% Change
AL	4,297	3,823	− 11.0	NV	3,037	2,033	− 33.0
AK	4,058	3,303	− 18.6	NH	2,615	3,014	+ 15.3
AZ	4,683	3,734	− 20.3	NJ	2,880	4,272	+ 48.3
CO	3,019	2,286	− 24.3	NM	4,922	4,494	− 8.7
CT	8,218	2,383	− 71.0	NY	4,034	2,226	− 44.8
DE	7,750	2,368	− 69.4	NC	3,918	3,997	+ 2.0
DC	5,768	2,499	− 56.7	ND	2,719	3,412	+ 25.5
FL	4,368	3,399	− 23.6	OK	3,110	3,802	+ 22.2
GA	5,933	3,338	− 43.7	OR	4,074	3,693	− 9.4
HI	5,790	2,103	− 63.7	RI	4,045	2,944	− 27.2
ID	3,403	2,493	− 26.7	SD	7,496	4,645	− 38.0
IL	2,295	3,583	+ 56.1	TN	5,010	4,232	− 15.5
IA	1,630	4,073	+149.9	UT	7,623	3,902	− 48.8
KS	3,157	1,981	− 37.3	VT	5,721	4,560	− 20.3
KY	2,086	1,966	− 5.8	VA	4,964	2,902	− 41.5
LA	4,131	3,496	− 15.4	WA	7,071	2,121	− 70.0
ME	4,153	3,985	− 4.0	WV	7,091	2,082	− 70.6
MI	1,399	2,430	+ 73.7	WI	2,836	2,160	− 25.7
MN	8,412	3,653	− 56.6	WY	4,529	2,181	− 51.8
MT	4,156	2,206	− 46.9				

III. High Concentration (Index over 5,000 in 1986)

State	1978 HI	1986 HI	% Change	State	1978 HI	1986 HI	% Change
AR	7,566	5,709	− 24.5	NE	3,512	5,400	+ 53.8
MS	4,656	5,150	+ 10.6	SC	2,060	6,256	+203.7

Source: *Best's Review*, 1979–1987.

Note: The A. M. Best Company publishes the percentages for only the top three reporting medical malpractice insurers in *Best's Review*. See the text for a discussion of our method for computing the Herfindahl Indexes.

market conduct (below) investigated this issue more closely. Based on the market structure of malpractice insurance, collusion does not look as plausible here. Physician-sponsored companies seem unlikely to collude in charging massively higher insurance prices to physicians (though they may wish to accumulate prudent amounts of surplus). In general, one expects collusion to take place and to persist (absent some form of coercive public intervention) only when it is in the interest of each voluntarily colluding firm. But the diversity of ownership forms in many states makes it difficult to envision a particular cartel pricing policy that could simultaneously satisfy such different companies.

Underwriting Standards and Product Definition

Are firms selling malpractice insurance selling the same product? It would be inappropriate to combine firms' market shares in particular market areas or compare their premiums if the firms differed appreciably in the risks they insure. Our Survey of Medical Malpractice Insurers, conducted during 1987 and early 1988, included several questions about underwriting standards (Table 4.4).

The firms surveyed were willing to insure virtually all of the physicians licensed to practice in the state. More specifically, all sold to all types of physicians in the state, although only one company was required to do so by state law. For these dominant insurers, the product is clearly malpractice insurance, not some subset of it.

However, almost half of the insurers had competitors that specialized in particular categories of physicians. Many of these were national plans specializing in a particular physician specialty, including risk retention groups (Chapter 3). The market shares of firms offering coverage to selected specialties tended to be far smaller than those of the companies we surveyed.

Companies sold to all types of physicians but not to every physician applying for coverage (Tables 4.4 and 4.5). No state required that insurers accept all physicians, irrespective of their claims history or other factor predictive of high future claims costs. (One state previously had such a requirement. This may account for the lack of new entrants into the malpractice market in that state.) Twelve of the 14 firms did not impose higher underwriting standards for physicians seeking higher amounts of malpractice insurance coverage.

Firms did in fact reject some applicants for coverage, but there is no evidence of market segmentation based on policyholders' expected loss. On average, the firms

Table 4.4. Underwriting Practices

		Responses		
Question (Verbatim)		Mutual-Reciprocal	Stock	Total
1. Does company insure all, or particular	All	11	3	14
categories, of physicians?	Part. cat.	0	0	0
2. If all, does state law require company	Yes	1	0	1
to offer insurance to all categories of	No	10	3	13
physicians?				
3. Do competitors specialize in particular	Yes	6	1	7
categories of physicians?	No	4	1	5
	No answer	1	1	2
4. Is company required by state law or	Yes	0	0	0
regulation to write medical malpractice	No	11	3	14
insurance for anyone licensed in [com-				
pany's home state]?				
5. Are more stringent criteria applied to	Yes	2	0	2
physicians seeking [the] higher	No	9	3	12
amounts of malpractice insurance				
coverage?				

Source: Survey of Medical Malpractice Insurers.

responding to our survey rejected 7.1 percent of new applicants in a typical year (Table 4.5). The range was from 1 to 29 percent, but the latter was due to unusual circumstances. The 29 percent company was severely limiting the number of new applicants because an important competitor had recently left its state; 29 percent rejection did not indicate unusually high underwriting standards. Physician-sponsored (mutual-reciprocal) companies appeared less selective on average—but only one stock company answered this question.

The mean rate of nonrenewal was much lower than that of initial rejection—only 1.2 percent for mutual-reciprocals, almost the same for stock companies, and with little variation by company. Ten of the companies listed the individual physician's claims history as the most important factor in screening applicants for coverage (Table 4.6). Less frequently mentioned were the professional qualifications of the physician, such as licensure and nature of the practice (e.g., unproven procedures being performed).

Two insurers noted their reluctance to reject physicians' applications for coverage out of a fear of antitrust suits. Having coverage is a virtual precondition to successful medical practice because hospitals require it (to avoid having to pay damages caused by an uninsured physician). So, a physician refused coverage might argue that his or her competitors on the board of a physician-owned company denied him or her coverage not for good insurance reasons but for illegitimate anticompetitive reasons. Many states and the U.S. Congress have immunized physicians participating in hospital peer review in good faith from such suits, but no such immunity protects malpractice insurers (Bovbjerg 1989).

Demand Curves Facing Individual Insurers

Another measure of the competitiveness of a market is the extent to which individual insurers possess market power. Market power can be assessed by the extent to which they can raise their premiums above the amount charged by competing sellers without losing large numbers of customers. We begin with indirect inferences about the plausible responsiveness of physicians to price differentials.

Persistence of Physician Insureds with Their Insurers

Our Survey of Medical Malpractice Insurers asked, "What persistence rate have you observed over the past three and five years?" The "persistence rate" is the percentage of insureds still with the company three or five years later. Reasons for leaving a company included death, retirement, and relocation, as well as dissatisfaction with the insurer's price and service. (Recall also that a little over 1 percent of insureds a year are nonrenewed, according to Table 4.5.) After three years, 88 percent remained with their company on average (Table 4.7), implying that less than 3 percent of all insureds voluntarily leave a given company in any given year. (It is difficult to think of death or disability as voluntary.) The means for the mutual-reciprocal and stock companies were similar, 89 and 86 percent, respectively. At five years, the mean persistence rate declined markedly, to 72 percent (73 percent for the mutual-reciprocals, 68 percent for the stocks). One mutual insurer had a persistence rate as low as 50 percent in an area where a stock company had entered its market with low premiums.

Why the decline should accelerate over time is unclear. One possibility is the

Table 4.5. Applicants Rejected or Not Renewed by Insurers (Percent)

	Mutual-Reciprocal				Stock				Total			
	Mean	Maximum	Minimum	N	Mean	Maximum	Minimum	N	Mean	Maximum	Minimum	N
Applicants rejected	6.7	29.0	1.0	9	12.5	12.5	12.5	1	7.3	29.0	1.0	10
Insured not renewed	1.2	2.5	0.5	10	1.3	1.5	1.0	3	1.3	2.5	0.5	13

Source: Survey of Medical Malpractice Insurers.

Note: N = number of responses to the questions. Not all companies responded.

Table 4.6. Important Factors in Screening Applicants for Coverage

	Listed 1st	Listed 2nd	Listed 3rd
Claims history	10	2	2
Professional qualifications, licensure	3	3	1
Nature and method of practice procedures	1	2	4
Disciplinary action		3	1
Physician disability, impairment, chemical dependency		2	1
Physician specialty		1	3
Prior coverage cancellation		1	
Competence			
Possible sexual problems with patients			1
Number of companies responding	14	14	13

Source: Survey of Medical Malpractice Insurers.

Note: The question was open-ended, and companies could list up to three factors in order of importance. One company did not provide a third factor.

timing of our survey, which meant that the latter two years of persistence occurred as the markets for malpractice coverage improved, increasing physicians' options for coverage (though seldom with the extreme effect of our 50 percent persistence insurer).

Over one-quarter of physicians thus leave a company within five years. But why do they switch? We asked each company: "What factors cause you to gain and lose physicians?" Eleven of the 14 companies stressed price. Of the remaining three, all mutuals or reciprocals, one did not answer the question. A second said it could not respond because it was a monopolist in its state. The third implied that physicians in its state do not select insurers on the basis of price. One insurer volunteered that young physicians were more price-conscious than their older colleagues. A cautious interpretation of these data is that the demand facing individual insurers is somewhat responsive to price.

It would certainly be wrong to conclude on the basis of such data alone that demand is greatly responsive to price, so that small premium differentials would cause widespread switching of insurers. Potential switchers may be concerned about how long any new entrant will remain in the market. Physicians badly need coverage and fear losing it. If a new insurer leaves, the old one may not take physicians back, at least not right away (as we saw where an insurer raised rejections to 29 percent after a competitor's departure).

Elasticity of Demand

"Elasticity of demand" is a ratio of the percentage change in demand for a good or service divided by the percentage change in the price. For example, if an insurer raises its price by 10 percent and the demand for insurance from this company drops by 5 percent, the elasticity of demand is 0.50 (the negative is understood). Ideally, to assess responsiveness to price, one would derive estimates of the elasticity of demand facing individual insurers. To do this precisely, one needs premium and loss data by line from all of the major insurers in particular market areas. Available resources did not permit primary data collection on this scale, even if individual insurers would release it. Nor were the requisite data available from secondary sources. We are able, however, to

Table 4.7. Persistence Rates of Insureds

	Mutual-Reciprocal				Stock				Total			
	Mean	Maximum	Minimum	N	Mean	Maximum	Minimum	N	Mean	Maximum	Minimum	N
Three years	89	98	80	6	86	87	84	2	88	98	80	8
Five years	73	90	50	5	68	72	64	2	72	90	50	7

Source: Survey of Medical Malpractice Insurers.

Note: N = number of responses to the question.

illustrate a likely range of elasticities, using a formula for the individual firm's elasticity of demand[6]:

$$\epsilon_i^d = \frac{\epsilon_m^d}{S_i} + \frac{\epsilon_j^s(1 - S_i)}{S_i} \tag{4.1}$$

where

ϵ_i^d = firm-specific elasticity of demand
ϵ_m^d = market elasticity of demand
ϵ_j^s = fringe supply elasticity
S_i = firm's market share

A smaller firm-specific elasticity of demand means greater market power of individual firms.

Lower market demand elasticity means a lower firm-specific demand elasticity (other factors constant). Although precise estimates are unavailable, the market elasticity for malpractice insurance is surely small. Hospitals typically require coverage, and insurer respondents to our survey indicated that 99 percent of physicians in their areas had coverage. For applying equation (4.1), we accordingly assumed a value of 0.05 for the market elasticity of demand (ϵ_m^d).

The fringe supply elasticity (ϵ_j^s) gives the percentage increase in supply of output by the firm's competitors for each percentage increase in price by the firm under study (firm i). For calculating the elasticity of the individual insurer's demand curve, we assumed values of 0.33 and 0.67 for ϵ_j^s. Higher fringe supply elasticity means a higher firm-specific elasticity of demand, holding other factors constant. As the firm's market share rises, so does its firm-specific elasticity of demand. We assumed market shares ranging from 0.10 to 0.90 (10 to 90 percent). Actual shares vary markedly among insurers and states.

As seen in Table 4.8, firms with market shares of 0.25 or less face substantial firm-specific demand elasticities (over 1.0). Such firms have little power to set prices on their own. By contrast, insurers with market shares of 0.50 and over have considerable market power, that is, the ability to set prices without colluding with their competitors. As Table 4.9 shows, in more than half of the states, over half of the office-based physicians are insured with a physician-sponsored company, of which there is

Table 4.8. Firm-Specific Elasticities of Demand[1]

| Firm's Market | Fringe Supply Elasticity | |
Share	0.33	0.67
0.10	3.47	6.53
0.25	1.19	2.21
0.50	0.43	0.77
0.75	0.18	0.29
0.90	0.09	0.12

[1]Based on equation (4.1), hypothetical elasticities, and market shares.

Table 4.9. Rank Ordering of Physician-Sponsored Company Market Shares, 1987

Rank	State	Market Share (%)	Rank	State	Market Share (%)
1	Oklahoma	"Market saturation"	25	Kentucky	55
2	Arkansas	95	27	Florida	50
2	Michigan	95	27	Washington	50
2	Tennessee	95	27	Wisconsin	50
5	Colorado	90	30	Georgia	45
5	Nevada	90	30	Hawaii	45
5	Ohio	90	30	Minnesota	45
8	Arizona	85	33	Connecticut	40
9	Alabama	80	33	Louisiana	40
9	Mississippi	80	33	Texas	40
9	New York	80	36	Idaho	35
12	Maine	75	36	Iowa	35
12	Montana	75	36	North Dakota	35
12	New Mexico	75	39	Indiana	30
12	Utah	75	39	Nebraska	30
12	Wyoming	75	39	Virginia	30
17	Maryland	70	42	Oregon	25
18	California	65	42	West Virginia	25
18	Illinois	65	44	South Dakota	5
18	Missouri	65	45	Delaware	—
18	New Jersey	65	45	Kansas	—
22	North Carolina	60	45	Massachusetts	—
22	Washington, D.C.	60	45	New Hampshire	—
22	Pennsylvania	60	45	Rhode Island	—
25	Arizona	55	45	South Carolina	—
			45	Vermont	—

Sources: Number of policyholders from the PIAA (1987) listing, supplemented with calls to individual insurers; number of office-based physicians from the American Medical Association (1986).

Note: Percentage market share = (number of physicians in the state obtaining medical malpractice insurance through a physician-owned company)/(number of office-based physicians in the state). Percentages are reported for some states that do not have a physician-sponsored medical malpractice insurer based in their state. Some physician-sponsored medical malpractice insurers wrote medical malpractice coverage in other than their home states. The unit of output for computing shares here is the policyholder—not premiums, as in Chapter 2.

typically only one per state (with some exceptions, such as California). Although many of the physician-sponsored companies appear to have market power, it is unclear that they would want to charge higher than competitively priced premiums to their policyholders, who are also the residual claimants.

Economies or Diseconomies of Scale

Where substantial economies of scale exist, new entry is made more difficult; at the extreme, economies of scale create a natural monopoly. We therefore sought to assess the presence of economies or diseconomies of scale. Again, available data fail to capture the full complexity of costs. What we could do was to specify and estimate cost equations, with the ratio of total expense to total premiums as the dependent variable. Explanatory variables included total premiums, share of premiums from different lines of insurance, organizational type, and measures of labor cost (see Box 4.2).

Box 4.2. Regressions on Cost

In the regression, total expense was defined as the sum of loss adjustment, underwriting, and investment expenses for the company as a whole; this was expressed as a fraction of total premiums. Loss expense was excluded.

The primary data source was A.M. Best's *Best's Insurance Reports— Property-Casualty* for the years 1979–87, which are issued annually. The data spanned 1978–86 and included 19 single-line insurers, all specializing in medical malpractice insurance, and 17 multiple-line insurers. The multiple-line insurers were all commercial stock companies.

We included these explanatory variables: total premiums and such premiums squared; fractions of total premiums from (1) medical malpractice, (2) Workers' Compensation, (3) multiple peril, and (4) other liability, with automobile liability the omitted reference group; binary variables for the mutual and the reciprocal-exchange organizational forms, with the omitted reference group being stock companies—both commercial and physician owned; and the mean weekly earnings in the insurance and banking sectors in the state where the company was domiciled. With the exception of the earnings variable, which came from *Employment and Earnings*, the data came from the *Property-Casualty Reports*. All monetary values were converted to 1986 dollars.

We obtained the following cost equation:

$$\frac{Total\ expense}{P} = 0.58 - (8.75\text{E} - 8)P + (1.21\text{E} - 14)P^2 + 0.26Pmm$$
$$[1.22\text{E} - 7] \qquad [2.37\text{E} - 14] \qquad [0.32]$$

$$+\ 0.033Pwc + 0.26Pp - 0.41Po$$
$$[0.25] \qquad\ [0.30] \qquad [0.34]$$

$$-\ 0.56^bM - 0.57^bRE + 0.00007W$$
$$[0.25] \qquad\ [0.25] \qquad\ [0.0002]$$

$$R^2 = 0.45 \qquad \bar{R}^2 = 0.41 \qquad F(9,120) = 11.0$$

(4.2)

where

P = total premium
Pmm = medical malpractice premium share
Pwc = Workers' Compensation premium share
Pp = peril premium share
Po = other liability premium share
M = mutual company
RE = reciprocal-exchange company
W = mean weekly earnings
[ ] = standard error of the coefficient
b = statistically significant at the 5 percent level (two-tail test)

Although the regression is limited by data availability,[7] several results are noteworthy. Most of the 36 firms in the sample operated at output levels at which there were economies of scale. The point of minimum average cost was substantially above the mean premium. Most of the single-line insurers were mutuals or reciprocal-exchanges. A few single-line insurers were physician-owned stock companies. The results suggest that companies not organized on a stock basis are comparatively efficient. Although there are scale economies, they are small: The decrease in average administrative cost per dollar change in premium implied by the regression below the point of minimum average cost is small. Comparing scale economies with the effects of ownership, it appears that most of the mutuals and reciprocal-exchanges are relatively efficient in spite of their small sizes. Thus, on the ground of administrative efficiency, it is not surprising that the small single-line medical malpractice insurers survive.

CONDUCT

The major concern about conduct is collusive, anticompetitive behavior.

Agreements Not to Compete

There do not appear to be explicit agreements not to compete in medical malpractice insurance. However, a large number of sellers do not compete for reasons of law, custom, and/or deliberate policy. Almost all physician-sponsored companies restrict themselves to one state. The majority either (1) most commonly have no desire to enter other states, (2) would enter a state only if requested to do so by the state's medical society, or (3) are prohibited by law from entering a state other than the one in which they are domiciled. In response to a question in our Survey of Medical Malpractice Insurers, one insurer stated that for it to enter another state, it would both have to be invited by the physician-sponsored company in that state to enter and also have the sponsorship of the medical society in that state. (At one time, the PIAA accepted as members only companies with medical society ties; this rule has been dropped.) With a few exceptions, most notably California, physician-owned companies rarely compete within other states.

This single-state pattern is evident from responses not only to our Survey of Medical Malpractice Insurers, but also from secondary data on where physician-sponsored companies do business, and from the fact that national commercial companies accounted for almost all entry and exit during the past decade.[8] Given that most physician-sponsored companies will not compete with sister companies, it is the threat of nonphysician insurer competition that provides some degree of market discipline over individual sellers of medical malpractice insurance.

Other Possible Forms of Collusion

Firms may not explicitly collude, yet implicitly achieve similar results.

Use of Same Actuaries

Actuaries are very influential in rate making and other key policy choices of an insurer. Thus, to the extent that competing companies use the same actuaries, certain decisions might be harmonized across companies. Our Survey of Medical Malpractice Insurers asked the companies whether they used in-house or outside actuaries, and to name any outside actuary they used. All three stock companies used in-house actuaries; one also used outside actuaries as expert witnesses in rate hearings. With one exception, the 11 mutual-reciprocals used outside actuaries, but five different actuarial firms were named. So, not only do the mutual-reciprocals typically have a policy against competing, but they also use various actuaries. They do compete against stock companies, but the latter all use in-house actuaries. Thus, use of the same actuaries does not appear to be a source of collusion among medical malpractice insurers.

Role of Rating Bureaus

Rating bureaus have developed in the property-liability insurance field for the purpose of collecting and processing expense information and, based on such data, computing suggested premiums (Brainard and Dirlam 1966). Such data collection and advice assist insurers, especially the smaller firms that do not have the loss and expense information base on which to develop rates on their own. In this sense, bureaus promote competition.

However, concerted rate making may also tend to suppress price competition. A report of the Department of Justice (1977) expressed a concern that, with the institution of rating bureaus, competing insurers may be able to publish industry rates collectively for future periods based on industry average costs, often without effective governmental supervision.

The same theme has been taken up in several academic studies (see, e.g., Joskow 1973 and Danzon 1983b). Use of rating bureaus may present a particular danger to competition in prior approval rate regulation states, where the insurance department may insist that individual insurers adhere to bureau rates. The most recent work on this issue by Danzon (1983b), which focused on passenger automobile insurance and reviewed much of the other literature, concluded that the empirical evidence on balance did not suggest that rating bureaus have been used to cartelize the industry.

Judging from the interviews we conducted, it appears that malpractice insurers rarely, if ever, use bureau rates.[9] Even if rating bureaus posed an anticompetitive threat to other property-liability lines, they do not appear to affect the pricing of medical malpractice insurance.

Role of Medical Societies

Medical societies have long played an important role in the market for malpractice insurance. Their role became even more important after the malpractice insurance crisis of the mid-1970s, with the rise of physician-sponsored insurers. In the majority of states, medical societies have helped organize physician-sponsored companies to provide medical malpractice insurance. The 1987 market shares of physician-sponsored companies (the percentage is defined as the number of physicians in the state obtaining insurance through a physician-sponsored company divided by the total number of office-based physicians in the state) ranged from nearly 100 percent in one state to zero in seven others (Table 4.9). With the exception of Michigan and Ohio, all of the states with physician-sponsored company market shares of 90 percent or more in 1987 were small or medium-sized markets. The only two small states without their own physician-sponsored company in the list of states with market shares of 90 percent and over are Nevada, which was served by California-based companies, and Arkansas, served by a Texas-based company.

The states with a dominant medical society-sponsored company had very little in common. Michigan has had a litigious climate, especially in the Detroit area. By contrast, in Tennessee, claims frequency and the mean dollar value of paid claims (severity) have been comparatively low. Several of the states without physician-sponsored companies in 1987 are in New England, where JUAs have dominated the markets in Massachusetts and Rhode Island.

The roles of the medical societies have differed among the states. In some cases, the medical societies supplied start-up capital. In others, the societies did not contribute equity or lend funds to the insurer, but rather assisted in organizing the companies. Analytically, these relationships between medical societies and physician-sponsored companies can be described as vertical combinations. Malpractice insurance may, in turn, be viewed as an input in producing physicians' services, hence the physicians' organized interest.

One way that medical societies have become involved is in sponsoring group programs—joint ventures between medical societies and insurers. One commercial insurer in responding to our Survey of Former Medical Malpractice Insurers stated:

> In the mid-70s we concluded that the only way that we could continue offering coverage to doctors would be through a State Medical Society sponsored program. This sponsorship mechanism gave us a vehicle to engage in Risk Management and Claims Management Activities; such Risk Management and Claims Management Activities could not be performed, in our estimation, when writing insurance on an individual doctor basis. Consequently, in 1976, we began a withdrawal from offering individual malpractice policies and subsequently limited our writings to members of state sponsored programs.

By endorsing the plan, the medical societies assisted the company in marketing insurance. Judging from the responses to the Survey of Medical Malpractice Insurers, one may infer that the risk management activities may have involved loss prevention seminars facilitated by the medical society, and local physicians may have helped to assess the quality of care rendered by physicians with problematic claims histories.

Both joint ventures and vertical combinations potentially reduce competition. They sometimes may be justified on the ground that the risks to insurance competition are more than offset by the efficiency gains to be obtained from the insurer-society relationship in marketing, underwriting, loss prevention, and claims management. The risks to competition are that association between a medical society and an insurer will deter entry of other insurers into the market.

The problem is not monopoly pricing, for no organization acting on behalf of physicians would want to set monopolistic prices for an input to medical practice. The true concern for competition lies elsewhere: By controlling the supply of an essential input, such arrangements may potentially influence entry of physicians, practice patterns, and modes of financing and organizing the delivery of health care services.

Insurer practice can also influence how physicians relate to alternative providers, like nurse midwives or chiropractors. If, because of special favors granted by medical societies to certain insurers, it becomes impossible for nonaffiliated insurers to compete, then many or all physicians will have to rely only on a society-influenced carrier for coverage. Such power may be used to deter disfavored conduct by covered physicians (perhaps testifying in malpractice cases or working with nurse midwives) or may serve as an entry barrier to innovative or other physicians not favored for one reason or another by organized medicine and its malpractice insurers.

We have no empirical evidence from the Survey of Medical Malpractice Insurers or other sources that any such anticompetitive practices prevail in this industry. In fact, two firms indicated their awareness of potential antitrust problems of this type in their responses. However, there is likewise no evidence that such anticompetitive practices never occur. And even if not used now, such arrangements may be used to limit competition in the future.

Interdependencies in Premium Setting

Our survey included a set of questions on interdependencies in premium setting among firms within a market. More specifically, we asked, "Have you observed instances of 'follow-the-leader' pricing?" Only four companies said "yes." In one case, it was stated that small companies do not have an adequate claims' database on which to forecast future losses. Hence they are forced to copy the premiums charged by others that sell malpractice insurance in the market area. Others ascribed the interdependencies to competitive pressures. One insurer stated that "when there are three firms trying to acquire a significant piece of a couple of thousand available insureds, competition can be intense." One physician-sponsored company responded that competitors tried to keep their premiums 5 percent below its own. Another physician-sponsored company denied that interdependencies in premium setting existed in its area but then stated that "small companies rely on our experience."

On the other hand, some companies stated that competitors had entered their markets with substantially lower premiums than theirs. These companies did not lower their premiums in response to the competition and did not lose an appreciable number of customers, but, as noted above, one company did lose a substantial number of policyholders to a lower-priced commercial insurer entrant. The difference in actions and reactions probably reflects differences in relationships among medical societies and insurers in the various states, the price of tail coverage, and the quality of the lower-priced insurer, as well as the commitment of the insurer to sell insurance in the state, at least as perceived by physicians practicing in the state.

COMPARISONS AMONG OWNERSHIP TYPES

In what ways does behavior differ, if any, between commercial stock insurers and physician-sponsored medical malpractice insurers? As already noted, we could detect no difference in underwriting standards by organizational form (above), but physician-sponsored insurers may be more willing to engage in loss prevention activities (see also Chapter 2).

Monitoring Physicians

Physician-sponsored companies may theoretically have a competitive advantage in monitoring the physicians they insure, for they have built-in expertise and professional credibility. To investigate this issue, we included several questions on loss prevention-risk management on our Survey of Medical Malpractice Insurers (Table 4.10). Virtually all companies provided information about loss control through mailings to their insureds. The commercial companies were less likely to sponsor seminars on loss control or to offer seminars for continuing medical education (CME) credit than the mutual-reciprocals. A minority of both types of companies gave premium discounts to participants in loss prevention-risk management seminars or required that new policyholders attend a loss prevention seminar. The premium discounts to policyholders for attending loss control seminars ranged from zero (four companies) to 22 percent.

Both the stock and the mutual-reciprocal companies also mentioned other loss control activities not specifically included in our questions. These included providing material to physicians for home study, on-site facility/office evaluations, office staff seminars, a loss prevention committee composed of physicians to review the records of physicians with large claims, and a team of nurses hired specifically to assess the record-keeping practices of physicians with liability problems.

The only real difference in risk management-loss prevention between the stock and mutual-reciprocals that we could detect was in the provision of seminars. However, since the efficacy of loss prevention seminars is not known, it is not possible to judge whether such seminars give a firm any competitive advantage. In fact, it might be argued that by giving physicians an opportunity to assemble, such seminars yield benefits to organized medicine, regardless of whether they reduce claims frequency or severity.

Defending Physicians

To determine whether physician-sponsored companies devote more resources to defending claims than commercial companies, we analyzed a file from Florida of almost

Table 4.10. Loss Prevention and Risk Management

		Responses		
Question		Mutual-Reciprocal	Stock	Total
1. Does your company provide information to insureds through mailings?	Yes	10	3	13
	No	1	0	1
2. Does your company provide information to insureds through seminars?	Yes	11	1	12
	No	0	2	2
3. Do physicians receive CME credits if they participate in seminars?	Yes	8	1	9
	No	3	2	5
4. Are premium discounts given to seminar participants?	Yes	3	1	4
	No	9	2	11
5. Are new policyholders required to attend a loss prevention seminar?	Yes	3	0	3
	No	9	3	12

Source: Survey of Medical Malpractice Insurers.

5,500 closed claims from late 1985 though early 1988. All claims closed in Florida must be filed with the Florida Department of Insurance. For each closed claim we knew, among other things, the company that defended the claim, defense cost, indemnity payment, severity of injury on a nine-point scale, plaintiff age, and the date the injury occurred in the year the case was closed. As a first step, we used regression analysis to compare the percentages of total payment (i.e., indemnity plus insurer defense cost) that were allocated to defense cost by type of company (holding other factors constant). We compared the percentages for commercial companies (both stock and mutual, a total of 2,229 closed claims) with various types of physician-sponsored companies. The latter included a physician mutual (11 closed claims), a physician reciprocal (1,000 closed claims), two companies classified as a "physician trust" (1,747 closed claims), and a "physician fund" (421 closed claims). A final category was self-insured plans (32 closed claims). Given the paucity of observations in the mutual and self-insured categories, comparisons between these categories and the omitted reference category, commercial companies, are not very interesting.

Holding year, severity of injury, and claimant age constant, there were no systematic differences between the percentage of the payment allocated by the physician-sponsored companies to defense and that of the commercial companies. The percentage for the reciprocal was 4 percent higher than the percentage for the commercial companies. However, the percentage for the trust was 4 percent lower. The percentage for the physician fund was 1 percent higher than the percentage for the commercial companies. Such differentials should be viewed as inconsequential.

Moreover, we did document that, holding constant factors such as severity of the injury, nature of the injury, and characteristics of the claimants and defendants, non-commercial insurers were more likely to pursue cases to verdict than were commercial stock companies. In this sense, they fought claimants harder, but they compensated claimants more often (Sloan and Hsieh 1990).[10]

Assuring Availability of Coverage

One of the questions asked at the beginning of the chapter was whether physician-owned companies fill a niche not occupied by the traditional for-profit insurer. It seems they definitely do. Many of these companies were started in the mid-1970s, when the availability of insurance became an issue. By having in place a single-line company, where money need not be diverted, either to lines experiencing trouble or to lines that are more profitable and do not need to make insurance decisions based solely on profits, the physician-owned companies ensure continuous availability of malpractice insurance.

CONCLUSIONS AND IMPLICATIONS

The relevant product market for our analysis is medical malpractice insurance, and the relevant geographic market is the state. So, malpractice insurance can be thought of as an industry. In certain regards, however, competition looms from potential entry by property-casualty insurers not currently selling malpractice coverage and from out-of-state malpractice insurers. Structurally, there are no large barriers to entering the market, although there are regulatory hurdles. Support of a state's medical society facilitates entry, but there is little hard evidence that lack of organized medicine's support has been an absolute entry barrier. Success in this line requires specialized data and knowledge, as well as a local presence. But such "barriers" do not call for government intervention.

The prevalence of claims-made policies may be one of the strongest competitive hurdles to overcome for a firm wishing to enter the market. As seen earlier, there is a high persistence rate in this industry. It is not known if the loyalty is due to satisfaction with the product or the need to purchase a tail policy, usually costing the equivalent of the latest year's premium, from one's current insurer before one can be accepted by a new insurer.

Tabulations show that there has been some exit and entry of medical malpractice insurers in the past decade. Commercial stock insurers have disproportionately been the firms entering and exiting, so it appears that they, rather than the physician companies, are especially sensitive to changes in expected returns. Disruptions associated with exit are understandably of concern to physicians and hence to their patients, and exiting insurers often bear some continuing expense after withdrawing from the malpractice insurance market.

In most states, the industry is highly concentrated, but the trend has been toward less concentration. High concentration is worthy of scrutiny to the extent that it facilitates collusion among sellers. However, it is clear that a physician-sponsored company would not want to charge physicians monopoly prices, and it is not clear why it would collude with a commercial stock insurer, which has different interests. Further, our investigation found no concrete evidence of collusion—agreements not to compete, use of the same actuaries, or use of rating bureaus. But some findings are troublesome, in particular, the policy of most physician-sponsored companies not to compete with sister companies.

Given the high insurer market shares in each state, individual firms may possess market power even in the absence of collusion. Insurers with shares of around 50 percent or more do have appreciable market power. Most firms in a position to exercise such power, however, would probably not desire to do so. We documented some economies of scale, and some small states thus will probably not support more than one firm in the long run.

Organizational form does not appear to influence underwriting practice. Nor have we been able to document important systematic differences in conduct among forms, specifically in loss prevention. In particular, none of the companies, commercial or noncommercial, were particularly vigorous in identifying, dropping, or surcharging physicians likely to incur disproportionate losses, an issue to be revisited in our analysis of experience rating in Chapter 8 and in some of our articles on the industry (Sloan 1990; Sloan and Hassan 1990). However, physicians clearly believe that doctor-sponsored companies are in business for the long haul, whereas commercials are more likely to leave the market. Indeed, most exits have been by commercials. Moreover, holding other factors constant, commercial stock companies had higher loss adjustment, underwriting, and investment expenses. And, as seen later in our analysis of premium-setting (Chapter 7), their premiums have been relatively high, holding other factors constant. Thus, the high market shares of noncommercial stock companies in many states are not at all surprising.

NOTES

1. See, for example, Scherer (1980, 3–5).
2. See U.S. Department of Justice (1984, 3).
3. Ibid.
4. One national insurance company responding to our Survey of Former Medical Malpractice Insurers (see the Appendix to Chapter 1 for a description) indicated that managing claims from afar was one of the mistakes they made.
5. Changes in rankings by company name were obtained from *Best's Review* (1979–87).
6. See Landes and Posner (1981, 939–51).
7. On the issue of how small a firm can successfully compete, one would like to know about the availability and cost of reinsurance to firms of varying sizes, as well as the one-time costs of new entry into a market that may deter a small firm's start-up. Unfortunately, these data are not available.
8. The exact state-by-state and year-by-year counts underlying Table 4.1 shows this. These data are not presented here to conserve space but are on file with the authors.
9. We thus confirm Danzon's assertion that the Insurance Services Office (ISO) remains of little importance (1985, 92–96).
10. A profit-maximizing insurer would allocate funds to defense up to the point where the dollar spent on defense saves a dollar in indemnity. This calculation ignores possible externalities, such as the likelihood that some physicians would be attracted by a reputation for tougher defense.

5

Reinsurance

Reinsurance is a way that insurers themselves share risk with another insurer. One insurer, the ceding company, transfers responsibility for some or all of the liability assumed under the policies it sells to the reinsurer, along with a share of the premium. Reinsurance generally involves a contract between a primary insurer that sells insurance to the public and a reinsurer; with very few exceptions, the reinsurer has no contractual obligations to the public. (Hence reinsurers are seldom regulated; see Chapter 3.) The reinsurer, in turn, frequently reinsures some of the loss exposure with other reinsurers. Such transactions are termed "retrocessions." Primary insurers typically do not cede all of their liability; rather, in insurance terminology, they "retain" part of the liability. Normally, reinsurance is sought especially against very large losses.

FUNCTIONS OF REINSURANCE

Reinsurance serves four principal functions, although more motives can be listed:[1] reducing the risk of insolvency, increasing capacity, obtaining technical assistance, and retiring abruptly from a territory or class of business.

Reinsurance and Solvency

Primary insurers attach high importance to remaining solvent. This motive is reflected in premium setting (Chapter 7) and in some of the ways they deal with risk (Chapter 2). Although changes in expected mean frequency and severity of losses can be accounted for in premium setting, insurers face random fluctuations that cannot be ignored. Annual aggregate claims experience always fluctuates around the mean; in particular, random variation also occurs from a few losses that are very large, relative to surpluses and reserves, and hence especially threaten solvency. Insurers employ a variety of methods for reducing the risk of bankruptcy due to such variations, such as adjusting surplus-to-premium ratios, the mix of lines and locations where insurance is sold, and underwriting standards, as well as the riskiness of their investment portfolios. Reinsuring also helps by covering part of the losses, especially those in the upper tail of the loss distribution. Often an insurer in a given market is not large enough to reduce the risk of random fluctuation to desirable levels. There are limits in the ability to pool large numbers of insureds to minimize fluctuation, especially in medical malpractice, where the market is a single state, often with relatively few physicians, and losses are high in severity relative to most lines of coverage.

Reinsurers also cover a larger territory than primary insurers. Therefore, they can more readily diversify away risk from localized losses arising from a single adverse event, such as a large fire, an earthquake, or an adverse judicial decision with broad effects on other claims. Moreover, primary insurers like to report reasonably stable earnings to investors, regulators, and others (Chapter 6), which would be disrupted by significant variations in year-to-year losses, even when solvency is not threatened. Thus, even if the probability of outright bankruptcy is low, loss sharing offers the advantage of stabilized reported earnings and a stabilized surplus.

Reinsurance and Capacity

One protection against insolvency is to maintain adequate capacity (capital or surplus) relative to exposure to risk (premiums). Indeed, one key indicator of fiscal health used both by regulators (Chapter 3) and by insurers themselves is the ratio of net premiums written to policyholders' surplus; regulators consider values above 3 to 1 "unfavorable" (Webb et al. 1984a). According to our Survey of Medical Malpractice Insurers, many companies prefer much lower ratios. Because net premiums are gross (or direct) premiums less the amount of premiums ceded to reinsurers, cessions to reinsurers increase the amount of coverage, including policy limits, that a primary insurer can sell. Sharing risk with others increases capacity. This can be especially important for a small, new entrant that would otherwise be unable to match the offerings of larger, more established insurers.

Technical Assistance from Reinsurers

Reinsurers sometimes provide technical assistance to primary insurers, including underwriting, premium setting, defending (large) claims, and financial advice (Strain 1980, 494–98). Reinsurers may be in a position to do this because of their experience in insurance (and financial markets) from various lines and geographic areas.

Dropping a Territory/Line of Business

When an insurer decides to cease selling a line or doing business in a territory, it may prefer to cede the premiums from the unwanted policies rather than cancel them outright. Reinsuring may avoid various costs of canceling policies, including bad will.

Empirical Evidence on Motives for Reinsuring

According to our Survey of Medical Malpractice Insurers, reducing fluctuations in large losses was an important motive for both the physician-sponsored mutual-exchanges and the commercial stock companies (Table 5.1). The commercial companies emphasized that, in contrast to the smaller physician-sponsored companies, assuring continued financial solvency was *not* a reason they reinsured. Eight of the physician-sponsored companies did indicate that financial viability was a major reason they ceded part of their premiums. Only four companies, all mutuals or exchanges, indicated that

Table 5.1. Major Reasons for Obtaining Reinsurance

Reason	Major Reason	Minor Reason	Not a Reason	No Answer
Physician-Sponsored Mutual-Exchange				
Spread risk of catastrophic loss over time	11	0	0	0
Eliminate/reduce total excess loss	8	1	1	1
Insure portfolio diversification decisions	0	5	3	3
Insure manager's underwriting criteria	1	3	4	3
Insure underwriting capacity	7	2	1	1
Insure viability of primary insurer	8	1	2	0
Commercial Stock				
Spread risk of catastrophic loss over time	2	0	0	1
Eliminate/reduce total excess loss	2	0	0	1
Insure portfolio diversification decisions	1	0	1	1
Insure manager's underwriting criteria	0	1	1	1
Insure underwriting capacity	1	1	0	1
Insure viability of primary insurer	0	1	1	1

Source: Survey of Medical Malpractice Insurers.

Note: Thirteen companies responded to this question.

they received some form of technical assistance from reinsurers (not shown in the table). None of the companies interviewed were in the process of dropping malpractice insurance as a line, meaning that reinsurance was not purchased to cover withdrawal from a market.

POTENTIAL IMPACTS OF REINSURANCE ON THE PRIMARY MARKET

Reinsurance is central to the operation of malpractice insurance markets. It must thus be central to our analysis as well. First and foremost, many of the sellers of malpractice insurance are essentially single-line companies operating in a limited geographic area with relatively low levels of capitalization. Many of these companies would probably not be able to compete if they did not obtain reinsurance.

Second, precisely because reinsurance is essential, reinsurers' practices affect the practice of many primary malpractice insurance companies: Decisions made by reinsurers on the terms and price of reinsurance are likely to affect the terms on which the primary insurers offer malpractice insurance "at retail."

CHAPTER OVERVIEW

The second section provides an overview of the reinsurance market and describes key elements of reinsurance contracts, including risk-sharing provisions and pricing. Much of this discussion applies to the property-liability insurance industry more generally. Motives for reinsuring are further detailed in the third section. In the fourth section, we present evidence on determinants of medical malpractice insurers' demand for reinsurance. Finally, in the fifth section, we analyze the influence of reinsurance on the market for medical malpractice insurance, including availability of coverage, premiums, and policy forms—availability of claims-made versus occurrence policies.

INSTITUTIONAL CONTEXT

The Reinsurance Market

The reinsurance market is international. One leading reinsurer illustrates this point well: Its full-page ad is headlined "American Re's services are only available at the above location"—under a color photo of the earth from space. Most of the reinsurance obtained by U.S. insurance companies comes from foreign sources, and while U.S. reinsurers also sell abroad, the United States is a net importer of reinsurance. In 1982, the ratio of premiums purchased abroad to premiums sold to foreign insurers was 2.2.[2] The five largest professional reinsurers (specialists in reinsurance) in 1981 were Munich Reinsurance (Germany), Swiss Reinsurance (Switzerland), General Reinsurance (United States), Gerling Group (Germany), and Mercantile & General (United Kingdom).[3] The U.S. market is composed of (1) professional reinsurers, (2) U.S. insurers or licensed alien reinsurers that sell principally to the public but have professional reinsurance departments, and (3) nonlicensed alien reinsurers.[4] In 1982, this last category provided almost 30 percent of the reinsurance sold in the United States; the professional reinsurers provided slightly over half.[5]

Reinsurance is typically placed by a reinsurance broker. The broker serves several roles: provision of information, often among companies based in different countries; negotiation and administration of reinsurance; and assistance in settlement of losses. Frequently, several companies write reinsurance for a single primary company. Brokers perform a necessary coordinating role.[6]

In contrast to direct insurance, reinsurance markets are unregulated. According to one account,

> Unlike direct insurers, reinsurers are often free of any regulatory control, nor do they have big overheads. Virtually anyone with a telephone, a telex and a business address could set up shop in the late 1970s. And lots of no-goods did. Many, describing themselves as reinsurers, took money through a reinsurance contract, kept part of the premium, then reinsured (or retroceded) much of the risk with another insurer. It was money for old rope. But it was a rope with which many were to hang themselves. (*The Economist* 1987, 11)

One respondent to our Survey of Medical Malpractice Insurers reported that it was unable to collect a payment due from a bankrupt reinsurer. There is some evidence of problems in collecting on reinsurance of property-liability insurance (Freedman 1987).

Types of Reinsurance

There are several ways to characterize reinsurance contracts. One key distinction is between "facultative" and "treaty" reinsurance. Under facultative reinsurance, the ceding company negotiates a separate reinsurance agreement for each policy it insures. Reinsuring on such a case-by-case basis is administratively costly and is limited mainly to unusual risks that might adversely affect the ceding company's overall operating results. Treaty reinsurance is far more common (86 percent of one survey of property-liability carriers).[7] As the name implies, treaties are standardized, ongoing reinsurance. Treaties set up formulas that apply to a number of policies.

Both treaty and facultative reinsurance may be either pro rata (proportional) or excess of loss (nonproportional). (See Figure 5.1.)

Nonproportional or excess loss reinsurance is much more common in liability (third-party) lines than is proportional reinsurance. Nevertheless, proportional reinsurance is sometimes written in liability lines in general and in malpractice in particular. Thus, we discuss both proportional and nonproportional types.

Proportional Reinsurance

Here the ceding company and the reinsurer agree to apportion both premium income and future losses according to fixed percentages. Proportional coverage may, in turn, be "quota share" or "surplus share." Under quota share, the parties have the same percentage participation in each risk; for example, they may split premiums and losses 50:50. Under surplus share, the two parties agree on a split of premium income and losses only above a dollar retention kept by the ceding insurer. Under surplus share, the parties start with a dollar value to be retained by the cedent. Only risks above this level ("surplus" ones) are then shared on agreed percentage terms. Surplus share reinsurance is sometimes built up in layers, with a different reinsurer for each layer. As for quota share, the split of losses tends to equal the split of premium income.

Proportional insurance performs well in providing primary insurers with added capacity to write insurance. However, it does less to protect against insolvency, for there is no upper bound on the primary insurer's losses. A surplus share arrangement is more effective than a quota share arrangement in providing the ceding company with capacity to write policies with high liability limits. An advantage of proportional reinsurance is that the reinsurer typically pays the ceding company a commission at the front end, in recognition of the latter's acquisition costs, including premium taxes.

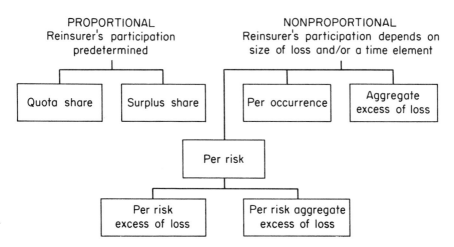

Figure 5.1 Reinsurance plans. Proportional insurance may be either "quota share" or "surplus share." Nonproportional insurance may be "per risk" excess, "per occurrence" excess (catastrophic treaty), or "aggregate" excess (also called "stop loss" or "excess of loss ratio"). Per occurrence and aggregate excess loss cannot be written on a facultative basis because they apply to a class of business, a geographic area, or the cedent's entire book of business.

Under excess loss reinsurance, commissions are usually not paid.[8] The commission contributes immediately to the cedent's underwriting profit and surplus and, principally because of the latter, to its capacity to write primary insurance (Strain 1980, 55–59).

Nonproportional Reinsurance

Here the ceding company and the reinsurer do not share premium income and losses in equal proportions. Rather, the reinsurer's portion of the loss depends on the size of the loss. The reinsurer covers losses only above a predetermined deductible on retention and up to a preset limit. The reinsurer typically covers all or almost all of the excess over the retention.

Again, several varieties of nonproportional plans exist. Under a "per risk" plan, each risk or subject of insurance is covered separately. Thus, for example, following an earthquake, the ceding company would be exposed up to the retention amount on each policy for which a loss from the earthquake was reported.[9] Under a "per occurrence" excess policy, on the other hand, the cedent obtains coverage for the entire earthquake, subject to only one retention.[10] Under "aggregate excess of loss" plans, the reinsurer pays when the losses for a collection of risk (e.g., all malpractice insureds of a company in a state) in the aggregate exceed a predetermined retention amount over a specified time (e.g., all claims in a year). In malpractice insurance, reinsurance tends to be written on a per risk basis, with coverage if the loss per risk per year exceeds a retention amount.

There are two major advantages of nonproportional (or excess of loss) reinsurance. First, the ceding company obtains protection for large losses over a certain amount. Above the deductible, its retention, coverage by the reinsurer is complete or nearly complete. Second, because the reinsurer has no liability for losses below the retention level, such reinsurance tends to be cheaper. The reinsurer need have no knowledge of the vast majority of smaller individual claims filed with the primary insurer.[11]

The reinsurance premium is generally stated as a fraction of the ceding company's premium income for the covered lines of business, but this premium bears no necessary relation to the primary premium. Instead, the reinsurer's premium is determined by negotiation between individual cedents and reinsurers and is a well-kept secret—not divulged to regulators (or interviewers, for that matter). (See Borch [1974] for a model of the bargaining process between a ceding company and a reinsurer.)

The reinsurance premium is set to cover (1) loss (including allocated loss adjustment expense), (2) expense, such as the marketing and acquisition costs of either the reinsurer or the broker, and operating expenses of the reinsurer, and (3) contingency allowance and a profit for the owners of the reinsurer (Simon 1980). The underwriting profit margin may vary from 5 to around 20 to 25 percent of the reinsurance premium. A higher underwriting profit is generally built into riskier policies.[12]

The reinsurance premium is often set in terms of a minimum and a maximum percentage of the ceding company's premiums for the covered line, depending on the cedent's actual loss experience. Initially, the cedent pays the mid-point of the range between the minimum and maximum rates, with final settlement depending on the actual loss experience. Primary insurers with more frequent penetrations of the initial reinsurance layer in the recent past pay higher provisional and actual minimum and maximum rates. Physician specialty category may be considered in addition to recent experience in setting reinsurance premiums (personal correspondence with Manny Buzzell, Corroon and Black Corporation, March 1988).

A variable premium scheme tries to reflect changes in loss exposure to the reinsurer. Alternatively, but apparently much less frequently for malpractice insurance, the reinsurer may charge a fixed premium payable in advance or in installments. In some contracts, to account for inflation during the course of the reinsurance contract, the primary company's retention is indexed—for example, by $25,000 per year.[13]

Financial arrangements between primary insurers and reinsurers are typically kept secret. For this reason, we did not include questions on this issue in our Survey of Medical Malpractice Insurers. Nor did we include a direct measure of the price of reinsurance in our empirical analysis of primary insurer demand for reinsurance.

Retention Amounts and Liability Limits

The percentage distribution of liability limits and retention amounts of primary malpractice insurers are shown in Table 5.2. "Occurrence" refers to amounts to be paid per claim. "Aggregate" refers to the total payments per policyholder per year. Data for the physician-owned companies come from *Best's Insurance Reports—Property/Casualty* and are for 1986. No data are presented on commercial stock companies because Best's does not publish data on retention and policy limits by line.

Most of the companies offered policies with per occurrence limits in excess of $2 million. None of the companies in the sample on which Table 5.2 is based retained as much as $2 million per occurrence. In fact, most retained less than $500,000. These data serve to emphasize the importance of reinsurance in a line for which single-line companies provide an appreciable share of the insurance. It is doubtful whether most of these small companies would have been willing to provide insurance with much higher limits than they did in 1986, or that it would have been prudent for them to do so. The vast majority of companies in the sample purchased nonproportional reinsurance or, in a few cases, a combination of nonproportional and proportional reinsurance.

Table 5.2. Liability Limits and Retention Amounts: Sample of Physician-Sponsored Insurers, 1986 (Percent Distribution)

Policy Limit or Amount Retained	Highest Policy Limit		Amount Retained
	Per Occurrence	Aggregate	Per Occurrence
<$500,000	8.3	0.0	65.2
$501,000 to 999,000	0.0	9.1	21.8
$1 million to <$2 million	16.7	13.6	13.0
$2 million to <$3 million	25.0	0.0	0.0
$3 million to <$5 million	8.3	36.4	0.0
$5 million+	41.7	40.9	0.0
	100.0	100.0	100.0

Source: A.M. Best Co., *Best's Insurance Reports—Property/Casualty*, 1987 edition.

Note: Data are for 24 single-line medical malpractice insurers. There were two missing values for highest policy limit aggregate and one missing value for amount retained occurrence. Aggregate amount retained was published for only six companies. Thus, a percentage distribution is not presented for aggregate amount retained.

Malpractice Premiums and Reinsurance Cash Flows

Data on cash flows in reinsurance appear in Table 5.3. These include data on *direct premiums* (premiums before accounting for amounts reinsured), *premiums ceded* to *and assumed* from other companies, *commissions received* from reinsurers for ceded premiums *and paid* to other companies for assumed premiums, and *reinsurance amounts recovered* during calendar year 1986.[14] The commercial stock companies included in this and other tables based on A.M. Best's data are those for which we obtained Convention Statements from 1978 to 1986. Additional companies are included in the regressions described below. Further details on the sample are provided in the Appendix to Chapter 1.

On average, the physician-sponsored insurers had $55.5 million in direct premiums, of which they ceded $7.3 million in 1986. Two of the 24 physician-sponsored and other noncommercial stock companies in the sample acted as reinsurers for other companies, leading to a mean value of $1.4 million in assumed premiums for the 24 companies overall. In the same year, these insurers received around $400,000 on average in commissions from the reinsurers for selling insurance to policyholders. They paid about $200,000 in commissions to primary insurers when they assumed premiums. The 24 companies recovered an average of $15.5 million in reinsurance payments compared to $7.3 million ceded. Although ceding and recoveries should balance in the long-run, in any given year, the two may be quite different.

The six commercial companies had appreciably higher values for all the items in Table 5.3. They ceded a much higher percentage of direct premiums (37.3 percent) than the physician-sponsored companies (13.2 percent). However, the mean values for the commercial companies obscure appreciable differences in ceding percentages among the companies. The St. Paul, by far the largest malpractice insurer, ceded relatively little—7.3 percent of direct malpractice premiums. By contrast, Farmers and Travelers ceded more than their direct premiums. Travelers had decided to discontinue the malpractice insurance line; it would appear that it had underpriced its line, in the eyes of the reinsurers taking over its business. In contrast to the physician-sponsored

Table 5.3. Malpractice Premium and Reinsurance Cash Flows, 1986 (Millions of Dollars)

	Cash Flows (Mean Values)[1]						
	Direct	Reinsurance		Net	Commissions		Reinsurance
Company Type	Premiums	Ceded	Assumed	Premiums	Received	Paid	Recovered
Mutual (11)[2]	62.9	8.7	0.0	54.2	0.7	0.0	11.3
Exchange (8)	66.2	8.4	0.0	57.8	0.2	0.0	28.8
Physician stock (5)	36.2	2.4	6.5	40.3	0.2	0.8	6.3
All physician- sponsored (24)	55.5	7.3	1.4	49.6	0.4	0.2	15.5
Commercial stock (6)	200.3	74.7	35.9	161.5	—[3]	—	22.2
All companies (30)	105.6	20.8	8.3	93.1	—	—	16.8

Source: A.M. Best Co., *Best's Insurance Reports—Property/Casualty,* 1987 edition.

[1]Mean values are unweighted.

[2]Number of observations in sample are in parentheses. One exchange did not report reinsurance recovered.

[3]Because of intracompany transactions, commissions cannot be computed for the commercial stock companies.

Table 5.4. Net Premiums Ceded as a Percentage of Direct Premiums, 1986

Percent of Premium Ceded	Type of Insurer (Percent Distribution)				
	Mutual	Exchange	Physician Stock	Commercial Stock	Total
<0	0.0	0.0	40.0	0.0	6.7
0	9.1	0.0	0.0	0.0	10.0
0.1–9.9	18.2	50.0	40.0	33.3	26.6
10.0–19.9	9.1	12.5	0.0	0.0	6.7
20.0–29.9	36.3	12.5	0.0	33.3	23.3
30.0–49.9	18.2	25.0	20.0	0.0	16.7
50.0+	9.1	0.0	0.0	33.3	10.0
Total	100.0	100.0	100.0	100.0	100.0
No. of insurers in sample	11	8	5	6	30

Source: A.M. Best Co., *Best's Insurance Reports—Property/Casualty*, 1987 edition.

companies, the commercial companies ceded much more than they recovered from reinsurance in 1986.

The frequency distribution of shares of direct premiums ceded (Table 5.4) shows the appreciable differences among companies in reliance on reinsurance. Over one-quarter of the insurers ceded more than 30 percent of direct premium net. By contrast, over 40 percent ceded less than 10 percent. Negative net ceding occurs when premiums assumed exceed premiums ceded.

To determine whether commercial companies with high amounts ceded and/or assumed in 1986 also had high values in previous years, we examined 1984 and 1985 data (not shown in Table 5.4). The net ceding percentage was very close in all three years: 19.6 percent in 1984 and 21.4 percent in 1985 versus 19.4 percent in 1986. The gross ceding percentages, however, were much lower in 1984 and 1985 than in 1986: 21.6 percent in 1984, 21.5 percent in 1985, and 37.3 percent in 1986. Companies with high gross ceding in 1986 also tended to have high corresponding values in the previous years. But there was substantial year-to-year variation among companies in the relative volume of premiums written.

WHY PRIMARY INSURERS REINSURE

This section considers empirical evidence on the four motivations for reinsurance already noted: solvency (and stabilization), increased capacity, technical assistance, and retirement from a territory or class of business.

Solvency Motive

Large Claims and the Distribution of Losses

Primary malpractice insurers face a frequency distribution of claims that is highly skewed toward large claims. Hence random variation is very threatening to their

Table 5.5. Percentage Distribution of Closed Claims by Claim Size, 1986

Company	Zero	$1–$49K	$50–$499K	$500K+	Total	No. of Claims $500K+
Mutual-Exchange[1]						
Company 1	80.7	9.4	7.2	2.7	100.0	21
Company 2	69.2	23.6	6.9	0.3	100.0	1
Company 3	77.3		20.9[2]	1.7	100.0	82
Company 4	63.5	25.8	10.0	0.7	100.0	11
Company 5	87.5	8.4	3.0	1.2	100.0	12
Company 6	64.1		35.5[2]	0.4	100.0	1
Company 7	91.2	5.0	3.5	0.3	100.0	2
Mean	76.2	14.4[3]	6.1[3]	1.0	100.0	19
Commercial Stock						
Company 1	74.0	18.0	7.6	0.4	100.0	9
Company 2	69.0	26.4	4.2	0.4	100.0	55
Mean	71.5	22.2	5.9	0.4	100.0	32
Mean, all companies	75.2	16.8[3]	6.1[3]	0.9	100.0	22

Source: Survey of Medical Malpractice Insurers.

[1] All mutual-exchange companies in this sample were physician sponsored.

[2] For Companies 3 and 6, these percentages are for claims closed with paid indemnities between $1 and $499,999.

[3] Mean excludes mutual-exchange Companies 3 and 6. All companies' percentages have been normalized so that the total equals 100.0.

solvency. Among the nine companies responding to the question in the Survey of Medical Malpractice Insurers on the distribution of closed claims by dollar amounts paid in 1986, 0.9 percent of closed claims involved indemnity payments of $500,000 or more (Table 5.5). In contrast, 75.2 percent of claims were closed with no payment and 16.8 percent with indemnity payments between $1 and $50,000. On average, the mutual-exchange companies had 19 claims with indemnities of $500,000 or more. Assuming a mean claim size for payments in this category of $800,000 (typical policy limits were $1 million/$3 million), total payments per mutual-exchange of paid claims in the $500,000 and over bracket were $12.8 million. The mean surplus for this sample of mutual-exchanges in 1986 was only $28.1 million. For some of the mutual-exchanges, the ratio of the value of large claims to surplus was much less favorable than this; in some cases, the amounts paid on large claims probably exceeded the company's surplus. Although companies can undoubtedly cover the expected number of large claims with premium income, large fluctuations in the number of such claims may often threaten company solvency.

A limited amount of information on annual fluctuations in large closed claims is available from the Survey of Medical Malpractice Insurers (Table 5.6). Mutual-exchange Companies 1 and 3 had the highest shares of claims in the $500,000 and over size category—2.7 and 1.7 percent, respectively (Table 5.5), and both of these companies experienced extremely high growth in large closed claims (Table 5.6). In 1982, Company 1 had 5 closed claims in the $500,000-plus class; by 1986, it had 21 such claims—a 35.9 percent annual growth rate in such claims. To the extent that the annual growth rates were reasonably constant, such increases could easily have been anticipated in setting premiums. But most of the growth was concentrated between 1984 and

1986. In the case of Company 3, the number of closed claims in the $500,000-plus bracket doubled from 1985 to 1986. The number of such claims for this company was lower in 1984 than in 1983. For both companies, the ratio of large to smaller claims rose appreciably between 1982 and 1986, as shown by the ratio of closed claims in the $500,000-plus category to closed claims in the $50,000 to $499,000 category.

Three of the mutual-exchanges in Table 5.6 also faced a threatening pattern of large closed claims of another type. Companies 2, 6, and 7 had only one or two large closed claims each year. For these companies, the problem in the upper tail was less unanticipated growth than the small number of such claims; even a change of one or two large claims could be large relative to the historical expected pattern. Excess loss reinsurance eliminates such risk by pooling. Such insurance is ideally suited for this purpose rather than for assuming the risk of larger companies experiencing a pronounced secular trend in large paid claims in fits and starts.

Hoerger, et al. (1990) in a separate part of this study, demonstrated conceptually that insurers with greater variability in losses and lower surplus have greater demand for reinsurance. "Loss variability" refers to variation around a mean value of losses. Thus, insurers with substantial trends in loss would pay for the trend by increasing premiums for policyholders. Variability around the trend, however, would provide a motive for reinsuring. Volatility of the insurer's total losses, that is, indemnity payments plus loss adjustment expense, was measured over the number of years for which loss data were available. Loss volatility was computed as the standard deviation of the first annual differences in losses for a time span of at least five years divided by the mean annual direct premiums written over the same period (a measure of expected loss) in 1983 dollars. In most cases, more than five years' data were available for computing insurer-specific loss volatility.

Table 5.6. Growth in Claims with Indemnity Payment Exceeding $500,000, 1982–86

| | Number of $500,000+ Claims/Year | | | | | Annual Percentage Change, 1982–86 | Ratios of No. of Claims $500K+ to $50–$499K | |
Company	1982	1983	1984	1985	1986		1982	1986
Mutual-Exchange[1]								
Company 1	5	7	8	13	21	35.9	0.167	0.368
Company 2	0	0	1	2	1	—	0.0	0.045
Company 3	18	33	23	41	82	37.9	—[2]	—[2]
Company 4	8	7	14	6	11	8.0	0.071	0.065
Company 5	0	2	3	7	12	—	0.0	0.235
Company 6	0	1	1	2	1	—	—[2]	—[2]
Company 7	1	2	1	2	2	17.3	0.125	0.087
Stock								
Company 1	4	8	7	8	9	20.3	0.074	0.065
Company 2	13	20	26	54	55	36.1	0.051	0.087
Total	49	80	84	135	194	34.4	0.064[3]	0.102[3]

Source: Survey of Medical Malpractice Insurers.

[1] All mutual-exchange companies in this sample were physician sponsored.

[2] Information on the number of claims closed in the $50–$499K category not available for the company.

[3] Does not include claims from the mutual-exchange Companies 3 and 6.

Table 5.7. Loss Volatility

Ratio of Standard Deviation of Losses to Mean Direct Premiums Written	Type of Insurer (Percent Distribution)				
	Mutual	Exchange	Physician Stock	Commercial Stock	Total
0–0.199	0.0	25.0	0.0	16.7	10.0
0.2–0.299	27.3	0.0	0.0	33.3	16.7
0.3–0.399	18.2	37.5	0.0	16.7	20.0
0.4–0.499	27.3	0.0	60.0	33.3	26.7
0.5–0.759	18.2	12.5	20.0	0.0	13.3
0.76+	9.1	25.0	20.0	0.0	13.3
Total[1]	100.0	100.0	100.0	100.0	100.0
Mean	0.43	0.46	0.61	0.29	0.44
No. of insurers in sample	11	8	5	6	30

Source: A.M. Best Co., *Best's Insurance Reports—Property/Casualty*, 1977–87 editions. The same data were used in the empirical analysis of demand for reinsurance in Hoerger et al. (1990).

[1]The total may not add to 100 percent due to rounding error.

Frequency distributions of loss volatility, with 1986 as the terminal year for the calculations, are shown in Table 5.7. Individual companies are the observational units. There is substantial variation in volatility within and between ownership categories. As anticipated, loss volatility was appreciably lower for the commercial stock companies, which not only pool far more claims nationwide but which also have predominantly nonmalpractice business, and hence lower severity exposure. The five physician stock companies in particular had extremely volatile claims experience. The loss volatility measure captures total loss for the company, not just for medical malpractice insurance, but only the commercial stock companies had more than a trivial amount of insurance business in lines other than medical malpractice.

Capacity Motive

Policyholders' Surplus and Solvency Regulation
Policyholders' surplus provides a cushion from which to cover losses that exceed anticipations. Even in the absence of regulation, insurers are generally concerned about their obligations to policyholders. The case for solvency regulation, however, is that policyholders cannot properly gauge an insurer's insolvency risk (Chapter 3).[15]

Regulators typically prohibit insurers from writing policy limits that could expose over 10 percent of their surplus on a single claim. Moreover, an insurer is considered to be overextended if its total premiums exceed policyholders' surplus by a ratio of more than 3 to 1.[16] This ratio is often called the "Kenney ratio." Reinsurance enables primary insurers to meet the market demand for higher limits and to underwrite more policyholders for a given surplus—which is desirable for pooling purposes. The reason is that the solvency benchmarks apply to net liabilities and premiums, that is, direct obligations or premiums minus amounts ceded to reinsurers. So, a primary insurer with a given amount of surplus can double its gross premium if it has a 50 percent proportional reinsurance treaty, for example. Reinsurance substitutes for surplus. Similarly, a primary insurer can write much higher limits with nonproportional reinsurance, for the large losses will be taken from the reinsurer's funds, not its own.

Insurer-Specific Measures of Policyholders' Surplus

Frequency distributions of surplus and premium-to-surplus ratios by company for 1986 are shown in Tables 5.8 and 5.9. Direct premium-to-surplus ratios (Table 5.9) represent the ratio of direct premiums to surpluses; net premium-to-surplus ratios reflect reinsurance transactions (net ceding). The data again are for the companies as a whole, not just for medical malpractice insurance. It is clear that many of the physician-sponsored and other noncommercial medical malpractice insurers would not have had much large-line capacity in the absence of reinsurance. The mean surpluses for the mutuals, reciprocal-exchanges, and physician stock companies were $25.1, $35.1, and $13.1 million, respectively. Four physician companies had surpluses of $5 million or less (one mutual and three physician stock), meaning that they could ordinarily write no more than $500,000 per single loss exposure. Ten were under $10 million, and thus were limited to $1 million limit—inadequate in today's market.

Half of the noncommercial insurers had direct premium-to-surplus ratios exceeding 3.0. In fact, the means for two of the three groups exceeded this benchmark. (The net ratios tended to be a little lower, but the mean for the entire sample exceeded 3.0.) Clearly, the conventional standard was not always binding on individual companies, although these companies appeared to have suffered in Best's rating when they were rated (not shown). It is apparent that reinsurance provided only a little relief, for the direct premium-to-surplus ratios were not appreciably different from their net premium counterparts. In fact, by assuming premiums from other companies, one company (Kentucky Medical Insurance Company) had a higher net premium-to-surplus ratio than a direct ratio, and another's (Physicians Insurance Company of Michigan) direct and net ratios were identical. Overall, reinsurance thus appears to have provided much more assistance to malpractice insurers in increasing large-line capacity than it has had in increasing aggregate capacity.

Commercial stock insurers' ratios were lower, with only one company's net premium-to-surplus ratio as high as 3.0 (Table 5.9). Physician mutuals and exchanges

Table 5.8. Policyholders' Surplus, 1986

| Surplus (Million $) | Type of Insurer (Percent Distribution) | | | | |
	Mutual	Exchange	Physician Stock	Commercial Stock	Total
0.0–4.9	9.1	0.0	60.0	0.0	13.3
5.0–9.9	27.3	37.5	0.0	0.0	20.0
10.0–29.9	27.3	12.5	40.0	0.0	20.0
30.0–49.9	18.2	25.0	0.0	0.0	13.3
50.0–99.9	18.2	25.0	0.0	0.0	13.3
100.0–999.9	0.0	0.0	0.0	16.7	3.3
1,000.0+	0.0	0.0	0.0	83.3	16.7
Total[1]	100.0	100.0	100.0	100.0	100.0
Mean	25.1	35.1	13.1	2,018.0	—[2]
No. of insurers in sample	11	8	5	6	30

Source: A.M. Best Co., *Best's Insurance Reports—Property/Casualty,* 1987 edition.

[1]The total may not add to 100 percent due to rounding error.

[2]The mean for the total is not noteworthy, given the large differences in surplus between commercial stock companies and the other insurers.

Table 5.9. Premium-to-Surplus Ratios, 1986

| | Type of Insurer (Percent Distribution) | | | | | | | | | |
| | Mutual | | Exchange | | Physician Stock | | Commercial Stock | | Total | |
Ratio	Direct[1]	Net	Direct	Net	Direct	Net	Direct	Net	Direct	Net
0.0–0.99	18.2	18.2	12.5	12.5	0.0	0.0	0.0	0.0	10.0	10.0
1.0–1.99	18.2	27.3	50.0	50.0	40.0	20.0	16.7	33.3	30.0	33.3
2.0–2.99	9.1	18.2	0.0	25.0	0.0	40.0	33.3	50.0	10.0	30.0
3.0–3.99	18.2	18.2	12.5	0.0	0.0	0.0	50.0	16.7	20.0	10.0
4.0–4.99	18.2	9.1	12.5	12.5	20.0	0.0	0.0	0.0	13.3	6.7
5.0–9.99	9.1	0.0	12.5	0.0	20.0	20.0	0.0	0.0	10.3	3.3
10.0–19.99	9.1	9.1	0.0	0.0	0.0	0.0	0.0	0.0	3.3	3.3
20.0+	0.0	0.0	0.0	0.0	20.0	20.0	0.0	0.0	3.3	3.3
Total[2]	100.0	100.0	100.0	100.0	100.0	100.0	100.0	100.0	100.0	100.0
Mean	3.9	3.2	2.5	2.0	6.7	6.9	2.9	2.3	3.8	3.3
No. of insurers in book	11		8		5		6		30	

Source: A.M. Best Co., *Best's Insurance Reports—Property/Casualty*, 1987 edition.

[1]Direct is direct premium-to-surplus ratios; net is net premium-to-surplus ratios.

[2]The total may not add to 100 percent due to rounding errors.

may be less exposed than stock companies, for they can withhold a dividend more readily and can often assess policyholders retroactively for shortfalls. The net premium-to-surplus ratios (or Kenney ratios) for the commercial stock companies were only slightly higher in the mid-1980s than during the previous decade (Table 5.10). However, net premium ratios were considerably higher for the physician-sponsored companies in 1985–86 than previously (Table 5.10). This is consistent with much larger increases in the price per policy than in the surplus, with no contraction in the number of policies sold. In fact, the net premium-to-surplus ratio was higher in 1985–86 than at any time since 1976, around the time that many of the physician-owned malpractice insurance companies were established.

Other Financial Indicators of Insolvency Risk

Another frequently monitored indicator of insurer health is the "net leverage ratio." This is the company's net liability divided by its surplus—a measure roughly equivalent to the debt-to-equity ratio used in financial analysis more generally. On this measure as well, the physician-sponsored companies show some deterioration over time in financial health (Table 5.10). In 1986, the physician companies as a group had a mean ratio of 14.1 (not presented), twice the ratio of multiple-line, commercial stock companies (7.70) and twice the value of the physician-owned companies themselves in the late 1970s and early 1980s.

Rather than focus on surplus or any other individual indicator alone, the A.M. Best Company performs comprehensive financial analyses of companies.[17] Five factors are measured: underwriting performance, management economy, reserve adequacy, adequacy of net resources, and soundness of investments. Grades range from "excellent" (A+, Contingent A+, and Contingent A) to "fair." Many companies are not rated because they have not been in business for at least five consecutive years, and

Table 5.10. Trends in Insurers' Risk-Bearing Measures, by Year and Company Type

	Mutual				Exchange				Physician Stock				Commercial Stock			
	Kenny Ratio[1]		Net Leverage Ratio[2]		Kenny Ratio		Net Leverage Ratio		Kenny Ratio		Net Leverage Ratio		Kenny Ratio		Net Leverage Ratio	
Year	Wtd[3]	UWtd	Wtd[3]	UWtd	Wtd[3]	UWtd	Wtd[3]	UWtd	Wtd[3]	UWtd	Wtd[3]	UWtd	Wtd[3]	UWtd	Wtd[3]	UWtd
1976	3.47	9.28	9.09	21.13	0.84	0.80	1.81	1.70	—	—	—	—	3.04	2.54	8.32	6.03
1977	3.32	5.13	10.91	16.65	1.03	1.01	2.69	2.55	—	—	—	—	2.74	2.54	7.66	6.77
1978	2.42	2.62	10.15	9.63	1.17	0.96	3.68	2.94	1.84	1.22	3.73	2.49	2.53	2.44	6.76	8.13
1979	1.98	2.15	9.72	9.38	1.07	1.00	3.94	3.51	2.35	1.10	6.52	3.07	2.37	1.99	5.49	5.85
1980	2.17	2.08	11.50	9.63	1.17	0.94	4.88	3.74	2.87	2.11	9.28	6.94	2.01	1.58	4.61	4.93
1981	2.25	1.58	12.96	8.64	1.29	1.26	6.22	5.33	1.91	1.50	9.26	6.56	2.10	1.60	4.70	5.27
1982	2.03	1.47	12.66	7.94	1.69	1.60	8.97	6.93	1.60	1.60	9.02	7.44	1.89	1.60	9.19	7.20
1983	2.18	1.65	15.59	9.88	2.25	1.89	14.80	10.35	1.69	1.90	7.03	7.31	2.30	2.03	7.71	6.91
1984	2.03	1.78	16.29	11.21	1.65	1.65	9.32	7.86	3.31	3.24	14.59	13.28	2.42	2.21	8.42	7.51
1985	3.79	2.85	22.54	14.09	5.04	3.17	30.81	17.51	4.99	4.47	20.94	16.52	2.51	2.58	8.40	8.44
1986	4.03	3.15	22.14	14.20	2.29	1.99	11.18	9.10	7.92	6.90	37.81	26.66	2.42	2.35	7.70	7.62
Mean	2.86	2.89	16.10	11.65	2.26	1.58	12.38	7.22	4.47	2.94	17.83	10.38	2.40	2.14	8.10	7.23

Source: A.M. Best Co., Best's Insurance Reports—Property/Casualty, 1977–87 editions.

[1] Net premiums divided by surplus.

[2] Net liability divided by surplus.

[3] Weighted by proportion of direct premiums written.

even longer for malpractice insurers (Troxel and Breslin 1983, 218). Thus, not being rated is not necessarily a bad sign.

As of 1986, all six of the commercial companies in our sample based on Best's data had Best's ratings of A or higher. By contrast, 14 of the 24 other companies in the sample were not rated, but the commentary on a few of these malpractice insurers in *Best's Insurance Reports—Property/Casualty* was not favorable. For example, Best's indicated that it would not have given the Medical Liability Mutual Insurance Company of New York a high rating if it had rated the company.[18] Eight of these 24 companies received "excellent" ratings (A or better). Each of these companies had very low net premium-to-surplus ratios. On the other hand, the Michigan Physician Mutual Liability Company, with a surplus of $5 million and extremely high premium-to-surplus ratios, had a rating of C (the only sample company with this rating).

Technical Assistance

As indicated above, few respondents to our Survey of Medical Malpractice Insurers indicated that they received technical assistance from reinsurers. Sample responses capture the flavor: One commercial company stated that reinsurers provided assistance in premium setting and in determining the capacity to sell insurance. The ceding company itself set premiums and underwriting standards, although reinsurers were aware of them and had the right of final acceptance. Up to the time of the survey, no reinsurers had requested any adjustments in underwriting criteria and only minor ones in pricing. The reinsurers did have a role in determining large-line capacity, that is, the policy limits offered by the responding company. The company also sought the support of its reinsurer(s) when considering entry into new types of programs or geographic territories.

Another commercial insurer indicated that its reinsurers offered assistance with regard to capacity, loss reserving amounts, and decisions about entering a new market. As far as loss reserving is concerned, reinsurers would get involved if the primary insurer incurred large losses in order to be sure that sufficient reserves were being set aside.

One company organized as a physician exchange stated that reinsurers "want us to handle the primary insurance. . . . We have a cooperation clause, but they've [reinsurers] never gotten involved in the defense of a single claim."

Others indicated selected situations in which reinsurers may offer some kind of assistance, but such help mainly serves the business interest of the reinsurer. That is, if a primary insurer's decision, for example, to take on another line and another geographic territory, appears to the reinsurer to be a poor business decision, the reinsurer simply would not go along with the decision. Giving advice would be just part of saying "no."

Retirement from a Territory or Class of Business

The final motive for reinsuring is to retire gracefully from some field of insurance. Rather than break contracts or relationships with policyholders, primary insurers may continue to maintain coverage while ceding the premiums collected.

STATISTICAL ANALYSIS OF DEMAND FOR REINSURANCE

The above discussion suggests several hypotheses about the determinants of insurer demand for reinsurance that can be empirically tested. First, firms faced with comparatively high loss volatility (and hence the risk of insolvency) should reinsure a higher share of gross premiums, holding other factors constant. Second, increases in surplus (capacity) and in premium income should, again holding other factors constant, make insurers want to reinsure less.

Both hypotheses are based on the notion that companies reinsure to reduce the risk of bankruptcy. The hypothesis linking surplus to reinsurance could also reflect the capacity motive. The two motives have the same effect on the demand for reinsurance. Third, we expected companies in weaker financial position to want more reinsurance.

Statistical Methods

To test these hypotheses, we estimated equations with several relevant measures—loss volatility (as presented in Table 5.7), Best's ratings (a measure of solvency risk), and capacity (measures of surplus and premium).

Two alternative measures of company demand for reinsurance served as dependent variables—(1) total premium ceded as a fraction of direct premiums written and (2) net premium ceded as a fraction of direct premiums written (Hoerger et al. 1990). The numerator of the first measure was the amount ceded. The numerator of the second measure was the difference between the premiums ceded and the amount (if any) of premiums assumed by the insurer from other companies.

The *net ceding* measure overstates the bankruptcy risk after two-way reinsurance transactions have been completed. Companies presumably reduce their risk by trading potential losses in the tails of their primary coverage for potential losses in the tails of other insurers' direct business. Otherwise, they would not engage in these transactions. However, the gross ceding measure understates the bankruptcy risk after reinsurance because it does not account for the additional risk assumed by primary insurers that also accept reinsurance. The primary data source was *Best's Insurance Reports—Property/Casualty*, 1977–87 editions, the same source and sample we used for other analyses.

Results: Solvency and Capacity Motives Confirmed

The empirical analysis, on the whole, supported the hypotheses, whether reinsurance was measured by gross or net amount ceded.[19] Insurers with more volatile losses tended to reinsure more, as expected. Also as anticipated, increases in both the insurer's surplus-to-premium ratio and the level of premium income led to decreased demand for reinsurance. Companies with high surplus and premium volumes have lower bankruptcy risk on average. Insurers with low Best's ratings may have wanted to reinsure more, but the statistical analysis showed that they in fact reinsured less rather than more. One explanation is that reinsurers refuse to deal with low-quality primary insurers or supply insurance to them only in limited amounts.

INFLUENCE OF REINSURANCE ON THE MARKET
FOR MALPRACTICE INSURANCE

Reinsurance has influenced the market for malpractice insurance both directly and indirectly. Single-line insurers have had an important share of the market since the mid-1970s. Such insurers would have had much more difficulty competing in a world without reinsurance. In particular, many single-line insurers would not otherwise have been able to offer high policy limits. It is inefficient for policyholders to obtain the desired amount of primary insurance by purchasing separate policies for different layers of coverage from different insurers. If the single-line insurers were not in a position to offer deep coverage, they would undoubtedly lose some customers to multiple-line insurers able to cover the upper tail of the loss distribution. Physicians understand that they may face a multi-million-dollar verdict and predominantly buy limits of $1 million/$3 million or more in most states (U.S. GAO 1986a). Reinsurance allows single-line insurers to offer higher limits, just like a larger, multiple-line company. In this sense, reinsurance has helped capacity and promoted competition. However, it appears that reinsurance has had little impact on aggregate capacity. This conclusion follows from the observations that the amount of premiums ceded is not large and that many insurers had high net premium-to-surplus ratios even after ceding.

Our Survey of Medical Malpractice Insurers included several questions on how changes in reinsurer capacity—the reported shrinkage in reinsurer capacity in 1984 and the reported increase in capacity in 1986—affected the capacity and premiums of the primary malpractice insurers surveyed. The vast majority reported no relationship between reinsurer capacity and their underwriting capacity, at least none they could document. One commercial insurer stated that "All the emphasis on capacity shrinkage [of reinsurers] can be misleading. Basically, carriers with soundly priced and underwritten books of medical malpractice business were able to secure reasonable levels of reinsurance. This was particularly true if the reinsurance relationships were with long-term, knowledgeable reinsurers, as in the case of our company." One mutual insurer stated that, in 1984, reinsurers indicated that they would no longer reinsure occurrence policies issued by the insurer, echoing reports heard in less formal conversations with industry sources.[20] Loss of reinsurance was also said to be a factor in persuading this company's state regulators to approve claims-made policies. (However, part of the respondent's problem may have been poor underwriting results.) Reinsurers certainly have special reason to be concerned about the long tail of traditional malpractice occurrence policies, which is considerably shortened by a claims-made policy form.

Some of the responding insurers did link changes in reinsurer capacity to changes in premiums charged policyholders. We asked the companies how much their premiums would decrease if the cost on their first level of reinsurance were to decrease by 10 percent. Only 7 of the 14 companies provided usable responses. The mean was 2.2 percent, with a range from 0 to 10 percent. Reinsurance premiums have some effect on malpractice insurance premiums, but the reinsurance premium is only a small proportion of total insurer expense, given the amount of retention typical in the industry.

What about the solvency of reinsurers themselves? Collectibility of reinsurance has been an issue faced by malpractice insurers. Most of the responding companies reviewed the prospective reinsurer's financial health as part of the contracting process or relied on a reinsurance broker to do so. In one case reported to us, a reinsurer

Table 5.11. Primary Insurers' Reinsurers, 1986

Primary Insurers	Reinsurers
Physician Mutual	
Mutual Assurance Society of Alabama	Underwriters of Lloyds
	CNA Reinsurance of London
	Insco Ltd.
Mutual Insurance Company of Arizona	Skandia America Reinsurance Company
	Kemper Reinsurance Company
	American Medical Assurance Company
	Prudential Reinsurance Company
Group Council Mutual Insurance Company	Prudential Reinsurance Company
	Denis Clayton & Company
	Turegum Insurance Company
Norcal Mutual Insurance Company	Underwriters of Lloyds
	Unionamerica Reinsurance Company
	CNA Reinsurance of London
Louisiana Medical Mutual Insurance Company	General Reinsurance Corporation
Medical Mutual Liability Insurance Company of Maryland	Kemper Reinsurance Company
	Underwriters of Lloyds
	Skandia Insurance Company
Michigan Physicians Mutual Liability Company	Clarendon National Insurance Company
Medical Liability Mutual Insurance Company (New York)	Kemper Reinsurance Company
	Metropolitan Reinsurance Company
	Skandia America Reinsurance Corp.
Medical Mutual Insurance Company of North Carolina	National Indemnity Company
	Union Insurance Company
	Skandia America Reinsurance Corp.
	CNA Reinsurance of London
	American Medical Assurance Company
	Underwriters of Lloyds
The P.I.E. Mutual Insurance Company	Underwriters of Lloyds
	General Reinsurance Corporation
State Volunteer Mutual Insurance Company (TN)	Underwriters of Lloyds
	Unionamerica Reinsurance Company
Physician Exchange	
Doctors Company	—
Medical Insurance Exchange of California	Underwriters of Lloyds
	Kemper Reinsurance Company
	Skandia America Reinsurance Corp.
Physician Exchange	
Southern California Physicians Insurance Exchange	Underwriters of Lloyds
	American Medical Assurance Company
	Terra Nova Insurance Company
Illinois State Medical Inter-Insurance Exchange	CNA Reinsurance of London
	Underwriters of Lloyds
	Skandia America Reinsurance Corp.
Minnesota Medical Insurance Exchange	Kemper Reinsurance Company
	General Reinsurance Company
	Hannover Reinsurance Company
	Underwriters of Lloyds
Medical Inter-Insurance Exchange of New Jersey	Unionamerica Insurance of London
	Underwriters of Lloyds
	CNA Reinsurance of London

(continued)

Table 5.11. *(Continued)*

Primary Insurers	Reinsurers
Utah Medical Insurance Association	Underwriters of Lloyds
	CNA Reinsurance of London
	Unionamerica Insurance Company
Washington State Physicians Insurance Exchange	General Reinsurance Company
Physician Stock	
Kentucky Medical Insurance Company	Underwriters of Lloyds
	Physicians' Insurance Co. of Ohio
	CNA Reinsurance of London
	General Reinsurance Corporation
	Terra Nova Insurance Company
Physicians Insurance Company of Michigan	Skandia America Reinsurance Corp.
	Physicians' Insurance Co. of Ohio
Missouri Medical Insurance Company	Kemper Reinsurance Company
	Belvedere Insurance Company
	Hannover Reinsurance Company
Physicians Insurance Company of Ohio	Fireman's Insurance Company
	Carter, Wilkio, and Kane
	Reliance Insurance Company
Pennsylvania Medical Society Liability Insurance Company	Kemper Reinsurance Company
	Hannover Reinsurance Company
	INA Reinsurance Company
	Union Insurance Company

Source: A.M. Best Co., *Best's Insurance Reports—Property/Casualty,* 1987 edition.

became financially insolvent, resulting in a loss of over $500,000 to the primary insurer.

The case for regulation of insurers stems essentially from two concerns: insolvency risk and market power. The same may apply to reinsurance. Reinsurer solvency is probably an important issue, judging from commentary in the media and from the insurers' responses to our survey. Causal statements made about reinsurers would imply that they have market power, individually or as a group. So, in a way, it is surprising that reinsurance is so little regulated. However, as a practical matter, it is hard to get jurisdiction over international operations or to monitor worldwide financial transactions. And the "consumers" arguably needing protection are large companies, which seemingly should be able to look after themselves and which may be politically less potent than the ultimate consumer-voters.

Twenty-four primary malpractice insurers' reinsurers as of 1986 are listed in Table 5.11 (derived from data published in *Best's Insurance Reports—Property/Casualty,* 1987 edition). The reinsurers listed in this publication are only the major ones; as noted, it is easy for new entrants at least to say that they are reinsurers, even if they do not stay for the long term. Nevertheless, it is apparent that insurers tended to obtain reinsurance from several reinsurers. Almost as many reinsurers as primary insurers are listed. There were many changes in reinsurers between 1985 and 1986 (not shown). It would appear that malpractice insurers have many choices among reinsurers and that this ability to choose is frequently exercised.

One might argue that the reinsurance market is cartelized by some more subtle mechanism, such as through brokers. However, entry into the reinsurance market appears to be easy, and there are few if any entry barriers imposed by regulatory agencies. (The same seems true for brokers as well.) Thus, it is difficult to see how cartel discipline could be maintained.

CONCLUSIONS AND IMPLICATIONS

Reinsurance provides an important tool for insurers to cope with risk. If reinsurance did not exist, the composition of sellers of medical malpractice insurance would look very different. Some of the single-line insurers would simply be unwilling and/or unable to write coverage with the malpractice insurance liability limits physicians demand. In particular, many of the physician-sponsored firms that have gained a foothold—and, in many states, the dominant market share—would undoubtedly not exist. When reinsurance capacity shrinks, there are almost inevitable effects on insurance markets. But over the period we observed, reinsurance appears to have had much more of an impact in enabling small insurers to offer policies with high liability limits than in boosting the aggregate capacity to sell medical malpractice insurance. Reinsurers have also influenced medical malpractice insurance more directly. Their role in causing the demise of occurrence policies is probably the best example.

The empirical evidence establishes a direct link between the risk of primary insurer bankruptcy and the demand for reinsurance. Limitations on the primary insurer's capacity to write insurance imposed by the state insurance department stem directly from the motive to protect the public from insurer insolvency.

Unlike primary insurers, reinsurers are virtually unregulated. The market is international, and exit/entry appears to be free. Thus, there is no justification for regulation of reinsurance based on market power arguments. Further, reinsurer insolvencies appear to be a minor problem. For the time being, the best public policy posture toward reinsurance seems to be one of benign neglect.

NOTES

1. See, for example, Bawcutt (1982), Carter (1983), Strain (1980), Johnson (1977), and Webb et al. (1984a).
2. Webb et al. (1984a, 359).
3. Ibid. (362).
4. Reinsurance is not subject to regulation of policy forms or rates (Chapter 3). This would be impractical, as reinsurance contracts are tailor made to specific circumstances and capacity is raised in international financial markets beyond the reach of state regulators. However, reinsurers are often encouraged to be licensed (or "admitted"), or at least "approved" or "accredited," by regulators' refusal to allow primary insurers credit for reinsurance. Using this mechanism, about half of the states require that a reinsurer be licensed in a state, meet surplus minimums, and get the commissioner's approval (Strain 1980, 615–20).
5. Webb et al. (1984a, 364).
6. On the role of brokers, see Carter (1983, 49–53).
7. Webb et al. (1984a, 334).
8. Carter (1983, 87).

9. A "per risk aggregate" plan is also recognized, under which a reinsurer participates in losses above the retention amount for the aggregated claims for a risk over a period of time.

10. Defining an occurrence can be tricky. When Hurricane Hugo hit South Carolina in 1989, the storm's damage on outlying islands came hours before damage on the mainland, making this two occurrences and subjecting primary insurers to two retention amounts.

11. Carter (1983, 172).

12. Simon (1980, 223).

13. See Simon (1980, 241–42) for a discussion of index clauses.

14. The recovered amounts exclude recoveries on incurred but not reported loss (IBNR)—estimates of claims yet to be filed—and unearned premiums. Companies for which IBNR or unearned premium recoveries were given but excluded for purposes of the table are identified in the table. Although it would be desirable conceptually to include IBNR recoveries, the amounts were extremely volatile, most likely reflecting recalculations of IBNR over a number of policy years.

15. See also Troxel and Breslin (1983) for a general discussion of solvency regulation and its implications for insurers.

16. Webb et al. (1984, 325).

17. See *Best's Insurance Reports—Property/Casualty* (1987) and Troxel and Breslin (1983, 217–21).

18. See the listing for the company in A.M. Best Co. (1986).

19. With a few exceptions, results for gross ceding were similar to those for net reinsurance. This indicates that the hypothesis tests did not depend critically on the choice between the two dependent variables.

20. This was also one of the allegations made by state attorneys general in a lawsuit against liability insurers.

6

Loss Reserving and Claims Management

Claims management and loss reserving can seem dry, technical, and inconsequential—matters best left to insurance clerks in green eyeshades. At least, so it may appear to outsiders. Certainly, underwriting and premium setting appear more linked to insurance crises, antitrust and regulatory decisions, and other matters with superficially more policy relevance. But before readers skip this chapter, they should note that claims reserving vitally affects rate making and the timing of profits, and that loss management is in fact critical to the short-run profits and long-run survival of any insurance company. These activities are most complicated in a line where a long claims tail and an unstable social and legal environment interact, as in medical malpractice.

Some early physician insurers' managements were misled by the normal buildup of cash in their early years of operation, when relatively few and relatively small claims are actually settled, whereas premiums are paid up front. However, large payments eventually come due, and good reserving is needed in anticipation. Serious mistakes in predicting and managing future losses can cripple an insurer.[1] It is not unknown in the industry for companies to abandon a line with large losses; for a PCF to run out of cash, having underpriced coverage (as in Florida); and for an entire state to be thought underreserved.

Insolvency always raises the specter of unfulfilled obligations to current policyholders. In geographic markets with few sellers of medical malpractice insurance, insolvency may also lead to serious problems of general availability, at least temporarily. Other companies may have insufficient surplus to underwrite a large expansion of premiums or may be unwilling to commit capital they deem better used in other markets. In other cases, special assessments on policyholders (allowed by some physician insurers and JUAs) may be needed for "bailout" money. The last resort is support from state guaranty funds supported by taxing insurers (Chapter 3). At least one major malpractice insurer, the Medical Liability Mutual Insurance Company (New York), is substantially underreserved (Corcoran 1988), as are JUAs in several states (Alliance of American Insurers 1988).

AN INSURER'S LIABILITIES

The two most important liabilities of an insurance company are reserves—for unearned premiums and for future losses and loss expense. Unearned premium reserves represent funds held on behalf of the policyholder for the unexpired term of the insurance policy. Such reserves are necessary because the period to which the premium applies does not typically coincide with the year in which the policy is sold. In principle, the unearned premium reserves should be sufficient to provide a refund to the policyholder in the event that the company goes out of business before the end of the policy year.

Loss reserves cover loss and allocated loss adjustment expense (ALAE) arising from policyholders' claims. ALAE is expense that can be specifically attributed to the resolution of a particular claim, such as the cost of investigation and defense. Not included in ALAE is unallocated loss adjustment expense (ULAE) or the general overhead of the insurance company. Loss reserves are divided into two categories. The first consists of losses on claims that have already been reported. Here the claim is known but its ultimate cost must be estimated. Or a claim may have been paid but remains open because all aspects of the case have not yet been resolved. The second is losses on claims that have been "incurred but not (yet) reported" to the insurer—that is, IBNR reserves.[2] The extent of such unknown claims can only be estimated from prior experience.

IBNR reserves are relatively more important under occurrence insurance policies than under claims-made policies. Under occurrence policies, the insurer is liable for any claims arising from any incident occurring that year, regardless of when the claim is reported. Only the legal statute of limitations determines the cutoff for how much later these claims may be filed. The time interval between the incident and its report may be substantial, particularly for medical malpractice, for medical injuries are often less obvious than those in many simpler cases of trauma (like auto accidents). Statutes in most states allow injuries discovered after many years to be sued upon, even though the statute of limitations would have run out on an obvious injury. Because of this long tail, IBNR reserves must be correspondingly large. Under claims-made policies, the insurer covers only claims reported in a particular year. Thus, the delay in any particular case can at most be a matter of months—the processing time for learning of a claim or lawsuit filed in a given year.[3]

Both categories of loss reserves are "soft." Reserves are not fixed obligations (unlike conventional liabilities such as debt), but rather must be estimated by claims managers, then periodically revised as knowledge about the case or other circumstances change. "Claims management" includes activities involved in establishing the initial value of a reported claim, updating that value as more information becomes available, and setting the value for IBNR reserves.

There are many reasons for policymakers and analysts to be interested in insurers' practices in these areas. The following subsections focus on these issues.

DO INSURERS DISTORT LOSS RESERVES?

It has been alleged that insurers vary loss reserves to improve short-term company earnings as reported to stockholders, or at least to smooth out variations in earnings over time. Another potential motive for distortion is regulation: Insurers may want to overreserve in order to demonstrate to state regulators that a premium increase should be approved because claims are high and returns inadequate. Alternatively, under-reserving may seem desirable to show regulators that the firm has the capacity to write larger amounts of insurance.[4] Changes in reserves also potentially could move profits from one time period to another for tax purposes. These observations have come not only from persons with practical knowledge of the insurance industry, but also from scholars who have studied loss-reserving practices more formally. Manipulating reserves is a plausible strategy. One study found that property-liability insurers with lower variability in earnings were viewed by investors as less risky (Foster 1977).[5] There are also reasons to expect errors in reserving apart from intentional distortion (see below).

Any distortions, intentional or not, are important because small percentage changes in the loss reserves recorded in an accounting year can have major effects on the earnings a firm reports on its income statements. Similarly, changes in loss reserves on the liability side of the balance sheet can greatly affect policyholders' surplus. Whether or not any such distortion occurs is accordingly of considerable significance for regulators and analysts alike.

OTHER REASONS FOR INTEREST IN LOSS RESERVING

Even if there is no deliberate attempt to distort, there are other reasons to be interested in loss reserving and claims management. The definition of what constitutes a claim may vary across malpractice insurers, as well as over time for a single insurer. A lawsuit filed definitely triggers a claim, but should an inquiry from a dissatisfied patient? A telephone call from a nervous insured physician? If practice varies, it will be difficult to compare claims frequency over time and among insurers. It also becomes difficult for a regulator or a policymaker to make comparisons across companies or geographic areas in the value of open claims. Closed-claims studies circumvent some of the potential problems of differing loss-reserving practices, but they have problems of their own. In particular, because of the long tail in a line such as medical malpractice, the closed-claim rate may differ appreciably from the current-claims frequency, and the level at which future claims are likely to be paid may be quite different. Also, it may appear that one firm pays an indemnity in a far greater share of cases than does another, when in fact the firm with the seemingly lower paid claim rate just has a lower threshold for opening a claims file.

THE LONG TAIL OF LOSS DEVELOPMENT AND RESERVING ERRORS

The relatively long loss development period for medical malpractice insurance is documented in Table 6.1. This table shows loss payments by year over the nine-year period 1978–86 for policies sold in 1978, assuming that all payments were completed during that period.[6] Malpractice losses are slow to develop; the table is a graphic illustration of the long tail of medical malpractice losses. Although malpractice policies sold were typically claims-made rather than occurrence, only 21.6 percent of the total loss on the 1978 policy year was paid within three calendar years. In contrast, 53.6 percent of automobile property-casualty and multiple-peril payments occurred within three years. By the sixth year, 77.5 percent of medical malpractice insurance

Table 6.1. Cumulative Proportion of Loss Payment by Line, 1978 Policy Year

Line	Payment Periods in Years								
	1	2	3	4	5	6	7	8	9
Medical malpractice	0.046	0.098	0.216	0.402	0.565	0.775	0.864	0.945	1.000
Automobile liability	0.241	0.434	0.536	0.590	0.625	0.972	0.987	0.995	1.000
Other liability	0.060	0.125	0.201	0.298	0.372	0.797	0.894	0.959	1.000
Workers' Compensation	0.182	0.361	0.469	0.528	0.564	0.930	0.959	0.983	1.000
Multiple peril	0.318	0.476	0.517	0.545	0.563	0.964	0.982	0.993	1.000

Source: Our computations are based on data from *Best's Reproductions of Convention Statements*, 1979–87, Schedule P.
Note: Column 9 is based on the assumption that all claims were closed by the end of that year; only nine years of actual data were available (1978–86).

payments had been made, while payments for auto and multiple-peril insurance were virtually complete. The development period for the "other" liability line was similar to that for medical malpractice insurance.

Even with no ulterior motive, underreserving or overreserving is more likely for a line with a long claims tail, like medical malpractice. The reason is that claims managers must base anticipated losses on common assumptions about anticipated inflation and expected changes in the social and legal environments. Such projections call for predicting the course of many events beyond the insurance company's control, and the larger the tail, the more such events can intervene between the policy year and the time the claims from that policy year are finally closed.

Although reserving mistakes in a long-tail line tend to be relatively big ones (because of corresponding errors in assumptions), there is no inherent reason to believe that companies will consistently over- or underreserve. In fact, a case can be made for cycles in reserving practices, as claims managers learn from their mistakes in the recent past.

LOSS RESERVES AND DISCOUNTING

One factor that may lead to systematic overreserving is the failure to compute loss reserves as a discounted present value of future liabilities. Traditionally, property-casualty insurers have not discounted, out of fiscal prudence and regulatory concern.[7]

The case for not discounting is to be conservative—to build in a margin of error, especially in view of the likely inflation of loss values over time. However, this margin is not knowingly calculated. The case for discounting is that any liability is worth more if it must be paid now than if it need not be paid until later. No one will pay $100 today for the promise of receiving $100 next year. As discussed in other chapters, there is room for argument about the specific choice of the rate for discounting but relatively little room for debating the legitimacy of discounting liabilities. Other companies routinely discount future liabilities (and assets), and insurers have been truly unusual in this regard. By not discounting, and thereby overstating reserves, other factors being equal, insurers reduced their corporate income tax. In the Tax Reform Act of 1986, Congress made discounting a requirement for federal tax purposes.

Of course, insurers may have been conservative in not discounting anticipated future loss obligations, but at the same time may have been lax in other assumptions about the future. For example, insurers may have had a consistently rosy view of future inflation in loss payments, and this may have been reflected in their loss-reserving practices.[8] If so, the margin of error was necessary. There is a "chicken and egg" problem in guessing which came first, the rosy view or the cushion that made it possible.

To date, there has been much discussion in textbooks and at seminars about procedures insurers should use in establishing loss reserves. However, there is now virtually no empirical evidence for medical malpractice insurance or other lines about how insurers actually establish loss reserves. Textbooks frequently describe the loss-reserving practices of insurers, at least in general terms, but this information appears to come from authors' practical experience rather than from surveys of insurers or other broad-based data. Nor is it known exactly how requirements imposed on insurers by statute or regulation affect loss-reserving practices.

POTENTIAL GAINS FROM SELLING SEVERAL TYPES OF INSURANCE

As in other aspects of insurance (Chapter 2), insurers may benefit in loss reserving by diversifying across lines. A multiple-line insurer has an advantage over its single-line competitor if loss reserve errors in different lines tend to offset one another (that is, if errors are negatively correlated across lines). The loss reserve error is the difference between losses as reserved and as actually paid. If, for example, the factors responsible for overreserving in malpractice simultaneously cause underreserving in Workers' Compensation, the malpractice insurer would gain by adding the Workers' Compensation line. Such a correlation might exist if Workers' Compensation claims rise during periods of high unemployment (as laid-off workers seek funds to tide them over), but these unemployed workers are also less likely to visit doctors and hence to have an injury leading to a malpractice insurance claim.[9]

CHAPTER OVERVIEW

This chapter covers the general issues just presented. The second section describes loss reserving and claims management as conducted by medical malpractice insurers. The empirical material is drawn from our Survey of Malpractice Insurers. Specifically, we answer the following questions: Under what conditions do insurers open a claim file, and to what extent does practice vary among companies? What information do companies use to value losses for reserves, and under what circumstances are values revised? How do claim valuation methods differ by company? Do companies discount anticipated losses, and what justifications are offered for discounting or not discounting?

The third section examines systematic errors in reserving, using company-specific data published by Best's. In recent years, have malpractice insurers as a group over- or underreserved? What types of companies have tended to over- or underreserve? Has over- or underreserving been more or less common in medical malpractice insurance than in other lines?

In the fourth section, we use Best's data to evaluate the hypothesis that insurers manipulate their loss reserves to make their earnings and equity position look more favorable. To do this, we extend recent work by Weiss (1985) and Grace (1990) on the factors responsible for variation in loss reserve errors over time and across insurers. To assess possible gains from diversification, we examine simple correlations in loss reserve errors across lines from a sample of multiple-line companies.

The fifth section summarizes the chapter's key findings, discusses public policy implications, and identifies related topics for further study.

MALPRACTICE INSURERS' LOSS-RESERVING AND CLAIMS MANAGEMENT PRACTICES

Opening a Claim

Claim files are opened under a variety of circumstances, and practice varies across companies. Some companies open a claim only after receiving notification that a formal suit has been filed, while others open a claim based on notice of any potential suit from a policyholder (Table 6.2).[10] State statutes may account for some differences. In eight states,[11] potential claimants are required to notify intended defendants of their intent to sue a specified period before actually filing—which gives insurers faster notice. It is unknown how much such legislation has affected the behavior of claimants and claims managers.[12]

Several companies in our survey indicated that they distinguish between incidents reported by policyholders and actual demands for money. Such companies create an incident file if notified by a physician but do not create an actual claim file until they hear from an allegedly injured patient or his or her representative. Monetary reserves are established only when a claim is opened.

Claims practice can also vary in how it treats multiple demands for money from a single occurrence: More than one person may indicate an injury (e.g., the birth of twins), and/or more than one insured may be involved. Our respondents noted that they generally open a separate file for each occurrence for each insured. This is important

Table 6.2. Action that Precipitates Opening a Claim File (Percent Distribution)

Claim Opened in Response to:	Mutual-Exchange Companies	Stock Companies	All Companies
Standard incident report filed by insured or insured's representative	35	67	42
Inquiry by claimant or claimant's representative	20	7	17
Receipt of suit papers or notification of intent to sue	40	26	37
Other	5	0	4
Total	100	100	100
Total number of companies responding	11	3	14

Source: Survey of Medical Malpractice Insurers.

Note: Each respondent provided a percentage distribution of the actions precipitating the opening of a claim file. The distributions in this table represent mean values of the responses by individual insurers.

Table 6.3. Most Important Factors in Establishing the Expected Value of a Claim

All Companies	Factor 1	Factor 2	Factor 3	Total
Degree of liability	5	8	2	15
Damages sought	2	3	2	7
Severity of injury	5	2		7
Coverage limits	1		1	2
Ability of plaintiff's attorney			3	3
Number of defendants			2	2
Venue			1	1
Emotional appeal			1	1
Claim or lawsuit			1	1

Source: Survey of Medical Malpractice Insurers.

Note: Thirteen companies responded. Because we collapsed response categories for presentation purposes, there are more than 13 responses on "Degree of liability."

when it comes to establishing a reserve, given that the individual insured's policy limit per occurrence sets the maximum indemnity normally payable.

Claims management departments vary considerably in the size and background of their staff. Among our respondents, staff sizes varied from 4 or 5, with very little hierarchy, to over 40, with multiple supervisory levels. The number of claims closed in 1986 also varied greatly, but it is hard to make comparisons of full caseloads without knowing the number of open, ongoing cases and the times from opening to closing. Except for one stock company, whose field agents both sell policies and service claims, the companies' claims staffs were devoted full time to claims functions.[13]

Establishing the Value of a Claim

What information is most significant in setting the loss reserve for a given claim? We asked respondents to name the three most important factors (Table 6.3). All companies said that the degree of policyholder liability was a factor. Over half of the companies also listed the severity of the injury and the amount of monetary damages sought. One of these three items were cited as the most important factor by 12 of the 13 respondents, with the other response being the policy coverage limits. Other responses were generally given with an explanation that each case is different, and that reserving must account for multiple claimant and state-specific characteristics.

The companies were asked what external information they gathered for reserving medical malpractice cases. None of the stock companies indicated that they systematically gather information on jury verdicts or on competitors' closed claims (Table 6.4). The response from the physician-sponsored companies was markedly different: Eight of the 11 said that they do gather information on court-determined malpractice awards, and six indicated that they collect information on the dollar amounts of settlements of other companies. None of the stock companies did so. Such information, however, was rarely incorporated into loss reserves in systematic fashion, even by the physician insurers.

Companies repeated that they are very slow to adjust their loss reserves following legislated tort reforms. Only three physician-sponsored companies and one stock com-

Table 6.4. Loss-Reserving Practices

	Responses								
	Mutual-Exchange			Commercial Stock			Total		
Questions	Yes	No	No Answer	Yes	No	No Answer	Yes	No	No Answer
1. Does your company gather information on the dollar amounts of court-determined medical malpractice amounts?	8	3	0	0	2	1	8	5	1
a. If yes, is this information systematically incorporated into loss-reserving practices?	3	5	3	0	0	3	3	5	6
2. Other than verdicts, does your company gather information on the dollar amounts of settlements of other companies?	6	5	0	0	2	1	6	7	1
3. Does your company immediately adjust its loss reserves following tort reforms?*	3	7	1	1	1	1	4	8	2
4. Prior to the Tax Reform Act of 1986, did your company discount expected losses when computing loss reserves?	4	7	0	0	2	1	4	9	1

Source: Survey of Medical Malpractice Insurers.

*Answers to this question on the survey instrument were "never," "sometimes," and "frequently." No company answered frequently. We converted "never" to "no" and "sometimes" to "yes" for purposes of this table.

pany said that they sometimes changed reserving practices. One reason cited was the difficulty of quantifying the expected results of particular reforms. For example, the rules defining expert witnesses may be tightened, but the legal language gives no clue as to the actual impact of this change. Moreover, our respondents indicated that tort reform can be a two-edged sword: Even if the intended result eventually occurs, the attention from the news media accompanying such reform puts malpractice before the public, and this increased publicity may cause a temporary increase in filings. In addition, reforms may never have the intended effect, as courts may rule them unconstitutional. Even where reforms are eventually upheld, companies are reluctant to ease their reserving practices during the years of judicial appeals, fearing severe underreserving.

We obtained very little information on how companies revise the value of a given claim over time. Some companies reported that they review all active claim files on a scheduled basis, while others reported that they update their loss reserve on a given claim as additional information becomes available. "Additional information" includes verdicts on parallel cases, filing of an actual suit and the venue chosen for the suit, the company's changing determination of the degree of the policyholder's liability, and the ability of the plaintiff's lawyer, once known. All of the physician-sponsored companies have physicians who volunteer their time to serve on a claims committee. Having access to contributed expertise may lower these companies' expense; the stock companies all reported having physicians on staff to review their insureds' liability.

We queried respondents about who determines the initial amount to offer as a settlement and who has final authority. Seven companies—including all three stock companies—indicated that the claims representative usually determines the initial settlement offer; five companies indicated that some combination of the claims management staff and a physician committee made this determination. One company failed to give an answer. Final authority, however, varied with the size of the claim for 12 of our 13 companies. In some instances, authority was clearly delineated by amount, with large claims referred to either a physician committee, the full board of directors, or the president/chief executive officer. The dollar values calling for different authorization varied, generally reflecting the number of claims above a given threshold.

In addition to the formal survey, we have had discussions with other current and former medical malpractice insurers. Several of the companies that dropped the medical malpractice line indicated that they found it impossible to manage claims in different states exclusively from corporate headquarters. From our discussions with various companies, almost all of the multistate companies that sold individual policies to physicians had regional or state claims personnel. Anecdotally, insurers may rely on on-site claims investigators to develop information, even for a centrally maintained claims file.

Discounting Future Losses

Our Survey of Medical Malpractice Insurers asked companies if they had discounted loss reserves prior to the Tax Reform Act of 1986. Of the 13 companies responding, only 4—all physician sponsored—said that they had done so (Table 6.4).

SYSTEMATIC OVER- OR UNDERRESERVING

Previous studies of reserving have noted a tendency of companies to err on the side of overreserving, although errors vary by year. Overreserving may occur as the insurer attempts to reduce its federal tax bill, since loss estimates figure in the computation of tax liabilities. By overreserving, the insurer postpones tax payments and thereby gains the use of the funds in the interim. An insurer seeking to maximize the present value of cash flows will achieve a maximum discounted cash flow at the point at which the marginal tax savings equal the marginal costs of increasing its reserves. Possible costs include adverse reactions of insurance regulators (and, for publicly traded insurers, the Securities and Exchange Commission) and, probably more likely, adjustments of the insurer's reserves by the Internal Revenue Service (IRS) (Grace 1990).[14] Systematic overreserving would suggest that the anticipated cost to insurers of adverse reactions by various public agencies is relatively small. Both overall reserves and IBNR reserves have been studied (Box 6.1).

To determine the accuracy of medical malpractice insurers' initial reserves, we used more recent Best's data to compute loss reserve errors for three loss development periods—two of eight years, four of six years, and six of four years. We defined the loss reserve error as the difference between the original amount reserved and actual loss plus allocated loss expense payments as of a certain date in the future, expressed as a percentage of the amount originally reserved. In each case, one calculation discounted reserves; the other did not.[18]

Box 6.1. Prior Studies of Reserving

Anderson (1979) investigated the adequacy of loss reserves for four lines of coverage—automobile liability, other liability, Workers' Compensation, and Schedule O.[15] For 1955 through 1964, automobile liability and other liability reserves were within the range that casualty actuaries feel is reasonable, that is, "within plus or minus five percent of the actual amount paid" (p. 591).[16] Workers' Compensation and Schedule O reserves were most overvalued. For all lines assessed, the difference between reserves and payouts was 4.5 percent, a value toward the high end of the "reasonable" range that suggested overreserving. Anderson noted that "the loss reserves of the [36] sample companies were, for the most part, overvalued during the ten years of the study. Previous studies have stressed the role which underevaluations of loss reserves play in depleting surplus" (p. 591).

Although there was an overall tendency to overvalue reserves, there was substantial underreserving in the automobile and other liability lines toward the end of the ten-year period. This (and other findings) suggests that reserve adequacy differs over time because of changing practices on the part of insurers, major unforeseen circumstances exogenous to the companies that affect actual payouts (such as unanticipated inflation), or a combination of the two. The shift from reserve adequacy (or slight overreserving) in the 1950s to underreserving in the 1960s has been confirmed in studies by Ansley (1979) and Balcarek (1975), with a change to greater adequacy in reserves in the early and mid-1970s (Balcarek 1975; Smith 1980).

Aiuppa and Trieschmann (1987) considered the magnitude and accuracy of IBNR reserves for five lines: automobile property-liability, other liability, medical malpractice, Workers' Compensation, and multiple peril. The study covered the period 1975–82, paying relatively more attention to 1975–79. Malpractice insurance could be studied because Best's began to publish line-specific data on medical malpractice insurance in 1975. The sample included 23 to 25 malpractice insurers, depending on the table and year, none of them physician sponsored.

Not surprisingly, in view of the widespread switch from the occurrence to the claims-made form, the ratio of the IBNR reserve to the reserve for reported claims fell substantially for malpractice insurance between 1975 and 1982, especially at the end of this period. Small medical malpractice insurers had large ratios of IBNR reserve to reserve for reported claims, and the ratios of nonstock companies generally exceeded those of their stock counterparts.[17]

The authors assessed the adequacy of IBNR reserves. For all five lines in 1975–79, IBNR was overreserved except in one year, 1975. The medical malpractice line's IBNR was substantially overreserved for the 1976 and 1977 policy years, seriously underreserved in 1975 and 1978, and slightly underreserved in 1979. Although the authors did not compute a summary measure of IBNR reserving adequacy for the second half of the 1970s as a whole, it appears that such a measure would reveal that reserves were roughly adequate. The companies appear to have overreacted in 1976 and 1977 to the 1975 experience, and then, after a relatively good experience in 1976 and 1977, put too little in IBNR in 1978. Of course, at the same time, some of the companies may have switched from an occurrence to a claims-made policy form, which would lower IBNR, though not necessarily change the direction of any reserving errors.

Trends in Reserving Error

In general, medical malpractice insurance was overreserved for policy years beginning in the late 1970s (Table 6.5). The most accurate measure for loss-reserve error for a line with a long tail such as medical malpractice insurance is the eight-year loss development period. (It would be desirable to have even longer periods given the long tail in malpractice, especially in light of the fact that insurance companies fight the large claims the longest.) The undiscounted loss reserve errors for 1978–85 and 1979–86 suggest that the companies overreserved by around 10 to 20 percent for these policy years. The discounted errors are over twice as high. An excess of reserve over payout of 10 percent or less should not be considered overreserving, since some losses remain to be paid in the ninth and subsequent years (Table 6.1). Estimated errors for the corresponding six- and four-year development periods (1978–83, 1979–84, and 1978–81, 1979–82) necessarily exceed those for their eight-year counterparts, since the initial reserve was the same, but a smaller value of paid loss was subtracted from the reserve. These six- and four-year loss reserve errors reinforce the conclusion that reserves were, at a minimum, fully adequate for the 1978 and 1979 policy years.

Reserves for later policy years appear to have been less adequate. In particular, reserves for the 1980 policy year seem to have been inadequate. Although the results for later years are fragmentary, the four-year estimates suggest that payments were higher relative to reserves for policy years 1982 and 1983 than for 1978 and 1979. The underreserving problem in 1980 was largely concentrated in the commercial stock companies. But even for the other ownership types, the reserve cushion tended to be lower for the 1980 policy years than for the other years.

There is no consistent pattern in Table 6.5 between loss reserving and company ownership. For example, the loss reserve errors for the eight-year development periods, which began in 1978 and 1979, indicate that the commercial stock companies tended to set higher reserves relative to paid losses. Yet, for the 1980 policy year, these companies substantially underreserved.

Company-specific loss reserve errors for 22 companies are shown in Table 6.6.[19] There was considerable variation in loss errors among the companies. For example, among the mutuals, Group Council Mutual Insurance Company, Michigan Physicians Mutual Liability Company, and P.I.E. Mutual Insurance Company were substantially underreserved for the 1979 policy year. By contrast, Mutual Insurance Company of Arizona and State Volunteer Mutual Insurance Company had reserves far in excess of paid losses. Most commercial stock companies, such as St. Paul, American International, and Travelers, overreserved by an appreciable margin. But Fireman's Fund substantially underreserved.

We computed loss reserve errors for four other lines for eight-year development periods for 11 multiple-line companies (Table 6.7). Whether losses were discounted or not, the companies substantially underreserved losses for each of the other four lines. While underreserving was a serious problem for the other lines, it was not for medical

Table 6.5. Loss Reserve Errors for Medical Malpractice Insurance by Ownership (Percent)

Loss Development Period	Mutual		Exchange		Physician-Owned Stock		Commercial Stock		Total	
	Not Discounted	Discounted	Not Discounted	Discounted	Not Discounted	Discounted	Not Discounted	Discounted	Not Discounted	Discounted
Eight Years										
1978–85	0.1	27.5	25.9	45.9	15.5	41.1	29.6	47.6	19.6	41.0
1979–86	−9.9	29.8	13.9	38.8	19.7	42.2	22.0	39.2	11.9	36.5
Six Years										
1978–83	25.6	42.3	37.0	52.4	42.9	57.5	34.8	52.7	32.4	49.6
1979–84	23.1	42.4	30.1	47.9	35.6	51.4	38.7	48.7	32.7	46.8
1980–85	17.4	41.1	−1.1	28.8	3.3	30.6	−211.5	−131.5	−103.5	−49.9
1981–86	−0.5	38.1	4.4	37.0	6.0	35.7	23.5	50.1	12.8	43.8
Four Years										
1978–81	63.9	69.9	66.0	70.0	76.9	81.1	61.0	67.9	63.0	69.2
1979–82	67.2	72.0	64.0	70.6	61.8	69.2	41.4	51.9	53.2	61.3
1980–83	56.4	65.1	44.8	57.2	43.2	55.0	−142.3	−94.0	−48.2	−18.5
1981–84	49.8	61.2	48.4	62.2	46.4	58.3	61.6	69.7	55.2	65.3
1982–85	49.6	60.4	54.0	65.0	34.6	55.7	42.2	54.6	44.6	57.5
1983–86	49.8	63.1	54.1	63.2	57.7	74.4	41.1	53.8	46.7	59.6

Source: A.M. Best Co., *Best's Casualty Loss Reserve Development,* 1979–87 editions.

Note: Data come from 28 to 49 firms, depending upon the time period. The first year given for the loss development period is the policy year.

Table 6.6. Loss Reserve Errors for Medical Malpractice Insurance by Ownership (Percent): Selected Companies

Company	Eight-Year Period, 1979–86	
	Not Discounted	Discounted
Mutual		
Mutual Assurance Society of Alabama	3.7	30.1
Mutual Insurance Company of Arizona	37.0	55.0
Group Council Mutual Insurance Company	−91.6	−19.8
Norcal Mutual Insurance Company	53.1	63.6
Michigan Physicians Mutual Liability Company	−67.4	−11.8
Medical Liability Mutual Insurance Company of New York	−12.8	27.7
Medical Mutual Insurance Company of North Carolina	−7.3	16.0
P.I.E. Mutual Insurance Company	−65.5	−20.1
State Volunteer Mutual Insurance Company (TN)	61.9	69.9
Exchange		
Medical Insurance Exchange of California	58.1	68.8
Southern California Physicians Insurance Exchange	22.3	42.8
Illinois State Medical Inter-Insurance Exchange	4.3	36.8
Medical Inter-Insurance Exchange of New Jersey	−29.1	6.7
Physician Stock		
Physicians Insurance Company of Ohio	6.5	30.2
Pennsylvania Medical Society Liability Insurance Company	32.8	54.2
Commercial Stock		
American International Group	80.0	82.9
Farmers Insurance Group	41.6	59.4
Fireman's Fund Insurance Companies	−127.4	−66.9
Hartford Insurance Group	41.9	58.9
Medical Protective Company	8.5	37.6
St. Paul Group	39.5	52.9
Travelers Group	79.8	83.4

Source: A.M. Best Co., *Best's Casualty Loss Reserve Development*, 1980–87.

Table 6.7. Eight-Year Loss Reserve Errors by Line[1] (Percent)

	Mean Loss Reserve Error			
	1978–85		1979–86	
	Not Discounted	Discounted	Not Discounted	Discounted
Medical malpractice	27.4	46.1	21.1	40.9
Automobile liability	−158.1	−89.4	−177.1	−103.3
Other liability	−244.3	−119.5	−468.8	−265.7
Workers' Compensation	−97.8	−42.1	−99.9	−43.7
Multiple peril[2]	−274.4	−182.2	−324.7	−222.3
Total[3]	−128.2	−60.4	−179.4	−93.1

Source: A.M. Best Co., *Best's Reproductions of Convention Statements*, 1979–87, Schedule P.

[1]Commercial stock companies only.

[2]Includes farm; home; commercial; boiler and machinery; and ocean, marine, and aircraft (all peril).

[3]Includes the five lines listed above.

Table 6.8. Six-Year Loss Reserve Errors by Line[1] (Percent)

	Mean Loss Reserve Error							
	1978–83		1979–84		1980–85		1981–86	
Line	Not Discounted	Discounted	Not Discounted	Discounted	Not Discounted	Discounted	Not Discounted	Discounted
Medical malpractice	34.2	52.0	36.7	47.6	−189.4	−114.8	23.7	50.8
Automobile liability	−155.3	−87.9	−174.5	−101.8	−177.0	−99.6	−175.0	−95.3
Other liability	−195.2	−92.6	−385.6	−221.8	−170.4	−75.4	−202.3	−85.6
Workers' Compensation	−87.2	−36.3	−89.1	−38.2	−91.9	−36.7	−90.9	−33.9
Multiple peril[2]	−272.4	−176.4	−315.6	−217.6	−332.2	−226.6	−328.0	−221.2
Total[3]	−114.7	−51.6	−152.8	−81.3	−193.5	−110.5	−130.6	−53.3

Source: A.M. Best Co., *Best's Reproductions of Convention Statements*, 1978–87, Schedule P.

[1]Commercial stock companies only.

[2]Includes farm; home; commercial; boiler and machinery; and ocean, marine, and aircraft (all peril).

[3]Includes the five lines listed above.

malpractice. Taking the five lines as a whole, there was still a large shortfall for each policy year.

Except for the 1980 policy year, the six-year loss reserve errors reveal a similar pattern (Table 6.8). After only six years, and with discounting, payments for loss and loss expense had exceeded the amounts originally reserved for all lines but malpractice in every policy year examined.

At least for the period 1979–86, the loss reserve error for medical malpractice was often negatively correlated with the loss reserve errors in the other lines (Table 6.9). The correlations above the diagonals (of 1.00) are based on loss reserve errors without discounting; the correlations below the diagonals are based on loss reserve errors with discounting. Discounting did not affect these correlations. Many of the correlations were not statistically significant at conventional levels because of the small sample size (11 firms). If these results can be replicated for other years, they suggest that selling other lines, such as automobile insurance, in addition to medical malpractice insurance, is advantageous in the sense that it reduces aggregate reserving errors.

Table 6.9. Correlations Among Lines in Loss Reserve Errors

	Eight-Year Loss Development Period (1979–86)				
	Medical Malpractice	Automobile Liability	Other Liability	Workers' Compensation	Multiple Peril
Medical malpractice	1.00	0.04	−0.13	0.03	−0.10
Automobile liability	−0.14	1.00	−0.13	0.95	0.59^c
Other liability	−0.21	−0.12	1.00	0.96^a	0.70^b
Workers' Compensation	−0.08	0.94^a	0.96^a	1.00	0.98^a
Multiple peril	−0.25	0.57^c	0.71^b	0.97^a	1.00
	Six-Year Loss Development Period (1979–84)				
	Medical Malpractice	Automobile Liability	Other Liability	Workers' Compensation	Multiple Peril
Medical malpractice	1.00	0.08	−0.15	0.05	−0.12
Automobile liability	−0.14	1.00	−0.13	0.96^a	0.58^c
Other liability	−0.24	−0.12	1.00	0.97^a	0.70^b
Workers' Compensation	−0.08	0.94^a	0.96^a	1.00	0.98^a
Multiple peril	−0.27	0.57^c	0.72	0.98^a	1.00
	Four-Year Loss Development Period (1979–82)				
	Medical Malpractice	Automobile Liability	Other Liability	Workers' Compensation	Multiple Peril
Medical malpractice	1.00	−0.92^a	−0.09	0.41	0.46
Automobile liability	0.93^a	1.00	0.08	−0.42	−0.36
Other liability	−0.10	0.09	1.00	0.64	0.49
Workers' Compensation	0.37	−0.35	0.64^c	1.00	0.51
Multiple peril	0.45	−0.34	0.48	0.47	1.00

Source: Computations based on *Best's Reproductions of Convention Statements*, 1980–87, Schedule P.

Note: Commercial stock companies only. Correlations above the diagonal came from loss reserve errors without discounting and those below the diagonal from errors with discounting.

^{a}Statistically significant at the 1 percent level, two-tailed t-test.

^{b}Statistically significant at the 5 percent level, two-tailed t-test.

^{c}Statistically significant at the 10 percent level, two-tailed t-test.

LOSS RESERVE "SMOOTHING"

Another insurer practice investigated by some studies in the insurance literature is attempts by management to reduce variability in reported earnings. Motives for reducing reported earnings may be to please equityholders, who may view investments in insurers with volatile earnings as exceedingly risky (in general, however, some risk should be diversifiable) or to please regulators, who dislike variability of returns and policyholders' surplus. As Grace (1990, 35) noted, few practices offer more income-smoothing potential than manipulating reserves. The anticipated gains versus costs of manipulating reserves to stabilize reported earnings can, like the overreserving calculation, be cast as an optimization problem (Grace 1990). Although loss reserves for a particular line, company, and policy year are based on reserves for individual claims, insurers do not compute aggregates by simply summing the values for individual cases. Thus, an insurer could adjust reserves without influencing valuation decisions by claims adjusters in individual cases. To the extent that they do this, insurers are no different from banks that adjust the timing of writing of bad loans, or from firms more generally that adjust the time phasing of depreciation expense.

The most detailed studies of this issue analyzed the automobile insurance industry for 1955–75 (Weiss 1985) and automobile and other liability and Workers' Compensation for 1965–79 (Grace 1990). Weiss concluded that the "results indicate that loss reserving errors do stabilize reported underwriting results" (p. 199). In our view, this

---

Box 6.2. The Weiss Study

Mary Weiss (1985) examined loss-reserving errors in automobile liability insurance based on a pooled, cross-sectional time series regression for the period 1955–75. She tested two hypotheses. First, reported financial results are smoothed by manipulation of loss reserves. Second, exogenous economic developments affect the accuracy of loss reserve estimates. The dependent variable was the loss reserve error, defined as the difference between originally reported incurred losses (reserves plus paid losses in the policy year) and losses that actually occurred four years after the policy year expressed as a ratio—the difference divided by originally reported incurred losses. Four-year development of losses captures a far larger share of ultimate losses in automobile coverage than in malpractice (Table 6.1).

To test the first hypothesis, Weiss included a number of explanatory variables. The basic variable for determining the extent of adjustment was the company's combined ratio in the year in which the policy was written. The combined ratio appears to have been defined as the sum of two ratios: (1) paid loss and loss reserves to premiums earned and (2) underwriting expenses to premiums written. (Premiums earned by the insurer are generally very close to the corresponding value for premiums written.) Weiss also included a variable for the company's automobile combined ratio in some regressions. She argued that a negative parameter estimate of a combined ratio variable would suggest that firms with a high loss experience (i.e., a high ratio) tried to improve their results for a given year by setting loss reserves for the line and policy year below the level at which the claims departments would set them. In defining the combined ratio, she noted that any error in loss reserving should appear in the numerator of the combined ratio, as well as in the dependent variable. Thus, a measurement error (say, a typographical error) could result in a negative correlation between the combined ratio and the loss reserve error even if there was no adjustment (our term). She tried to correct this problem, but her method for correcting appears to be flawed.

Weiss included several other explanatory variables to test the first hypothesis. To the extent that companies attempt to stabilize earnings, she argued that the motive should be important for stock companies, which have shareholders, but not for mutuals. (By "mutuals," she may have meant nonstock insurers.) She distinguished between property-liability insurers that are owned by a holding company from those that are not. She included the Kenney ratio, defined as net premiums written to policyholders' surplus, on the ground that companies with high ratios may want to reduce them because, otherwise, regulators would worry about their possible future insolvency. To reduce the Kenney ratio, companies boost their surplus (in the short run only) by underreserving.

Several other variables were included to test the second hypothesis. First, if insurers accurately forecasted inflation, this would be incorporated in loss reserves as initially established. However, unanticipated inflation in claims costs would not be incorporated in initial loss reserves. (Weiss used an adjusted Livingston forecast of future inflation rates. The Livingston forecast has been criticized on the ground that it is inconsistent with rational expectations formation.) The interest rate at the time the loss reserve was set was also included. Weiss argued that when interest rates are high, insurers may accept a lower underwriting return by taking underwriting risks that in other times they would regard as unacceptable. If the loss reserve estimates do not completely reflect the effects of the relaxed underwriting standards, insurers may end up underreserving.

We do not find Weiss' argument compelling, since it relies on the assumption that insurers systematically underestimate the potential loss of risks they usually regard as unacceptable. This is a logical contradiction, even if different departments of the company are involved. But a case can be made that the interest rate should appear in an equation with the loss reserve error as the dependent variable, since when the interest rate is high, at least some firms must take account of the fact that a dollar reserved now is worth more later.

The coefficients on the combined ratio variables were consistently negative and statistically significant at conventional levels. Weiss took this as evidence in favor of the first hypothesis: that insurers do alter reserving to smooth financial results. However, for a reason mentioned in the second paragraph above, we suspect that the observed relationship may be spurious. Ownership—mutual versus stock and holding versus nonholding company—did not have consistent and statistically significant effects on loss reserve error. In three of the four regressions presented, the coefficient on the Kenney ratio had the negative sign Weiss expected, but the relationship was statistically significant in only one regression. High unanticipated inflation led to underreserving, as anticipated. High interest rates led to underreserving.

conclusion should be regarded, at best, as tentative (Box 6.2). Grace (1990), using somewhat different measures and a different sample, reached essentially the same conclusion for much of the time period she studied (Box 6.3).

We conducted an empirical analysis of loss reserving practices of 40 single-line malpractice insurers (Box 6.4).

Explaining Errors

The findings of our analysis appear in Table 6.10. First, there is suggestive evidence of some systematic manipulation of loss reserves. Companies with high combined ratios

---

Box 6.3 The Grace Study

Elizabeth Grace (1990) estimated the following equation with a sample of 70 property-liability insurers:

$$ERROR = a + \beta_1 TAX + \beta_2 SMOOTH + \beta_3 MISEST + \beta_4 MUTUAL + \beta_5 HOLDING + \mu$$

where

$ERROR$ = sum of reserving errors in automobile liability, other liability, and Workers' Compensation in a given year

a = intercept

TAX = sum of underwriting income, investment income, and net premiums earned for all lines of the insurer's business divided by net premiums earned in all lines of business in the year

$SMOOTH$ = sum of average reported underwriting income and investment income for the three years preceding the year for which ERROR was defined divided by net premiums earned in the year

$MISEST$ = difference between actual inflation and projected inflation as measured by changes in the weekly wage index

$MUTUAL$ = 1 if the company was a mutual

$HOLDING$ = 1 if the insurer was a member of a holding company

μ = equation's error term

A major difference between Grace and Weiss is that Grace's measure of smoothing uses values in the numerator from past years, thereby omitting the measurement error problem arising in Weiss' specification (Box 6.2). Grace's measure TAX was designed to test the hypothesis that insurers with substantial income to shield overreserve. Among her main conclusions were that, for most of the period studied, insurers smoothed reserves to reduce earnings, volatility and insurers with high potential tax obligations increased reserves to lower their effective taxable income.

Box 6.4. Regressions to Explain Loss Reserve Errors: Data and Methods

Given the long tail for medical malpractice insurance, we limited our analysis to eight-year loss reserve errors. The policy years examined were 1978 and 1979. Since we used data for only these two policy years, it was possible to assess differences by insurer (i.e., cross-sectional variation) in loss reserve errors, but our ability to assess the effects of temporal changes, such as real interest rate changes, was very limited. Our data came from *Best's Insurance Reports—Property/Casualty*.

We defined two dependent variables as measures of error: (1) the difference between the amount reserved and the actual payment for loss plus loss adjustment expense divided by the amount reserved and (2) the absolute value of this variable. The latter dependent variable was designed to measure the accuracy of loss forecasting that might occur even in the absence of systematic "diddling." To deal with the spurious correlation problem described in Box 6.2, we lagged the ratio by one year. In addition to Weiss' variables (Box 6.2), we added two independent variables not considered by Weiss. One measured whether the company had the power to assess policyholders in the event of a premium shortfall. Given assessability, the company might have less reason to be careful in forecasting losses. Another gauged the effect of company size on loss reserve error through a measure of company premium volume.

We also used a different variable for inflation. In determining reserves, companies must forecast claims inflation rates. Errors in such forecasts will lead to loss reserve errors. Inflation error is the difference between actual and expected inflation rates. For actual inflation, we used the Consumer Price Index. For anticipated inflation, we used annual expected inflation rates published in Hamilton (1985) through 1981. Hamilton computed anticipated inflation rates from actual nominal interest and inflation rates using a Kalman filter process. We extended his series through 1986 using equations in his article. This measure is conceptually superior to the inflation measures used by Weiss (1985) and Grace (1990).

---

had lower loss reserve errors (regressions 1 and 2). This finding is consistent with Weiss's and Grace's work (Boxes 6.2 and 6.3). The result for the combined ratio applies to the loss reserve error but not to its absolute value.

Second, larger companies (by premium volume) had smaller absolute errors on average. This is a plausible finding because, holding other factors constant, the variance in losses for larger companies should be smaller relative to the expected value. The findings did not hold for errors not measured as an absolute value, implying that there was no systematic "diddling" in one direction or the other.

Third, there were no other statistically significant relationships. In particular, the Kenney ratio has no effect on loss reserve error. We found no effect of unanticipated inflation or of real interest rates (the latter result not shown) on the error. This may be due to the fact that we used data from only two years. Finally, the ability of insurers to

Table 6.10. Loss Reserve Errors: Regression Results

Explanatory Variable	Error		Absolute Error
	Number 1[1]	Number 2	Number 3
Mutual[2]	0.037	0.076	−0.24
	(0.203)	(0.225)	(0.15)
Exchange	0.37	0.37	−0.35
	(0.28)	(0.28)	(0.18)
Kenney ratio	0.077	0.076	−0.064
	(0.068)	(0.070)	(0.045)
Combined ratio	−1.79[a]	−1.86[a]	0.63
	(0.87)	(0.91)	(0.58)
Inflation error	−0.020	−0.011	−0.029
	(0.071)	(0.074)	(0.047)
Assessability[3]	—	−0.18	0.19
	(—)	(0.35)	(0.23)
Real premium (mil. $)	—	−0.0006	−0.0036[a]
	(—)	(0.029)	(0.0017)
Constant	1.71	1.79	0.13
	(0.88)	(0.92)	(0.59)
	$R^2 = 0.16$	$R^2 = 0.16$	$R^2 = 0.22$
	$R^2 = 0.03$	$R^2 = -0.02$	$R^2 = 0.06$
	$F(5,35) = 1.3$	$F(7,33) = 0.9$	$F(7,33) = 1.3$

Sources: A.M. Best Co., *Best's Insurance Reports—Property/Casualty*, 1978–87, and *Best's Casualty Loss Reserve Development*, 1978 and 1987.

[1]The first equation replicates Weiss' (1985) work, the second equation adds assessability and premium volume as explanatory variables, and the third equation uses the absolute value of the error as the dependent variable.

[2]"Mutual" and "Exchange" are dummy variables for ownership, coded either 1 or 0. The omitted comparison group is "Stock company."

[3]"Assessability" is a dummy variable.

[a]Statistically significant at the 5 percent level (two-tail test).

assess policyholders extra in the event of a premium shortfall (assessability) had no effect.

FURTHER DISCUSSION AND CONCLUSIONS

It is never correct to treat any firm's balance sheet as if the underlying data were totally scientific. Even when accepted accounting techniques are employed, firms have some latitude in measuring key variables. This truism applies, if anything, with greater force to an insurance company, for a major part of its liabilities are contingent claims of policyholders. Especially in a long-tail line such as medical malpractice, current liabilities for future claims payments must necessarily be educated guesses at best.

Viewed after the fact, insurers' estimates are bound to have been wrong, either too high or too low. Understandably, we found errors in reserving for every year we were able to analyze. Initially forecasted losses on medical malpractice insurance policies sold in the late 1970s were 20 to 40 percent too high (the latter if future losses are reduced by discounting to current values). The loss reserve errors varied markedly by year but not systematically according to the company's organizational form. Judging from the pattern of correlations among loss reserve errors by line, loss reserve errors in medical malpractice are partly offset (in multiple-line companies) by errors in the opposite direction in other lines. Multiple-line insurers thus have an advantage in diversifying their risk of error relative to single-line malpractice insurers (which physician-sponsored companies are).

We also found evidence that insurers vary reserves to decrease the year-to-year volatility of reported earnings. To the extent that such manipulation reduces the price of capital supplied to such firms by reassuring investors, such manipulation is understandable. Furthermore, policyholders might be worse off without such tempering of year-to-year swings in expected losses. If insurers adjusted premiums for every change in estimated loss, insureds would find themselves hampered by unpredictable expenses for premiums. The one systematic source of loss reserve error identified is the failure to discount anticipated losses before 1986. At least to outsiders, the insurers' argument for not discounting is unpersuasive.[20]

NOTES

1. For example, substantial underreserving was responsible for the near insolvency of Geico (Loomis 1976).
2. Hafling (1981) expanded loss reserve categories from two to five: (1) case reserves; (2) reserves for development in the case reserves; (3) reserves for claims that will be reopened; (4) reserves for claims that have been reported but not recorded; and (5) reserves for incurred but unreported claims. Although only the fifth type is strictly IBNR, Hafling indicated that many insurers also put categories (2) through (4) in their IBNR reserves.
3. Most insurers provide tail coverage to cover claims against physicians who become disabled, die, or retire. The tail policy has an IBNR reserve associated with it.
4. Webb et al. (1984b, 275–76); Smith (1980, 311).
5. See Chapter 2 for a discussion of nondiversifiable risk.
6. The Appendix to Chapter 1 lists the 14 companies' data we used for the calculations. Because 1987 was the last year for which we had Convention Statements, we assumed that all payments due on 1978 policies were paid by the end of the ninth year. In fact, malpractice claims may be settled more than nine years after a policy year (NAIC 1980; U.S. GAO 1986b).
7. Troxel and Breslin (1983, 112) described discontinuing practices of property-casualty insurers as of the early 1980s: "Loss reserves generally are not discounted to their present value. Both statutory accounting practice and generally accepted accounting principles require that the insurer reserve a whole dollar for future payment of every dollar of unpaid losses. An exception is made for certain claims that are settled with periodic payments of specific amounts; these types of loss are discounted with conservative interest assumptions (e.g., four percent) and included in loss reserves at their present value."
8. The "rational expectations" school of macroeconomics rejects the view that decision makers form biased forecasts, although in any given situation, the decision makers may be proven wrong. See, for example, Sargent (1987).
9. There is empirical evidence that high unemployment lowers the demand for physicians' services (Sloan and Bentkover 1979), but the link between unemployment and malpractice claim frequency and severity has not been established empirically.

10. Medical malpractice insurance policies typically specify that the policyholder must report incidents likely to result in claims to the insurer. This provision is seldom if ever enforced because of the difficulty of proving that the policyholder knowingly withheld information on incidents from the insurer.

11. The eight states that required notice of intent to sue during the time period of this study are Arkansas, California, Florida, Maine, Pennsylvania, Texas, Utah, and Virginia. New Hampshire enacted similar legislation in 1977, but it was declared unconstitutional in 1980. This information comes from our survey of medical malpractice legislation. See Bovbjerg (1989).

12. Any incident report is typically a claim under claims-made coverage. If the policyholder changes insurers before the suit is filed, the suit remains the responsibility of the former insurer.

13. We asked participant companies about the backgrounds of their claims personnel. All but one company reported hiring people with several years of property-casualty claims management experience and/or a legal background. The one exception hires only lawyers. All of the companies gave new staff extended in-house training, and some companies reported having sufficient confidence in their programs to hire inexperienced people. While information was not systematically gathered on turnover in the claims staff, certain physician-sponsored companies anecdotally reported that some of their staff had joined the company at its inception, and one person reported that the only claims person who had left the company did so on retirement. Clearly, such limited turnover on top of good training provides these companies with a wealth of historical and institutional knowledge for valuing claims.

14. The IRS in the past has used as a general guideline the criterion that reserve estimates could not exceed developed losses by more than 15 percent without IRS intervention. Overreserving in excess of this would result in the IRS imposing an increase in federal taxes on the insurer. See Grace (1990).

15. Schedule O in the Convention Statement primarily includes property (first party lines), such as fire, earthquake, and burglary and theft. These lines tend to have shorter loss development periods.

16. He arrived at this range by speaking with "numerous" actuaries in the casualty field.

17. The nonstock companies were all nonphysician-sponsored, multiple-line companies.

18. When we discounted, we used the rate of interest on 20-year U.S. government bonds. We based the calculations on published data from Best's *Casualty Loss Reserve Development*. We started with a sample of 49 firms. However, for particular policy years, the sample was less than 49 because of missing data. The smallest number of firms for any period was 28. Although we disaggregated by insurer ownership type, the number of observations in any ownership category was typically small. Because discounting by a positive interest rate must reduce the loss payment stream, the loss reserve error with discounting was always necessarily higher than its nondiscounted counterpart.

19. We included a larger number of companies in the regressions presented below than in Table 6.6.

20. The not dissimilar issue of including a factor in rate making for interest earned on reserves is considered in Chapter 7.

7

Development of Premiums
for Malpractice Insurance

STAGES IN THE RATE-MAKING PROCESS

Rate making begins with claims data and ends with a market test. In between come actuarial science, business judgment, and regulation. How does the full process translate past claims experience into premiums offered to physician insureds to cover future losses? What factors most affect projections of losses and hence rates? To what extent do prospective investment earnings influence premiums? Is competition or regulation more important as a further influence on rates? Might they both contribute to insurance cycles in premiums and availability? This chapter explores such issues.

Figure 7.1 presents a schematic view of how premiums are set. The starting point is the relevant claims experience of physicians. The frequency of claims (number per exposure) and their severity (dollar cost per claim) are presumably influenced by numerous medical, legal, and social trends—none of them very well understood. Indeed, insurers have very limited control over claims experience: They can control whom they insure by using underwriting standards that are more or less selective of physician insureds, but there is disagreement about how predictable an individual physician's future loss may be (Chapter 8). Similarly, they can attempt, through risk and claims management, to reduce the number of claims and payouts on them.

Insurers can do little, however, to influence the underlying social attitudes or to affect directly the legal rules that drive patterns of litigation and insurance settlements. Even so, some insurers have sought to affect public attitudes through opinion advertising; others have lobbied for legislative change in legal rules and processes. Interestingly, the largest single malpractice insurer, a national stock company, has remained neutral on tort reform. In contrast, many physician-sponsored companies have actively sought reform legislation; their trade association, the PIAA, has even developed a new administrative alternative for resolving medical injury claims (PIAA 1989). One may speculate that the physician companies are acting mainly in the interest of their stakeholders, much as does the American Medical Association, (AMA), for example, another vocal advocate of legal reform (AMA 1984a, 1984b, 1985, 1988). Insurers per se, after all, have no vested interest in whether claims are high or low, so long as they are predictable and someone will pay the needed premium.

Whatever the exact nature of the claims process, claims results are an input (Figure 7.1, right arrow) into the next stage of rate making, namely, developing an

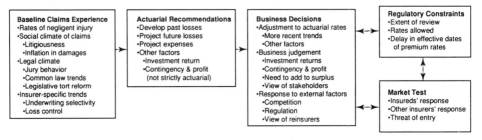

Figure 7.1 Stages in the development of medical malpractice insurance premiums.

actuarial recommendation on rates. Actuaries use past experience to project future costs and set premiums that will be adequate under given assumptions, for example, about loss trends, as well as needed profits and a contingency allowance. Then, business judgment is applied about whether to modify actuarial recommendations. Thereafter, outside influences come into play—regulation in states that review rates and market reactions in all jurisdictions. More dynamically, expectations about these reactions feed back into calculations at an earlier stage. Hence the arrows go both ways between the boxes in Figure 7.1. Insurer claims-reserving practices have just been discussed (Chapter 6). They contribute the basic rate-making data.

CHAPTER OVERVIEW

This chapter next turns to an overview of the fundamentals of actuarial methods (second section). The importance of actuarial techniques and judgment is generally appreciated, but information on them is not generally accessible to nonspecialists. This section discusses basic principles, with examples, so that policymakers can better appreciate the actuarial issues amid the broader disputes about the accuracy of rate making and the fairness of profits. We then present survey evidence on the importance of various actuarial concerns and of influences on rates other than actuarial recommendations (third section). Thereafter come the results of our empirical analysis of numerous factors thought to influence premiums, using multivariate regressions (fourth section). The fifth section concludes the chapter.

ACTUARIAL METHODS

Actuaries predict future premium needs based on past experience, various assumptions, numerical extrapolations, and professional judgment. The goal of rate making is to establish an adequate premium for a particular policy sold to particular insureds in a given state during a given year. Rates must be sufficient to cover three types of costs. The first type is future claims losses, plus closely associated expenses. The latter are the costs of investigation and defense that can be allocated to a particular case, such as fees paid to outside attorneys or court costs, plus similar but unallocated costs, such as overall expenses of the claims department. Insurance jargon calls these costs "loss adjustment expense (LAE)" (Chapter 6).[1]

Box 7.1. A Thumbnail Sketch of Actuarial Practice

Perhaps the salient feature of insurance is that its price is set before its cost is known; its price, moreover, varies less by expenses of "production" than by who buys it (and their expected losses). Hence, predicting future losses by category of insured is central to the business, but it is inherently an uncertain process. In medical malpractice, prediction is especially difficult, for losses take a long time to "run off" even once a claim is made. Many factors affect costs that are beyond the control of the insurer and subject only to general estimation of the actuary.

Greatly simplified, the process is as follows: The key problem is to estimate what the costs will be and hence what premium is needed to cover them. To do so, actuaries first assemble historical data on claims experience with which they feel comfortable. When their data base is large enough and consistent enough, they term it "credible" for purposes of rate making. Data for each past policy year are arrayed separately, for each "vintage" of policy had its own premium and was subject to the same social, legal, and economic factors affecting claims and losses. Older coverage periods have longer run offs of claims experience to observe than do more recent ones. The actuary thus looks at sets of data with one year of experience, two years, three years, and so on—much as a grower of Christmas trees looks at a field with saplings of various ages.

Second, actuaries predict what the losses will ultimately be for each of the past policy years when all possible claims are fully run off. They call this "developing" the loss experience to "ultimate." The Christmas tree grower would call it estimating the eventual average height of the harvestable crop—a key factor when consumers pay by the foot. Actuarial projections may be rather mechanistic extrapolations or may contain more sophisticated judgmental adjustments for various anomalies in the data (just as the grower would adjust expectations from observed patterns when an unusually dry year had stunted past growth). Using these ultimate values, actuaries next calculate how these developed losses related to premiums as loss ratios (losses as a fraction of premiums) or pure premiums (amount of premium needed to cover one "exposure" or base-rate-class physician).

Third, they "trend" loss ratios or pure premiums into the future period to be covered by the premiums being set. They may take various types of information into account in deciding on the proper trend factor(s) or statistical methods of projection. The tree farmer, too, cannot automatically use past experience to project the growth of the crop planted this year, for important influences may change in the future—the nature of seeds, fertilizer, irrigation, and the like. Actuarial science thus relies on three central technical considerations: credibility, development, and trending of losses.

Having predicted losses as loss ratios or pure premiums, actuaries finally determine what premium is needed to cover them, as well as other costs that must be loaded onto losses for the insurer to remain in business. Of course, variations on these basic actuarial themes are commonplace (see text).

Second, various types of other expenses not directly associated with settling claims must be accounted for. These include expenses of "production," that is, costs associated with conducting business, including commissions paid to agents and brokers, if any; costs of the field staff involved in business production, advertising, printing, and so on; general expenses, primarily home office costs; and taxes, including premium taxes. Profit, including an allowance for contingencies, is the third cost. The second and third items together constitute the "loading" factor that must be added to losses on claims if an insurer is to continue in business.

The major problem facing actuaries in a long-tail line such as medical malpractice is that losses and expenses must be forecast far into the future. The delay from the time the premium is collected to the time payouts may have to be made may be seven years, eight years, or even more (Chapter 6). Determining the profit also involves complex issues, but we leave the discussion of profitability to Chapter 9. The competitive underwriting profit depends in part on the yield on investments (Chapter 2).

We next discuss the steps that actuaries take to make these determinations in more detail. For a quick summary, see Box 7.1.[2] This discussion assumes that an insurer develops rates based primarily on its own data, which is now standard practice. The industry rating bureau, the Insurance Services Office (ISO), traditionally developed rates for use by members, but few companies now use it for basic calculations.[3] Problems arise in fully pooling data from different insurers, necessitating adjustments where claims reserving and expense reporting vary company by company.

Data Bases and Credibility

What Data to Include

Actuaries begin by assembling data—principally on losses, premiums, and exposures, from claims and underwriting departments. Exposures give the number of units insured (i.e., physicians), by rating classification. Past premiums and exposures by class of insureds are known with certainty, but past claims experience is not: Data on past claims include both closed claims and those still open, on which the ultimate cost is not known, only the current amount of claims reserves. Coping with this uncertainty is a key problem, and claims experience gets most of the attention in the following discussion.

The first task facing actuaries is to establish a "credible" data base for a particular calculation. Just what is required for full credibility of data is not completely agreed on, and different approaches exist (Philbrick 1981). Actuaries still have to decide what data to include in their data bases, how to array the data, and what they can extrapolate from the data, with credibility in mind.

For a liability coverage in a small line, such as medical malpractice, a logical geographic unit for compiling data is the state, given that legal practice varies by state and that social attitudes probably have a geographic component as well. (Where experience differs markedly in one or more large urban areas from elsewhere in the state, and the data base is large enough, rates may also be made for subareas within the state, normally by applying a relativity factor to statewide rates.) However, there are very few physicians in a state (compared, say, with automobile drivers or homeowners); moreover, the variation in experience is relatively large for malpractice. Again here, the nature of malpractice as a low-frequency, high-severity line affects insurance practice. Nonetheless, most states' experience is considered to be fully credible for basic rate-making purposes.[4] For very small states (and for computing certain projection factors), however, an insurer may use a credibility mix—with a calculation partly based on state data, partly on the experience of other states deemed comparable or the nation as a whole. (Historically, the ISO played a more substantial role here as a rating bureau.) Actuaries also need to be concerned about whether the nature of their insureds was consistent over time; if underwriting standards have changed, past experience will be less reliable.

Nor is there agreement among the technicians as to how many years of experience should be included in a data base. A longer time period gives more observations and hence more credible results. And the more variable the loss distribution, the longer the time period desirable.[5] But where underlying risk of loss or trend factors may be changing over time, older years' data may be "stale" and thus less reliable than more recent experience. Actuaries have several responses to this dilemma. One is to use different time periods of data for different purposes, such as base rates and higher limits. Another is to give more weight to more recent data, either judgmentally or through a statistical model.[6] A third response is to shorten the premium period and hence to increase the number of observational units being analyzed; a six-month premium is projected by one large company, although year-by-year analysis and rate making is the industry standard.[7]

Actuaries must also decide what groupings of physicians' experience are desirable for their data base. All physicians are not alike; clearly, different specialties have different expected losses, which is the basis for risk classification (Chapter 8). Moreover, the trends in losses over time may also differ among physician classes. So, there is a case for estimating each class's expected losses from its own separate data base. But, almost universally, all insured physicians within each state are pooled together. Thus, actuaries use pooled data on all physicians and develop a year's premiums for a base risk class, normally the one with the most insureds (typically a low-risk class, like general practitioner, no surgery).[8] Exposures and premiums therefore have to be normalized into base-class equivalents. Rates for other specialties are then set as multiples of the base rates, using relativities developed from longer time periods of data. This practice puts more observations into the data base, which improves credibility. It also results in less variation in year-to-year premiums charged to insureds, which might drive away customers. Moreover, computing rates first in the aggregate for all physicians, and then apportioning the total among subgroups also reduces the likelihood of a premium shortfall; any undercharge to one specialty is automatically balanced by an "overcharge" to another.

Actuaries also decide whether to group data from claims-made and occurrence policies together or to analyze them separately. Because claims-made is now the industry standard, and because for most states there are now many years of claims-made experience, this decision is of declining importance, although it still exists.

Another choice about the data to be included relates to the policy limits and sizes of losses to be examined. Losses at higher limits (say, above $100,000 per claim) are less frequent and more variable than those at lower limits. For one insurer known to us, less than one-fifth of losses are above this amount even in high-loss states. (See also, Chapter 6 on this point.) As for specialty premium differentials, actuaries normally first develop base rates for basic limits—traditionally $100,000/$300,000 but more recently $200,000/$600,000 or some higher amount. Expected losses and premiums for increased limits are, again, derived as a proportion of basic rates, using a larger data base.

As noted above, insurers' claims losses consist not only of direct payments to claimants (or reserves in expectation of such payments) but also of LAE. At least the allocated portion of ALAE for medical malpractice is normally included in the data base, along with claims losses. The rationale for this is that ALAE is very high for medical malpractice cases, which are expensive to investigate and defend. ALAE for malpractice is more than double that of other lines (Bovbjerg et al. 1989, 926, note 94). Moreover, ALAE and claims are thought to be subject to similar inflationary influences. Unallocated LAE may be included here or estimated separately from a different data base. An additional minor concern in analyzing claims data is what level of claim should be included. Some incidents never have a claim brought or any ALAE spent on investigation (Chapter 6); these may be excluded from projections. It is also possible to do separate calculations for claims closed with and without indemnity payments.

How to Array the Data

Having decided on what data to include in an analysis, an actuary must decide how to array the data for the relevant pool of insureds whose rates are being calculated. A basic actuarial tool is the "loss triangle." Table 7.1 shows a simplified, hypothetical loss triangle that illustrates loss development. Its size is determined by the length of

Table 7.1.   Hypothetical Loss Development Triangles

Panel A. Hypothetical Losses as of 12/31/89

Historical Coverage Period	Losses (in $ Thousands) by Evaluation Point (in Months)					
	12	24	36	48	60	Ultimate
1985	1,397	4,074	5,752	6,717	7,020	
1986	1,663	4,920	6,957	8,131		
1987	2,597	7,694	10,900			
1988	3,788	11,236				
1989	4,307					

Panel B. Hypothetical Development Factors

Historical Coverage Period	Ratios at Evaluation Points (in Months)				Estimated 60 to ultimate
	24/12	36/24	48/36	60/48	
1985	2.916	1.412	1.168	1.044	
1986	2.960	1.414	1.166		
1987	2.963	1.417			
1988	2.966				
Selected period-to-period ratios	2.962	1.413	1.167	1.044	1.015
	ult/12	ult/24	ult/36	ult/48	ult/60
Cumulative factors	5.178	1.748	1.237	1.060	1.015

Source: Adapted from Tillinghast (1987) by permission.

time to be included in the data base for basic premium development. The hypothetical shell for 1991 rates being developed in 1990 shows losses for five historical coverage years, 1985–89 (arrayed down the vertical axis), each tracked at 12-month intervals (across the horizontal axis). The earlier years have more years of claims history to observe—five for 1985, four for 1986, and so on, down to one for the most recent year, 1989. Hence the triangular shape of the array.

Actuaries need to track the developing claims experience of each historical period separately. Each year has its own mix of policies sold, accompanying exposures, and premiums, and the premiums need to cover subsequent expenses or the insurer will fail. So, actuaries want to compare how well historical premiums covered later losses attributable to the coverage those premiums bought. With the passage of time, more and more losses are known as payments on closed claims become larger and open reserves for unclosed claims smaller. So, actuaries compile loss data on a year-by-year basis (or other period) for each historical period. But different choices are possible about what historical periods to track. For medical malpractice, it is common to use a "notice year," that is, to compile together information on all claims reported to the insurer during the year.[9] In the hypothetical example of Table 7.1, Panel A, losses develop rapidly over time, as casual inspection will verify.[10] The next actuarial step is to quantify how rapidly claims grow over time.

Developing the Historical Experience of Claims

To set rates for an upcoming year, an insurer wants to know how well it is doing under past and current rates. Have they been adequate to cover claims? Because of the long payment tail, complete information on the historical pattern of claims is not available to the insurer for recent policy years. Under a claims-made policy, the insurer knows relatively quickly about the existence of claims that it must pay from a given year's premiums but not about the amounts at which they will ultimately close. There is still a long delay to settlement for many claims, especially larger ones (Chapter 6). So, information about the cost of recent claims is disproportionately an estimate—the amounts at which claims departments have set reserves on open claims. These amounts change over time. Extrapolations thus are necessary to analyze recent performance as if all claims were resolved; one needs to know the "ultimate" value of each year's losses when finally settled. Actuaries call such projections "developing" the data to ultimate values.

To perform this task, the actuary works with the same type of loss triangle just described (Table 7.1, Panel A). Once the data are arrayed in a triangle, certain adjustments may be needed before developing losses. For instance, it may be noted that the claims department systematically over- or underreserved in a given calendar year (which would show up in a diagonal in the triangle, for example, 2,597 to 4,920, to 5,752—each of which values comes from experience during notice year 1987).

Once any adjustments are made, the actuary must square the triangle. Typically, this is done by calculating "link ratios" between the numbers in adjacent columns—how much larger amounts are in the second developmental period than the first, in the third than the second, and so on. There could also be a decline over time—for example, if the triangle covered claims-made experience with incurred losses, i.e., including reserves. These ratios can be done in different ways, with a final selection of one to apply. Table 7.1, Panel B, shows one actuary's hypothetical development factors of the triangle in Panel A. Panel B is also a triangle, but is smaller by one column because it is composed of ratios for values in adjacent columns. Each ratio shows how much a historical period's losses grow from year to year. Then the actuary must decide judgmentally which link ratios seem most plausible in order to derive multiplicative factors for developing each vintage of losses to its ultimate value. In essence, the multipliers times the most-developed known losses for each historical period fill in the blank cells in the triangle of Table 7.1, Panel A, although the key developed data are in the column to the far right, the ultimate values, which lie beyond five years' experience in malpractice.

Hence the last development factor, shown at the lower right in Table 7.1, Panel B—the estimated factor for increasing 60 months' experience to ultimate. This factor must be derived from a larger data base, as by definition it goes beyond the five years of development illustrated. A higher multiplier to ultimate is naturally needed for a historical coverage period with only 12 months of development to date (5.178 in Table 7.1) than for a period nearing completion (1.060 for 48 months).[11] Development thus moves from left to right in the triangles, toward the far right-hand column of ultimate values, calculated by multiplying the figures in Panel A by the factors in Panel B. (Again, with incurred losses on claims-made policies, development could be down as well as up.) But knowing what losses on past periods will ultimately be is not enough. The key is what future losses on next year's coverage will be.

Trending Claims Experience into the Future

Therefore, the next task is to "trend" past experience into the future. Trending is necessary to account for inflation and other factors that may make future losses higher (or lower) than past ones. As already noted, the actuary is likely to examine more information on trend factors than on development—typically going beyond his or her own company's data as a source to Insurance Services Office data, figures from other insurers, and general economic indices (for example, the Consumer Price Index).[12]

To what date does the actuary trend past results? To the average loss date of the future policy year whose premiums are being set. Typically, the assumption is that policies will be sold uniformly throughout the policy year and that claims will likewise occur at a uniform rate, so that the average will be the midpoint in each case. (For example, if the policy year begins on January 1, 1991, the average policy will be sold on July 1 and will be in effect through June 30, 1992; the average claim will be made on December 31, 1991, so trending will go to then.) Trend factors extrapolate from results in each past year forward—vertically down the ultimate column in a developed triangle (Table 7.1, Panel A). However, trending is normally done not on losses alone, but rather on a comparison of losses to premium.

There are two main ways of doing such trending—the "loss ratio" and the "pure premium" approaches. Under the loss ratio approach, the actuary calculates a ratio of losses to aggregate premiums for each past historical coverage period, using nominal dollars for developed losses and current rate level premiums (i.e., the amount that would be charged under today's rates).[13] The result is a progression of loss ratios derived from the column of ultimate losses. Alternatively, the pure premium may be calculated for each year, that is, ultimate claims losses (including adjustment expense) divided by exposures—the amount of premium per period needed to pay for the losses of one normalized exposure. Again, the result is a progression of figures, analogous to developed losses but compared to exposures.

In either case, the next step is to fit a curve to the series of loss ratios or pure premiums. The simplest "curve" is, of course, a linear projection. Alternatively, an exponential or quadratic equation may be chosen as most appropriate. In trending a pure premium (which is frequency times severity divided by exposures), the actuary may examine frequency and severity trends separately. This is logical where, as seen in malpractice, frequency has ups and downs but severity rises more consistently over time.[14] One clue to frequency and severity trends may be whether or not there is a close fit between actual and estimated losses in the triangle and whether or not there are trends in goodness of fit. The actuary also examines trends in actual company data for trends in claims severity and frequency and, when possible, reviews data from other companies judged to be comparable for trends in these variables. In many lines of property-casualty insurance, regression analysis relating losses to time raised to an exponent is used to fit a trend in claims severity (Webb et al. 1984b, 94–95).

In addition to statistical calculations of trend, the actuary may consider other information, such as pertinent legislative changes to tort law and economic changes not captured in development or trend factors. The projection is then modified—by how much is an empirical question. Individual actuaries and the insurers for which they work vary in how much rate-making credence they give to tort reform (third section) before seeing results in patterns of claims reserves (Chapter 6). Of course, where reforms have their intended effects of reducing claims or payment levels, the reforms' effects will eventually be captured automatically in the development of losses, but not for premiums already collected.

Final Calculation of the Recommended Premium

Base Premiums

To convert a loss ratio or a pure premium into a premium, loading factors have to be included. Expenses (other than the loss-adjusted expense already in the loss ratio or pure premium), profit, and contingency factors need to be added and any discount or allowance for interest subtracted. One way to calculate a discount is to figure how much each dollar of pure premium will earn before it is paid out in claims. Some interest rate must be selected—say, returns on risk-free government bonds of maturities consistent with the pattern of loss development—and the time of investment must be estimated. The actuary generally does a full cash flow analysis of losses, although some may simply assume that all dollars are paid out at the average time of settlement. Expense loadings may be a simple percentage based on past averages (e.g., allow 20 percent for expenses) or a more complex calculation that takes into account that some expenses are fixed (e.g., the regulatory cost of operations in a given state), while others may vary with different factors (e.g., premium taxes by premiums, policy issuance expense by number of policies sold, claims department costs by volume of claims); moreover, different expenses occur at different times in relation to receipt of premiums (e.g., agents' commissions soon after the sale of a policy, the portion of unallocated LAE at the date of final settlement). The actuary may or may not load in reinsurance expense. Basic limits are unlikely to be reinsured, but every reinsured loss has a basic limits component, so developments at lower levels do affect claims experience at upper levels and loading makes sense. Logically, it should vary by risk class because of the variation in expected penetration of reinsured layers of coverage. Beyond operating expenses come profit and contingency allowances. These loadings are more judgmental.

In the pure premium approach, the pure premium is divided by 1 minus a fraction representing the loading. The result is the dollar premium to be charged to the exposure class that has been calculated. Alternatively, using loss ratios, the actuary adds expenses to the numerator of losses to create a new loss ratio and then compares it to the target loss ratio, given allowances for interest income, profit, and contingencies. If it is too low, current premiums must rise, and vice versa.

Setting Other Premium Rates

The base premiums just calculated need to be adjusted for different rating classes of insureds, as already noted. The class relativities are calculated separately, from a larger data base, but with not dissimilar techniques. Similarly, rates must be calculated for increased limits above base limits. Again, larger data bases are used. The St. Paul, for example, computes increased limits rates for three groupings of states—low-, medium-, and high-rated states. A state's classification can change over time. Thus, two determinations are involved: first, the national trends for those groupings and, second, the grouping that includes the state being rated. (Expense loadings may be calculated separately as well, especially by a larger insurer, given different classes' premiums and expected loss.)

Similarly, factors must be calculated for increased limits coverage. A company may sell coverage to a limit beyond the actuary's confidence to compute a rate with statistical methods like those described here. This is one reason for the importance of reinsurance (Chapter 5). Rates for higher limits (say, above $1 million/$3 million) would then be set by the terms of the reinsurance agreement (e.g., where the reinsurer assumes the entire risk) or by the primary insurer using more judgmental techniques.

For claims-made coverage, a separate premium must also be set for "mature" policies (generally defined as those in force with the company for five or more consecutive years), for earlier years (one through four), and for tail coverage (or "reporting endorsement," as the St. Paul dubs it). Because of the lag between incidents of alleged malpractice and reporting to the insurer, few claims are made in the first year of coverage (those made based on earlier incidents are the responsibility of a prior insurer). More claims can be anticipated in each successive year as the backlog of incidents become filed as claims. The actuary uses data on the extent of these lags between incident and filing to compute factors for the rates on nonmature claims-made coverages. By the fifth year, the flow of claims is deemed to be in a steady state, with no further year-to-year increase due to delayed filing. Mature rates apply until a physician leaves a claims-made insurer, whether to change companies or to retire from practice. Thereafter, the tail coverage applies. Its claims rate can be expected to fall from year to year as the backlog of incidents from the years of active practice is exhausted.

Finally, certain other premium adjustments may apply. An insurer may have merit-rating discounts or surcharges (Chapter 8). Alternatively, lower rates may apply to physicians who have teaching positions or who are semiretired. A discount may also be given where all physicians in a group practice buy coverage from the same insurer (which facilitates both marketing and defense of claims), even though each policy is an individual one. Such adjustments are quite judgmental, and for each lowering of one set of rates there needs to be an offsetting rise elsewhere, since in any particular state the actuaries have calculated the total amount of premiums needed.

Actuarial Technique in Perspective

As the foregoing sketch should make clear, actuarial science involves considerable art. Actuaries' basic data are "soft" in that they include much information on reserved claims as opposed to settled ones, especially in a long-tail line. Moreover, the most recent period has very little actual loss development to examine; most dollars from recent claims are estimates, that is, still in reserve, not paid. There is also a considerable lag between the last data observed and the period for which rates are being made, which complicates projections.[15] To be more confident in their projections, actuaries rely on rather long time series of data, giving considerable weight to data five or more years old, especially in long-tail lines that have a greater degree of volatility. Their general reliance on at least five-year development triangles and trend periods means that their rate projections will react to upturns and downturns in experience (notably, in claims frequency) only with a lag.

Actuaries, like sales personnel, need to "know the territory" so as to distinguish expected variation in these data from adverse underwriting experience, that is, from the start of a new trend. Actuaries do not earn their salaries or fees by being right for every specialty every year, just by being right in the aggregate and over time. They need to be above and below overall trends in equal measure.

Market considerations, such as the effect of premium levels on market share and on the mix of insureds, are not a direct concern of the actuary. Nor is the likely regulatory reaction to the indicated rate. As discussed further in the next section, medical malpractice insurers sometimes modify the actuary's recommendations based on market considerations or regulatory concerns.

EMPIRICAL EVIDENCE ON PRICING PRACTICES FROM THE SURVEY OF MEDICAL MALPRACTICE INSURERS

Our Survey of Medical Malpractice Insurers asked several questions about insurers' actual practice in pricing malpractice insurance policies. This section discusses these results, together with relevant information from other sources.

The Importance of Actuaries

Our survey asked respondents to check which one of listed departments takes the lead in setting the insurer's general pricing policy. Underwriting and senior management (including the board) got the most mentions here (7 of 13 responses for the former, 6 for the latter, with one company checking both). Almost half of the respondents checked two departments or added an explanation that the process was collaborative or committee oriented. Only one physician-sponsored company had an in-house actuary (see below), so actuarial department was not an option for 10 of our respondents. One multiple-line commercial stock company listed its professional liability department.

Nonetheless, all of our respondents rely heavily on actuaries, although only one cited such a department; several mentioned departments' working from the (outside) actuarial report. A follow-up question asked what department worked with an actuary to assist with the more specific task of premium development. Unprompted this time, eight respondents listed underwriting, four claims management, three finance, and one professional liability (including some double counting).

As just noted, we also asked whether the companies used an in-house actuary or an outside consultant. The national commercial stock companies used in-house actuaries. With one exception, the mutual-exchanges used outside actuaries. One of the companies with an in-house actuary also occasionally employed an actuarial consultant for special projects or for an independent view. Among the outside actuaries, there was considerable overlap among insurers in the particular consulting firms used. During the five years preceding the survey, the vast majority of insurers had not changed actuarial consultants. Comments written in various parts of the survey questionnaire indicate considerable satisfaction with actuarial performance. None of the companies noted any reliance on actuarial advice from the ISO, the leading rating bureau for all lines of property-casualty insurance, much less on advisory rates historically available from the ISO. This reflects the ISO's much diminished role in today's marketplace (Danzon 1985, 92–96).

Not all the information that actuaries consider in framing their recommendations is, strictly speaking, actuarially derived. Some comes from management, and some is quite judgmental. As our above discussion of actuarial technique showed (second section), there clearly is room for back-and-forth discussion between actuaries and others about the various elements of premium development. Our Survey of Medical Malpractice Insurers asked what information other than company loss and exposure information companies supply to actuaries for purposes of premium development. Responses were unprompted, and the typical respondent mentioned four items. Most frequently mentioned, in descending order, were prospective investment yields (by 6 of the 11 usable answers), company expense information (including commissions) and the price or "load" of reinsurance (4 each), information on competitors' premiums and loss data from other companies or for the industry more generally (3 mentions each), and the potential effects of tort reform (2). Numerous other factors were mentioned a single time. The 13th company said that it was "not aware of other relevant information" beyond company loss and exposure data.

One physician company drew an interesting distinction about actuarial credibility in different eras of an insurer's existence: "When the company was young, during the first five years, they would look at experience of other, similar companies, and those working in-state or nearby to see what rates were being charged." Another comment distinguished between rates for lower limits, determined by the company's own experience, and rates for "coverage over $1 million [where] they would look nationally at the premium rates for such coverage." We did not ask about the weight attached to each of the supplemental items in the actuaries' premium calculations because we did not believe we could obtain accurate responses.

Actuaries may provide point estimates for premiums or, instead, a broader range. Clearly, there is less need for overt intracompany disagreement over rates where a range is indicated. Our survey specifically asked whether the actuaries produce a "point value" or a "range." Most checked "point value"; moreover, except for one response, a point value is indicated, although in four of these cases, actuaries suggested a preferred value with reference to a range, such as the midpoint of a range or an accompanying range for use under certain scenarios. Only one company said that its actuaries gave a pure range, and no company mentioned a broader range than 5 to 10 percent. So, any divergence of opinion about actuarial recommendations must be resolved in the process of actuarial calculations or by overtly revising the actuarial rate once recommended, to which we now turn.

Companies' Revisions to Actuarial Recommendations

Another way to look at actuarial versus other influences on rate making is to ask how often management overrides actuarial preferences. During the five years preceding our survey, 6 of the 12 companies responding to this question had altered the actuary's proposed premium at least once. The revisions included both increases and decreases for various reasons. Three other managements indicated that they work very closely with actuaries; thus the question's assumption of subsequent review of actuarial work was not relevant. One physician-sponsored company put it well: "We don't modify. We're part of the development process."

Nine companies volunteered various unprompted reasons for making revisions or otherwise intervening. (The form gave space for three reasons.) The most common rationale offered was various versions of what one might call "second guessing" of actuaries: Six responses from five insurers cited points like "uncertainty of actuarial rates," actuaries considered "conservative," "interpretation of the dollar amount," and "more current data available," as well as "frequency" and "severity" of claims. Four different companies, including both national commercial stock and physician-sponsored insurers, remarked on the importance of "competition" or "market reaction," often with great emphasis. One company wrote: "Competition—the marketplace is the important determinant of what to charge." Another opined, "Competition has been a positive driving force." In contrast, in response to a different question, one physician insurer stated that it "bases premiums on experience, on the marketplace. In [our state], we drive the market."

Tort reform or legislative climate also drew four mentions. Here only one company gave it much commentary. Two companies—both national stock companies—cited negotiations with state insurance departments. Two physician companies also mentioned regulation. One said that it was definitely not a factor in changing actuarial rates, noting that the relationship "is not adversarial in [our state]." The other physician company, in sharp contrast, noted that its insurance department has forced large reductions in recommended rates (those recommended both by actuaries and by management). A few other reasons were cited by only one company each, one of which deserves notice. One physician company raised premiums once, 2.5 percent above the actuary's recommendation, in order to "recoup surplus." This company was the dominant medical malpractice insurer in its state.

One thoughtful overall response summarized that management had routinely modified its actuaries' estimates slightly downward in the past because of (1) more current loss data that subsequently became available, (2) negotiations with insurance depart-

Table 7.2. Importance of Factors in Setting Premium Rates
(Other Than Actuarial Recommendations)

Factor	Number of Responses		
	Not Important	Somewhat Important	Very Important
The company's recent underwriting experience	1	0	11
The company's recent return on investments	0	5	7
Projected inflation rate	1	4	7
Anticipated cost of reinsurance	2	4	6
Rate of expected earnings on reserves	3	2	6
Percent of risk covered by reinsurance	5	1	5
Need to increase surplus	3	5	4
Premiums charged by competitors	5	3	3
Expected regulatory reaction	4	7	1
Reports from sales personnel or agents	6	5	0

Source: Survey of Medical Malpractice Insurers.

Note: Other, write-in responses, all rated "very important"; tort reform (three insurers), percentage
carried by company (two), profit strategy (one).

ments, and (3) simple disbelief within the company that future losses would be as high
as projected. But this insurer's unanticipated losses led it to reverse this pattern because
of "increasing belief that the actuaries suggestions are accurate."

In a more structured format, we asked insurers to rate the importance for premiums of listed factors other than actuarial recommendations (Table 7.2). The dominant concern is recent underwriting experience, ranked "very important" by all but one
company. The next most important factors were returns on investments, projected
inflation rate, cost of reinsurance, and expected earnings on reserves (technically, on
funds held in reserve). Other factors trailed behind, including some "write-ins" added
by respondents. Regulatory reaction got only one "vote" as very important; given the
strong comments by more than one company about regulation elsewhere in the survey,
this relatively low showing should probably be interpreted as meaning that the companies worried most about regulation are not inclined to lower premium requests to
ease approval.

We included a question elsewhere, in the reinsurance portion of the survey, to
assess more directly the link between the price of reinsurance and premiums: "If the
cost on your first level of reinsurance were to drop by 10 percent, what effect would
this have on your capacity and on your premiums?" The vast majority of companies
responded that their premiums and their capacity to write insurance would change not
at all or only very slightly (0.5 to 2.5 percent).

Further Discussion

Responses from the survey suggest the following. First, actuaries' predictions are vital,
but they consider more information than strictly actuarial claims frequency and losses.
Given the vagaries of claims trends and the difficulties of projection, this is not
illogical. Actuaries presumably want to develop accurate premium recommendations
in the insurer's best interest, if only because they want to keep their jobs or (for outside

consultants) be rehired. Recommendations that are systematically too high or too low would cost their companies profits. To be accurate, actuaries must consider other information, including estimates on prospective investment yields and the company's competitive position. The survey shows that the companies indeed supply such information to actuaries; that they act on it is shown by the results: Insurers generally are well satisfied with actuarial performance; few have changed outside actuarial consultants, and many survey respondents offered complimentary asides about their actuaries.

Second, companies sometimes modify an actuarial rate recommendation, but any modifications are modest, and our respondents reporting a change say that they now give even more credence to the actuaries. The fact that many companies do not modify their actuary's rates does not necessarily mean that competition among insurers or regulation is not a factor in premium setting, for such factors may already be reflected in the actuary's recommendations, depending on company practice. Indeed, insurers cited both competition and regulation as reasons to alter or intervene in actuarial determinations.

Third, a handful of actuarial firms handled much of the malpractice insurers' outside actuarial work. In a way, this is not surprising, for medical malpractice has become a very specialized line of insurance. Potential concentration of actuarial expertise raises two major issues: For one, if a small number of actuaries give the same (well-meaning but wrong) advice on trends to many clients, their errors would affect more insureds, and their recommendations might exacerbate premium cycles (Chapter 2). This effect could occur even without actuarial concentration, because insurers want national data for trend factors and often look to industry data from the ISO, to publicly available information from the St. Paul, the largest carrier, and to competitors' calculations.

Another potential issue is that a small fraternity of actuaries working for competitors could theoretically foster conscious or unconscious collusion among otherwise rivalrous insurers. The problem with this hypothesis is that the physician insurers seldom compete head to head in any case. Arguably, some desirable innovation might also be stifled by the conventional wisdom of a few actuaries, who are in any case, by inclination and training, very conservative people. We found no evidence of any such problem, but concentration raises the issue. On the other hand, concentration of actuarial expertise may have the beneficial effect of allowing pertinent information to be shared, not necessarily through statistical pooling of data bases but rather mainly as a matter of actuarial "feel" for the data and emerging trends. With broader experience, an actuary's recommendations for one company may avoid being fooled by statistically influential but anomalous "blips" in a given company's data.

Fourth, judging from the survey responses, beyond underwriting experience, economic expectations—return on investments and anticipated inflation—are the most important factors in premium determination. The price of reinsurance, the desire to increase surplus, estimates of the likely effect of tort reforms, and anticipated regulatory reaction are, at most, of secondary importance. The unimportance of the price of reinsurance can be explained in terms of (1) the low share of this component of cost in the total cost and (2) the company's ability to adjust liability limits on policies in light of changes in the price of reinsurance and its availability. According to the way we posed the question, the motive to increase surplus could only apply in situations where the insurer has unexploited market power, that is, was not charging the profit-maximizing premium before the premium increase to boost surplus.

As explained in Chapter 2, surplus may also be a factor in premium setting in competitive markets, and our survey did not provide information on this. The fact that actuaries and client companies seem not to give tort reforms much weight in premium setting may reflect the uncertainties about the likely effects of such reforms on future payouts. We discuss this issue in greater depth in the next section.

DETERMINANTS OF MEDICAL MALPRACTICE INSURANCE PREMIUMS: REGRESSION ANALYSIS

Two recent studies used regression analysis to examine the influence of various factors on medical malpractice insurance premiums. Both studies emphasized the role of tort reforms enacted by the state on premiums. The second study, but not the first, included a parallel analysis of the influence of the same independent variables on claims frequency and severity (loss per paid claim). This allowed the authors to ascertain whether changes in premiums and in losses are responsive to changes in the same set of factors.

Sloan (1985) assessed determination of premiums charged physicians in three fields—general practitioners who do no surgery, ophthalmologists, and orthopedic surgeons—for $100,000/$300,000 coverage. The independent variables consisted of a set of variables for tort reforms enacted by states; variables thought to be associated with differences in the pool of cases and in the propensity to sue—personal per capita income, surgical operations, lawyers, and patient care physicians, all expressed as ratios to 1,000 state population; and binary variables for years and for each state. The observational unit was the state and year. The years covered by the analysis were 1974–78. All monetary variables were expressed in real terms, that is, deflated by a price index. Although the premium levels differed, premiums among the specialties were highly correlated, as one would expect, given actuarial techniques (second section). None of the tort reforms had systematic impacts on premiums. Because many of the tort reforms were enacted only during the mid-1970s, however, the observational period may have been too early to capture any meaningful effects of tort reforms.

More recently, Zuckerman et al. (1990), as part of this study, examined medical malpractice premiums for $100,000/$300,000 occurrence and claims-made coverage over a much longer period, 1974–86. The specialties selected for analysis were general practice, general surgery, and obstetrics/gynecology. In many respects, the equation specification was similar to Sloan's, but the analysis included a longer list of nontort explanatory variables, several of which are particularly pertinent to this industry study of medical malpractice insurance.

A few tort reforms were found to reduce premiums below the level they would have reached in the absence of the statutory changes. The reform that tended to reduce premiums the most was dollar limits on physicians' liability, either for pain and suffering and other intangible losses or for the total loss. Reforms of statutes of limitations on commencing lawsuits, which aimed to reduce the time plaintiffs have after an incident to file suit, also reduced premiums. Except for pretrial screening panels, none of the other reforms had statistically significant effects on any of the three premiums.

As anticipated (Chapter 2), increases in the real interest rate reduced premiums—as earnings on investment boost profits. To measure the effect of seller concentration on premiums, the study included a Herfindahl index based on premiums—the same index described in Chapter 4. The index had no effect on premiums and was dropped from the final specification. Stock companies charged higher premiums than mutuals, reciprocals, and JUAs. However, the difference between stock and mutual insurers was not statistically significant at conventional levels. JUAs tended to have the lowest premiums.

States with more insurance regulation had lower premiums. Specifically, the implementation of "prior approval" authority for a state's insurance department (Chapter 3) was found to be associated with substantially lower premiums in the long run than requiring no filing of rates with the regulatory agency.[16] Premiums in states requiring filing, but with no requirement that the changed rates be approved prior to implementation of the change, were lower than those in states with no filing requirement, but the difference was not statistically significant at conventional levels. We do not know the mechanism by which regulation exerts influence: Insurers may submit lower rates for approval to begin with, or regulators may actively disapprove or delay higher rates. Nor is it certain how the lower rates are achieved—by actually lowering losses or expenses or by forcing companies to absorb higher loss ratios or to maintain inadequate reserves. The survey responses (above) did indicate that more than one state was believed to have generally inadequate reserves. In this case, saving money on premiums in the short run could cause availability problems in the longer run. Prior studies of regulation in property-liability insurance have reached mixed conclusions about the effect of regulatory approaches as opposed to competitive rating.[17]

The study included several explanatory variables to measure differences among states in the pool of cases and in the propensity to sue. Percentage of population in urban areas was unrelated to premiums, controlling for jurisdiction and other relevant factors. (This result is contrary to Danzon's [1986] finding that urbanization raised claims frequency, without controlling for jurisdiction.) The authors speculated that the difference in results may reflect differences in equation specification or estimation method. Premiums increased with growth in the percentage of population over age 65, real personal per capita income, and rate of surgical utilization. However, for reasons that are difficult to explain, premiums are lower in states with high physician-to-population ratios. Perhaps having more physicians means more quality competition or sufficient informal monitoring among doctors, so that malpractice losses are lower. Alternatively, having more physicians may lead to lower prices (including time costs) and more usage of better care.

The results for claims frequency and severity did not correspond to those for premiums. This lack of correspondence was most striking for the tort reforms. In particular, reforms that have been found to reduce severity in other studies (see particularly Sloan et al. 1989a)—mandatory collateral source offset, caps on noneconomic loss as well as on total loss, and costs awardable provisions—had no effect on premiums in the Zuckerman et al. (1990) study. Lack of correspondence between claims frequency and premiums may be attributable to weaknesses in the data on frequency and to the need to use data from different insurers on premiums versus frequency and severity. Furthermore, there were differences between estimated effects on claims and on premiums for many of the nontort variables. For example, the percentage of the population over age 65 raised premiums but, inconsistently, lowered frequency and severity. So did real income per capita population.

CONCLUSION

Rate-making uses past claims experience (Chapter 6) and actuarial techniques to estimate future losses. Insurers in our Survey of Medical Malpractice Insurers reported
that they rely heavily on actuarial recommendations in making decisions on premiums,
although they freely note that competitive and regulatory circumstances play a role as
well. Especially in view of the importance of actuarial judgment, the concentration of
the market for actuarial services (particularly specialized malpractice actuarial work)
potentially has troublesome policy implications. However, we found no evidence of
collusion or other adverse effects. And with the decline in importance of ISO-made
rates and the rise in insurers' own rate making, arguably more actuaries make key
recommendations than historically was the case.

Our empirical analysis implies that the state's regulatory regime has an important
impact on malpractice premiums. Implementation of a more regulatory review of
premiums significantly lowered premiums in the long run, according to our regression
results. This result stands in contrast to findings from most previous studies of insurance regulation.

On the other hand, the measure of competition used (market concentration measured by the Herfindahl index) showed no statistically significant effect. In general,
tort reforms had little effect, either, apart from ceilings on recoveries. This finding may
help explain why survey respondents said that they give little actuarial credence to
reforms before claims data confirm any effects they may have.

In policy terms, the big question about rate making is how well it performs its
main social roles of bringing overall insurance premiums into line with underlying
costs and of bringing individual groupings of physicians' premiums into line with their
contribution to losses. Historically, complaints were frequent that insurers (largely
commercial insurers) often overcharged physician insureds. Today, with the presence
of dominant physician insurers, there is little reason to suppose that such overcharging
occurs. We did find that, if anything, commercial insurers charged more than physician-sponsored insurers. We could not analyze the accuracy of rate making per se; our
data on claims experience did not match our premium data. We can, however, address
the level of resulting insurer profits (Chapter 9).

Another traditional complaint is that insurance vitiates the intended deterrent
function of tort law by insulating insureds from the financial consequences of their
errors. On its face, this concern has more validity. We have no independent way of
addressing these questions with regard to premiums per se because we lack sufficiently
detailed company-specific data on claims experience and premiums. However, these
are important enough policy issues to call for further analysis. Chapter 8 considers
deterrence in the context of experience rating.

NOTES

1. See the discussion below for the distinction between allocated and unallocated LAE.
2. Our discussion draws mainly on informal interviews with malpractice actuaries and on
   attendance at a seminar run by consulting actuaries. Hossack et al. (1983) provides a good
   general discussion, as do Roddis and Stewart (1975, 1290–97) for malpractice. For earlier
   ISO practice in physicians' coverage, see Kendall and Haldi (1973, 529–33).

3. Danzon (1983b) discusses the role of rating bureaus in the U.S. property-liability insurance industry.

4. For other purposes, notably deriving trend factors and physician class relativities, national data are desirable, as discussed further later in this section.

5. For setting rate differentials among physician specialty classifications, one insurer in our survey (third section) told us that it examines 12–15 years of experience.

6. Insurers often mentioned more recent data than actuaries use as a reason for modifying actuarially recommended rates (third section); some reported that they had cause to regret this decision later.

7. Once again, our Survey of Medical Malpractice Insurers generated relevant data; with one exception, all of the responding insurers computed premiums annually. The one exception routinely computed rates every six months; another computed rates twice during 1985 only.

8. Our Survey of Medical Malpractice Insurers (third section) asked whether respondent insurers calculated a base premium from aggregate data or, alternatively, calculated rates separately for each specialty/geographic risk class. All 14 companies surveyed used aggregate data. One commented, "Aggregate data must be used to calculate overall rate levels. Classification or territorial relativities are derived using countrywide or industry data, plus judgment and competitive data. The data for the class on its own, or the relativities derived only from the particular state involved, is not enough to use in medical malpractice, due to the risk (or variation in results) involved." As stated in note 5, one physician company looks at 12–15 years of data aggregated by specialty.

9. Other possibilities include calendar year, accident year, and policy year. Insurers have to compute losses at the end of each calendar year for financial reporting purposes, so these data could be readily and inexpensively used for rate making as well. However, calendar year data are unreliable for malpractice because so little information comes in that quickly; even with claims-made coverage, malpractice remains a long-tail line. On an accident-year basis, losses are included in the array as of the year in which the incident with potential liability occurred. This is more appropriate for occurrence policies, in which the company's liability attaches with the incident, whether or not a claim is filed that year. Policy year is another choice, but it cannot end neatly on December 31 each year; one policy year in fact spans two years, for policies sold throughout the year (starting January 1 the first year) themselves run for a year (so the last one does not expire until December 31 the second year).

10. In Table 7.1, losses develop rapidly. The exact pattern shown in an actual loss development triangle is a function of a number of factors. Occurrence policies develop more "aggressively" than claims-made policies because, for the latter, virtually all claims are known at the end of the reporting period. Similarly, data on paid claims develop more quickly than on incurred claims, for the latter include estimates of the amount at which all current claims will ultimately settle. For claims-made policies and incurred losses, loss development can actually proceed downward, as claims can be overreserved in early years. However, just how incurred losses will develop depends on the reserving policy of the company involved; some companies create only nominal reserves when first notified of a claim.

11. Ratios may be computed for each historical coverage period separately, as shown in Table 7.1, Panel B. Alternatively, ratios can be calculated for all available years jointly; then the factors are computed as ratios of the sum of losses in adjacent columns. In Panel B, for instance, the 24/12 ratio could be computed by summing the four loss values for 1985–88 for 12 months and dividing that sum into the sum of 1985–88 for 24 months. This would give an aggregated figure for 24-month development of all four historical coverage years. Analogously, for the 36/24 development factor, the ratio would be set by summing 1985–87 at 24 months and dividing into 1985–87 at 36 months. This "chain ladder" method is in widespread use in the insurance industry for filling in the unknown losses in the triangle

(Hossack et al. 1983, 209–21). Obviously, this approach relies on a number of simplifying assumptions—no change in the time pattern of loss generation, stable inflation, constant mix of risks being insured, and no meaningful change in the legal environment. To the extent that some of these assumptions are not thought to be valid, it is sometimes possible to modify the chain ladder method, for example, to account for changing inflation rates in claims severity (mean paid claims size), considered more thoroughly below.

12. In our Survey of Medical Malpractice Insurers, many respondents mentioned such sources of data on trend. Interestingly, for trend, as for other large-data-set issues, more than one insurer noted that it examined data from the St. Paul, the largest single malpractice insurer, along with other sources. Because the St. Paul reports to the ISO and many companies do not, a large share of ISO data are St. Paul data.

13. Premiums may be expressed as current dollars either by multiplying past exposures by current rates or by using aggregate adjustment factors—one multiplier per year.

14. One clue to frequency and severity trends may be whether or not there is a close fit between actual and estimated losses in the triangle and whether or not there are trends in goodness of fit. The actuary also examines actual company data for trends in claims severity and frequency and, when possible, reviews data from other companies judged to be comparable for trends in these variables. In many lines of property-casualty insurance, regression analysis relating losses to time raised to an exponent is used to fit a trend in claims severity (Webb et al. 1984b, 94–95).

15. One respondent to our Survey of Medical Malpractice Insurers noted: "Rating and reserving have so many 'soft' issues. We [the company] have to make assumptions on investment income and trends. The actuaries gather the data and we assist with joint development of assumptions."

16. The percentage change implied by the coefficient was implausibly large but strongly negative.

17. Ippolito (1979) concluded that regulation in automobile insurance did not significantly affect loss ratios for either liability or property damage coverage. Hiebert (1976) concluded that average loss ratios are higher in states with some form of rate regulation than in states without it because of regulatory rigidities. Others have suggested that the influence of more regulatory approval authority is uncertain (Cummins et al. 1980; Peterson 1981; D'Arcy 1982; Pauly et al. 1986). Harrington's (1984) extensive review of such research on the property-liability insurance industry concluded that there is no strong support for the hypothesis that regulation creates lags in premiums or that average loss ratios and prices vary according to regulatory approaches. For further discussion, see Chapter 3.

8

Risk Classification

Insurance rates are based on experience. That is, actuaries examine historical claims patterns to predict future rates for particular insured groups or classes of individually rated insureds. Normally, the experience of an entire insured group or a whole class of individuals is used for basic prediction, but the past claims history of an individual may also be used, a practice known as "experience rating." Experience rating (or "merit rating") is common in automobile coverage, for example, where having one or more chargeable accidents in a base period typically affects the premium charged (Mehr and Cammack 1980). Surcharges or discounts based on a driving record, for example, are thought to improve the accuracy and fairness of the rating system and to provide an incentive to avoid accidents.

Common wisdom holds that malpractice insurance, mainly of individuals rather than of groups, generally does not base rates on a physician's claims history because claims are very volatile in this low-frequency, high-severity line. (However, coverage may be refused by the insurer's underwriting department.) Commentators have frequently urged more use of this rating tool (e.g., Rolph 1981).

This chapter discusses the issues of risk classification and experience rating. The following sections answer such questions as these:

- What risk classes are used and how are they developed?
- What is experience rating?
- Why is it thought desirable?
- What forms can it take?
- Currently, how extensively is it used?
- What explains current patterns of use?
- What public role, if any, is there in such rating practice?

How insurers use claims information in rating is important because it is through insurers' practice that the fiscal signals of tort law are transmitted to physicians. If the deterrent signals are garbled in transmission, an important justification of the traditional approach to personal injury law is undercut. Rating practice is also important on equity grounds. For some specialties, malpractice premiums have become a notable fraction of physician expenses; assuring fair and accurate assessment is very important to the profession. Because there is some evidence that the incidence of premiums affects physicians' behavior with regard to which patients they see for which services, there is a public interest as well (Sloan and Bovbjerg 1989; Institute of Medicine 1989a, 1989b).

The next section covers basic principles of rating. Thereafter, we discuss choices in designing rating plans, provide case studies of experience rating plans, and give information on the extent of such plans from our survey. We conclude with a discussion of the policy issues.

PHYSICIANS AND RISK

The Risk of Loss

Malpractice claims do not strike at random, like lightning. When it comes to the risk of malpractice claims, all physicians are not created equal. Some types are sued more often than others. Insurance companies know this, of course, and classify insureds by degree of risk. For medical malpractice, as already noted (Chapter 7), the principal classes are defined by medical specialty and sometimes also by operative procedures performed or by location within a state (generally, large urban area versus other). Variation of claims experience is well accepted both by insurance actuaries and by physicians as a basis for predicting loss and determining rates.

However, there is also strong empirical evidence of appreciable variation among individual physicians in losses within risk classes.[1] These results and their implications for insurance are more controversial. For example, over a six-year exposure period, 5 percent of Florida's anesthesiologists and obstetrician-gynecologists incurred 69 percent of the losses. Similar results prevail for surgical specialties (orthopedic, plastic, and neurosurgery) in the same state. Losses for internists were even more concentrated (Sloan et al. 1989). These findings go beyond earlier research and suggest that if relatively few physicians could be removed from the pool (or induced to change their conduct), whether by regulatory intervention, underwriting, or differential pricing, perhaps premiums to the others could be appreciably reduced.

Such findings need to be interpreted with some caution. Concentration of losses does not necessarily imply that policyholders within a risk class have different expected losses, especially if the observations come from a short time period. Policyholders may actually be homogeneous in their risk; yet losses may be concentrated if the adverse outcome has a low probability of occurring and a high associated loss—precisely the case in low-frequency, high-severity lines of insurance, such as for medical malpractice. But empirical evidence from several studies indicates that expected losses of physicians within typical malpractice risk classes indeed vary widely (Rolph 1981; Ellis et al. 1990; Nye and Hofflander 1988; Cooil 1989; Sloan and Hassan 1990).

Classifying Risks

A good risk classification system has the following desirable properties.[2] First and foremost, the classifying factors used to establish rating categories need to be demonstrably good predictors of future loss. In practice, this means that the factors need to be statistically related to losses across a credible base of experience. Beyond such actuarial justification, it is desirable that the factors be intuitively plausible.[3] Second, policyholders classified in the same risk class should in fact be homogeneous with respect to expected loss. Third, the system should achieve separation in expected losses across the various classifications it creates. The difference in expected losses between two adjacent insurance risk classes should be sufficiently large to warrant charging the two groups different premiums. Thus, the actual requisites of a classification scheme are that the members of a class should naturally cluster together in their predicted experience and that each class is noticeably distinct from its neighbors. The same principle applies not merely to insurance but also to other classification systems, such as Medicare's payment for hospital care by DRG classes.

Fourth, the variables used to define the risk classes should be reliable predictors. An unreliable predictor is subject to gaming or outright falsification, which is not amenable to ready detection by the insurers (and fellow insureds). Fifth, risk-classifying factors should motivate policyholders to prevent losses. Driver age may be a good predictor of automobile accident rates, for example, but using it will not motivate young adults to be more prudent. Basing premiums on accident experience or on taking specific precautions known to work, on the other hand, may help lower the incidence of accidents. Risk class variables beyond the control of the policyholder may be accurate as predictors but may fail as incentives. Sixth, risk classification factors must not only predict future loss well but also accord with social norms. This is the "admissibility" criterion. Race is the prototypical example of a factor that may be actuarially sound for certain purposes but socially unpermissible. Even short of this, certain factors may be a "hard sell" politically or in the market. An example is physician gender; females are sued less often in some specialties (Cooil 1989; Sloan et al. 1989).

No risk classification system can be perfect on all of these criteria, and there are some inherent conflicts among the criteria. Although some variables may be good predictors, and hence rank well in terms of separation, the cost of verifying the information may be high or the variable may be inadmissible. A completely accurate system may achieve homogeneity within risk classes, but at the cost of no longer adequately performing the insurance function because there are so many risk classes.

The Case for Experience Rating

Malpractice insurers rate physicians primarily by specialty. What does it matter that certain physicians have worse than expected experience? Should not all physicians share alike, at least by specialty? Persistently different experience conflicts with the ideal requisite of homogeneity of risk within classes.

Heterogeneity is undesirable for several reasons. First, lumping together physicians with expected losses known to be different is simply inaccurate. Second, merging low with high risks is unfair to the physicians with relatively low expected losses. Such physicians (and their patients, depending on how the added premium costs are shifted) are being asked, in effect, to cross-subsidize the premiums of the relatively high-risk physicians within the risk class.

Third, to the extent that the inaccuracy in their rates is known, the good risks may refuse to remain pooled with the bad risks, instead dropping out to form their own groups of insureds with relatively good risks. As more and more better risks leave, the cross-subsidy grows, increasing the motivation for others to follow (Rothschild and Stiglitz 1976; Priest 1987). Such "unraveling" of the insurance market accords with economic theory; there is some indication that it has not happened in medical malpractice insurance, for reasons that are difficult to explain. One frequent justification of differences in losses is that some physicians perform more risky procedures than others or treat more litigious patients. From the standpoint of insurance, this justification is not relevant. Insurance should be priced in relation to expected loss, regardless of the reasons for that loss. Because it falls indiscriminately on insureds, the cross-subsidy is both inequitable and provides misleading signals for loss prevention.

Fourth, not recognizing higher risks within a class reduces any incentive the tort system may create for loss prevention. Where losses are covered in full by insurance (financial losses, anyway) and premiums do not vary at all with prior experience, negligent physicians have much less to lose. They do, however, still have something to lose; insurers may not renew their coverage.

An additional deterrent is that the cost of the time spent in litigation is not insurable, nor is a lost reputation stemming from adverse publicity about the case (Danzon 1989). The time cost factor seems to be relatively small (Reynolds et al. 1987), but the cost of a lost reputation may be considerable.[4]

The foregoing discussion assumes an accurate, known divergence in risk within a rating class. But risk of loss is not perfectly predictable, and errors can occur (Palfrey and Spatt 1985). For example, a nonnegligent physician wrongly adjudicated as negligent or a competent physician who inadvertently made a mistake could, under experience rating, pay the same appreciably higher premium as a routinely incompetent physician (Sloan and Hassan 1990). Depending on how sensitive future premiums are to past experience, a risk-averse physician fearing misclassification could overprotect, drop certain procedures of value to patients, or leave the field entirely. The challenge in designing an experience rating plan is to provide proper incentives for loss prevention and to achieve equity among insureds while simultaneously avoiding risk classification error and its harmful effects.

Risk classification may be based on predictive variables that are independent of the policyholder's actual previous claims record, on the policyholder's experience, or on a combination of the two. Analytically, it is useful to consider the two pure types separately, as we do in this chapter.

NONEXPERIENCE-BASED RISK CLASSIFICATION

Our Survey of Medical Malpractice Insurers provides some information on the risk classification practices of insurers. No company charged a uniform premium to all physician policyholders.[5] All insurers used specialty in establishing separate rating groups. Physicians designated their own specialties; in some cases, there were sub-specialty assignments to a given risk class, depending on specific procedures performed (e.g., whether obstetric deliveries were performed). Of the 13 companies responding to this question, 3 had 8, 3 had 9, and the remainder had 11 or more specialty rating categories (Table 8.1). We did not obtain information on geographic rating groups for the stock companies surveyed. Five of the nine physician-sponsored companies had between two and four geographic rating groups in the state (or primary state) in which they operated. Four had one rating area for the state as a whole. Thus, taking into account both specialty and geographic territories, there were often 20 or more rating categories.[6]

Table 8.1. Rating Categories and Territories
Used by Companies Writing Medical
Malpractice Insurance

Specialty Categories		Geographic Territories	
Number of Categories	Number of Companies	Number of Territories	Number of Companies
8	3	4	1
9	3	3	3
11	1	2	1
13	3	1	$\underline{4}$
14	1		9^2
15	1		
21	$\underline{1}$		
	13^1		

Source: Survey of Medical Malpractice Insurers.
[1] One company did not respond.
[2] Responses only from physician-sponsored companies.

The companies generally reviewed the physician specialty groups annually. Only one company reviewed the appropriateness of these groups once every two years. Several companies reviewed the geographic categories as often as once a year.

The companies did not believe that there were enough cases to allow insurers to develop premiums separately for each category. Thus, they computed a base premium from aggregate data. The geographic and specialty rates were normally established using multipliers (relativities) based on each class's experience—claims frequency and severity—over time.

In addition, eight of the insurers employed some sort of discount factor based on physician hours of work, type of work (e.g., residents and teaching physicians received discounts), number of years with the insurer, number of years in practice, attendance at loss control seminars, and size of the physician group.

CHOICES IN THE DESIGN OF AN EXPERIENCE RATING PLAN

An experience rating plan uses claims or losses to help set premiums in some way. Several basic choices must be made in designing a plan. These will now be discussed.

Experience Rating Unit

What should be the unit for experience rating? Generally, the unit is the individual insured, but there are alternatives, ranging from medical partnerships to a hospital or its medical staff (Steves 1975; Sloan 1990; Sloan and Hassan 1990). Where individual insureds are rated as part of a larger institution, the group obviously must allocate premiums in some fashion by individual, whether directly or indirectly, thus raising the pricing problem in a new context.

Prospective versus Retrospective Rating

Should the plan be prospective or retrospective? A prospective plan establishes a future premium based in part on the insured's past loss experience. A retrospective plan allows for end-of-year rebates to insureds who had a relatively favorable experience during the premium year.

Basis for Experience Rating

Base periods and rate periods may vary in length. If an experience rating plan is prospective, should experience be gauged by frequency of claims, by severity, or by some combination of the two? Actuaries are often more comfortable with frequency, which is less volatile. Should experience be judged from open claims or just closed claims? It takes a long time for some claims to close, especially large ones. But the fresh information of open claims may not be accurate when the case is not resolved, especially if severity is used.

Calculation of Experience

It is easy for abstract discussion to gloss over just what "experience" means. In practice, plans must specify what experience counts as experience for premiums or rebates. For a start, over what time period should prior experience be calculated, and for how long should the rates computed from this experience apply in the future?

Should all claims be counted or should some be eliminated, and if so, what criteria apply? Some prefer only to charge for "meritorious" claims—whether paid or not. Adjustments can also occur, for example, to ignore claims with an indemnity payment below a certain dollar threshold. Should associated loss expense be part of the calculation, or should only indemnity paid (or incurred) on behalf of the policyholder be considered? Considering associated loss expense would markedly affect the frequency of claims, for many claims settle with no indemnity, but with some expense for investigation or defense.

Role of Peer Review

What role should peer review by physicians play in determining whether a claim counts as experience? Specifically, how should any such peer review of open and closed claims be organized and conducted? If open claims are to be included, some judgment as to their merit is called for to make them equivalent to closed claims. Should disciplinary actions of physicians by hospitals and other organizations be included as part of the experience rating system, and if so, what weight should such actions be given?

Relationship of Experience Rating to Other Policies

To what extent should a statistically determined set of rates, based on actuarial principles, be tempered by market and other considerations? An accurate and defensible premium may simply fail to sell. How should an experience rating be combined with nonexperience-based classification variables, such as subspecialty, procedure mix, and location?

How does the experience rating plan, or lack of one, relate to underwriting policy, loss control, and other practices? Should the "worst apples" be underwritten out, rated up, or somehow controlled? From the vantage point of other organizations, including the public sector, how does experience rating relate to other attempts to influence safety, such as licensure and discipline?

Mandatory versus Voluntary Program

Governments may decide whether insurers should experience rate and with what procedures. To date, state governments have rarely become involved, except occasionally to approve plans proposed by individual insurers.

There are three potential reasons for government involvement. First, if unraveling occurs because of the pooling of heterogeneous risks, insurers could be threatened with insolvency. Second, there may be a public interest in equitable premiums. Third, an experience rating system needs good information. Large numbers of physicians and a large baseline of data may be needed. However, loss experience is typically information privately held by individual insurers, and many states are too small for separate pools of data to be credible. Thus, there must be a mechanism for pooling information among insurers for experience rating to work well. One approach is private data sharing (under immunity from antitrust litigation). Another alternative to satisfy the need for pooled information would be a data bank operated under government auspices. The Health Care Quality Improvement Act of 1986 requires that such a public data bank be established, but only for closed medical malpractice claims—rather stale data for rate-making purposes. A few states (Florida, Indiana, and Wisconsin) also collect information on closed medical malpractice claims. For experience rating, information on open claims is desirable.

CASE STUDIES OF EXPERIENCE RATING

The following case studies illustrate how physician plans have actually approached the foregoing choices. They show great variation in design and implementation.

New York's Mandatory Program with Peer Review

By statute, New York required that the Department of Insurance promulgate a regulation establishing a uniform "merit rating" plan in New York to take effect on January 1, 1986 (Insurance Law, Sections 201, 203, and 2343(d)). Merit rating meant a system of surcharges and credits based on the individual insured's history of liability claims relative to the average insured in the insured's specialty and geographic area and on disciplinary actions by hospitals or licensing boards against the insured. The merit rating system was to be "revenue neutral," with income from surcharges to some physicians offset by discounts to others. The department issued its original merit rating plan in December 1985, to surcharge about 10 percent of the physician insureds. The initial plan was vigorously opposed by physicians for using open claims and paid loss adjustment expense as factors in the rate calculation.

In view of this opposition, the department's new regulations of June 1986 utilized paid claims only. The new plan used a point system based on "chargeable" losses paid during the previous ten years and disciplinary actions against the insured during the previous five years. A loss was defined as chargeable if the sum of all indemnity payments against the physician arising from an incident exceeded a given amount ($15,000 for incidents before July 1981 and $30,000 for incidents thereafter), with each chargeable loss counting as one point. A published schedule translated points into surcharges. The relationship between points and surcharges varied according to the physician's specialty classification and geographic location (downstate versus upstate). The surcharges were limited to a maximum of 200 percent; no physician could be charged more than three times the base rate. The regulation contained an appeals mechanism and a provision for refunds if an open claim was later closed for less than the threshold amount. Individual insurers could propose their own alternative plans but had to demonstrate the need for an exception. This modified plan was intended to surcharge only 2 to 3 percent of physicians.[7]

This plan also provoked opposition, but less generally: Two groups of high-risk physicians filed suit. The suit charged that the plan unfairly based surcharges on "old" claims and unfairly penalized physicians in high-risk groups who already pay high premiums.[8] Moreover, the state's largest medical malpractice insurer, the physician-run Medical Liability Mutual Insurance Company of New York (MLMIC), was granted permission by the department to substitute its own plan. The key feature of this plan was the use of peer review to examine individual case histories as opposed to the automatic surcharges specified in the department's regulations. MLMIC's plan gave specific criteria for review of a physician's claims experience and automatic review based on disciplinary actions. Adverse claims experience triggered peer review, but the final decision to surcharge came only after an adverse finding by the reviewers. (In contrast, the state's chargeable losses were automatically calculated.) Both open and closed cases could trigger a review. If the physician was a member of the state medical society, the review was performed by a committee of the society. Otherwise, the review was performed by a committee of the company. Disciplinary action review occurred automatically if (1) the insured's license was revoked or suspended in the state, (2) the insured was put on probation in any state, or (3) the insured's privileges were revoked, suspended, or restricted by any hospital. The department accepted MLMIC's plan. As of April 1, 1988, the department had received one statistical report from MLMIC. Only 83 physicians (0.6 percent of the total) were being surcharged by the plan.

Based on a review of this experience, the New York Department of Insurance concluded: "Physicians are unalterably opposed to merit rating. It is unrealistic to apply a merit rating plan, or any individual-risk rating plan, to a low-frequency, high-severity coverage. Due to the length of time claims are open, it is difficult to have enough meaningful data for merit rating of medical malpractice. A merit rating plan is not intended to be used to remove poor doctors by pricing them out of business."[9]

Massachusetts' Experience Review Plan

All insuring organizations are required by law (Chapter 175A sect. 5C) to set up a review committee to evaluate claims experience of individual physicians. Half of the panel members must be physicians. The other members are from the insuring organization. If there is a 50–50 split of the vote on an individual case that goes according to a bloc vote (physicians versus others), the nonphysician group's vote is decisive. Each insuring organization is to develop its own experience review plan. The JUA is the only insuring organization currently affected by this law. What follows are some key provision's of the JUA's plan (Medical Malpractice Joint Underwriting Association of Massachusetts, 1990).

The plan, implemented on July 1, 1990, requires that physicians with the following claims records during the past five years be reviewed by a screening panel: physicians—two reported claims; surgeons not otherwise listed—three reported claims; and high frequency surgeons—four reported claims. Other supplementary approaches exist for identifying physicians for review. If at least one screening panel member finds that further review is warranted, the case is to be referred to the JUA's Experience Review Committee. Remedial actions listed in the plan include: risk management consultation; risk management audit; additional medical education; supervision or consultation as a condition for coverage for a specified area of practice; imposition of copayments involving claims arising from certain areas of practice or settings; and surcharges. The surcharge option is only used if the physician fails to comply with other remedial actions. The JUA cannot refuse to provide coverage.

Earlier, the legislature had required that the Department of Insurance develop an actuarially-justified experience rating plan.[10] A plan, which incorporated surcharges was developed, but encountered strong opposition from organized medicine.

The JUA developed an experience rating plan that was to have begun on a one-year trial basis starting July 1989. The Massachusetts Medical Society opposed the commissioner's authority to impose an experience rating plan but submitted its own plan to base any experience rating on peer review. The State Rating Bureau proposed to levy formula-based surcharges on physicians with multiple claims within the past five years, both open and closed.

This is the plan the Rating Bureau submitted in September 1989. Physicians with more than one claim during this time period were being surcharged, according to a schedule of points for frequency and severity of claims. The point system ($4,000 in increased premiums per point) allowed physicians to be charged up to 140 percent of the base premium for the risk class. Each of the 18 risk classes was priced separately. All extra revenue generated was credited to the nonsurcharged physicians in the same risk class. In the face of political opposition, the plan was never adopted.

One unusual feature of Massachusetts was that its experience rating plan was for a JUA. The JUA cannot refuse to provide coverage. Therefore, there was a problem of what to do about a physician with claims well beyond the amounts needed to reach the maximum surcharge.[10]

Pennsylvania Medical Society Liability Insurance Company's (PMSLIC) Three-Tier System

With approval of the state department of insurance, PMSLIC implemented a three-tier individual experience rating plan effective July 1, 1986. Physicians in Tier 1 were charged the base rates. Those in Tier 2 paid rates 10 to 40 percent above Tier 1 rates. Those in Tier 3 paid premiums over 40 percent above Tier 1 levels, and then only on a "consent to write" basis. There was no stated maximum for any Tier 3 surcharge, but in practice, most surcharges did not exceed 200 percent. When the claims experience indicated a surcharge of over 200 percent, the company considered not renewing the insured. Under special circumstances, PMSLIC continued to provide insurance to such insureds, and the highest surcharge applied as of July 1989 was 500 percent.[11]

Both closed and open claims counted toward surcharges. The formula varied by specialty (of which there are 12) and geographic classification (of which there are five). Claims were subjected to peer review by physician board members of the PMSLIC. The plan distinguished between "defensible" and "nondefensible" claims. Fewer points were levied against defensible claims. More points were assigned to nondefensible claims with higher loss (indemnity and loss expense) than to smaller claims. Some very minor claims were not counted. As of September 1987, 11 percent of insureds (751) were being charged Tier 2 rates and 2 percent (158) Tier 3 rates. An additional 113 Tier 2 physicians had canceled their policies by that date, although some of the cancellations were due to death or retirement.[12]

PIE Mutual's Quality Rating Program

In 1986, PIE Mutual switched its policy form from occurrence to claims-made. Rather than offer a discount for the first three or four years of claims-made coverage, the company set premiums for the first year's claims-made coverage at the full mature rate, thus accumulating available funds for premium credits in future years. Physicians with favorable loss experience records over four years received up to a 30 percent discount on the base premium. The maximum discount went to physicians with no losses of $5,000 or more involving culpability on the part of the insured. Claims counted whether closed or open (using the reserved amount for calculations). Claims were reviewed by regional physician boards for purposes of operating the Quality Rating Program. The program covered all insureds in the five states in which the company operates. One major competitor implemented a merit-rating program in response, according to PIE.[13]

Princeton Insurance Company's Surcharge Program

Since April 1979, the New Jersey Medical Malpractice Association and its successor, the Princeton Reinsurance Association, have operated a surcharge program based on chargeable claims. A claim or suit was considered chargeable (1) if the loss involved $5,000 or more for nonsurgeons and $10,000 or more for surgeons (either actually paid or reserved for an open claim) and (2) if the loss was determined by a Medical Review and Advisory Committee to be a deviation from accepted standards of medical practice. The amount of the surcharge rose with the number of chargeable claims. Two chargeable claims resulted in an annual premium surcharge of $2,500 and four in a surcharge of $10,000. Insureds with more than four such claims may have paid even more, but such surcharges were not fixed by a formula. Once applied, the surcharge was in force for a period of three years.

State Volunteer Mutual Insurance Company's Retrospective Dividend Plan

State Volunteer Mutual Insurance Company, the dominant writer of medical malpractice insurance in Tennessee, began a new experience rating program in January 1989.

The physician-sponsored mutual had been paying annual company dividends since 1982. Prior to 1989, the dividend to the policyholder was proportional to the amount of premium paid during the previous five years. Thus, a policyholder who paid premiums totaling $20,000 received twice as large a dividend as one who had paid $10,000—regardless of personal claims experience.

In the revised plan, one-half of the declared dividend was distributed according to the five-year loss experience of the policyholder. For each insured, the company subtracted all indemnity paid on the insured's behalf (defense cost was excluded) from the premium paid during this period, with the difference not permitted to be less than zero. Then the same computation was done for all policyholders as a whole. Finally, a ratio of the two (each policyholder's premiums minus losses) determined each policy-holder's merit dividend (the ratio times 50 percent of the declared dividend). The other half of the declared dividend was paid as a general dividend. The latter was computed just as it had been before 1989, in proportion to the premium paid. This combined dividend was then paid as a reduction in premiums in the following year. Physicians who discontinued coverage through the company got no dividend. The overall dividend pool available for distribution depended on the financial position of the company in a particular year. A five-year base period for claims and premiums was selected as a device for smoothing out year-to-year variation in experience.

The company chose this retrospective approach to avoid having to convince poli-cyholders that their past losses predicted their future losses. Physicians who believed that their past experience did not accurately indicate future performance could thus be promised that they would benefit directly from any improvement in their own records. The plan rewarded good physicians, but only those who stayed with the company. The great majority of insureds did qualify for the merit dividend. In contrast, those with the worst records and lowest dividends were encouraged to leave.[14]

The St. Paul's Surcharge Plan for Physicians and Surgeons in Georgia

At the request of the Georgia Department of Insurance, the St. Paul Group developed an experience rating program applied briefly during 1986. Points were calculated based on the previous five-year's experience with the company. A prespecified schedule based points on the amount of indemnity plus associated loss expense for closed claims and on the severity of injury for open claims. Higher losses and severity levels were assigned higher point values. Claims costing less than $4,000 in indemnity plus associated loss expense were excluded. Surcharges ranged from 10 to 200 percent over the base premium, and the additional revenues were used to lower the base premiums of others. The plan was dropped by the company after only three months because it offered little financial incentive to physicians with favorable records (physicians with the most favorable records saved only 6 percent in premiums) and was complex to administer.

Medical Protective's Surcharge System

The Medical Protective Company initiated a medical malpractice insurance experience rating program in the late 1970s. At its peak, about one-third of its policyholders were surcharged in all states where Medical Protective wrote policies. By 1989, the program had been abandoned in all but one state.

The company based surcharges solely on the number of claims filed, rather than on the number of claims paid or the amount paid or reserved per claim. Statistical analyses of its insureds indicated that policyholders with one claim filed against them were 30 percent more likely to have a new claim filed against them than were policyholders who were claim free. This factor was chosen on the theory that the company has no influence over the filing of a claim. It does, however, have some control over the resolution of a claim—whether to settle and the amount of the settlement. The program proved to be unsatisfactory because surcharged physicians switched to companies willing to offer them coverage at a lower price.[15]

The Doctors' Inter-Insurance Exchange

The Doctors' Inter-Insurance Exchange currently provides medical malpractice insurance to doctors in 44 states. The company's board experience system rates physicians on the basis of their claims history with the company. Physicians with multiple small claims are assigned a mandatory deductible, ranging from $3,000 to $10,000. Individuals with high loss records are assigned a mandatory surcharge, ranging from 25 to 100 percent. Less than 1 percent of the company's policyholders pay either a deductible or a surcharge.[16]

EXTENT OF EXPERIENCE RATING IN MEDICAL MALPRACTICE: EVIDENCE FROM THE SURVEY OF MEDICAL MALPRACTICE INSURERS

How widespread is experience rating for medical malpractice insurance? The case studies give only partial evidence for selected states and companies. More systematic indications of prevalence come from our Survey of Medical Malpractice Insurers, along with information on the characteristics of plans and their practical experience. The survey sample of 14 firms was selected to be nationally representative, without regard to the use of experience rating, but we included several questions on this topic.

In one sense, we found experience rating to be fairly common in medical malpractice. Only 1 of the 14 companies had never implemented an experience rating program of any type. However, the majority of firms had either completely abandoned experience rating by the date of the survey or maintained a program of limited scope. Most of the plans were company initiated rather than forced by state statute or regulation.

The one company that had never implemented any plan maintained that experience rating is inappropriate for a low-frequency, high-severity line of insurance. The argument was that, given low frequency, one cannot tell whether a single claim is an isolated random event or part of a high-risk pattern. This company did use prior claims experience for underwriting purposes. Although a single claim did not necessarily disqualify a physician, a severe one, or a high frequency of minor claims, might do so. The company gave discounts for participation in loss control seminars and for number of years with the firm, thus perhaps indirectly rewarding factors hoped to relate to good experience.

The typical insurer in the survey operated an experience rating program on a limited basis. In several cases, the program had been cut back from its prior scope. Nine of the 14 insurers set premiums prospectively based in part on the physician's

Table 8.2. Experience Rating Practices

		Responses		
Question		Mutual-Exchange	Commercial Stock	Total
1. Does the company apply any form of experience rating to doctors with claims histories?	Yes	8	1	9
	No	3	2	5
2. Has the company tried other plans, such as retrospective rating or dividends?	Yes	2	1	3
	No	9	2	11

Source: Survey of Medical Malpractice Insurers.

claims history (Table 8.2). Three insurers employed some type of retrospective rebate system ("retrospective rating or dividends"). Some of the rebates went to groups rather than to individual physicians based on their individual claims histories.

The programs were limited in the following dimensions: First, very few physician insureds were typically affected. In several cases, less than 1 percent of physician enrollees paid more than standard rates because of adverse prior claims experience. Second, the surcharges were generally not substantial. They ranged from around 10 percent to 200 percent of the base premium. Although 200 percent may seem a large number, the variation in paid losses per exposure year within specialties tends to be far greater than this (Sloan and Hassan 1990). Surcharges tended to be imposed on policyholders for a two- or three-year period. Third, rather than affecting premiums through a strict, mechanistic formula, the physician's track record was often modified by peer review with an appeals mechanism in the event of an adverse decision.

One company applied deductibles ranging from $3,000 to $10,000; only losses above these thresholds potentially counted against the physician. A rationale for such deductibles was that physician liability may be negligible in cases of small dollar losses. Such losses may consist entirely of the cost of investigating or defending the claim, with no indemnity paid.

Another company only counted open claims that occurred within a recent time interval. Medical malpractice claims often take many years to close. Yet, to the extent that claims frequency measures the physician's quality or level of preventive effort, it is difficult to accept an event that occurred many years ago as indicative of the physician's current practice. For this reason, and because the frequency of open claims is not under the insurer's control, insurers in our sample tended to use open claims for experience rating purposes. The disadvantage of open claims is that neither physician liability nor the dollar amount of loss has been established. Thus, there is a valid argument for peer review of liability if open claims are used. To the extent that loss per open claim is used in experience rating, surcharges must be based on insurers' estimates of future losses, which understandably are subject to considerable error.

The companies differed in whether they counted claims filed or dollar amounts of loss. Claims frequency is often used in experience rating plans because the severity of the injury incurred by injured parties is thought to be beyond the control of the policyholder (Lemaire 1985). This point of view is certainly true in some lines of insurance: For instance, when a careless driver hits another vehicle, he or she has no control over whether the victim is a fragile, rich executive driving a new sports car or a sturdy, unemployed worker in an old wreck, and the law dictates higher payments to the former. However, frequency of claims and severity are not independent in medical malpractice; the physician's procedure and the patient mix may influence damages per claim. In fact, in medical malpractice, there is a positive correlation between a physician's frequency of claims and the dollar loss per claim (Sloan and Hassan 1990).

None of the respondents had "hard" empirical evidence that use of experience rating helps control the frequency or severity of claims. Some mentioned opposition to experience rating from physician insureds. We heard that physicians would rather pay a higher community rate than penalize physicians who have had the misfortune to be sued. Many physicians believe that claims, like lightning, strike randomly (Bovbjerg 1986). Medical societies, which represent the collective interest of physicians, could understandably take this community-oriented view. In recent years, medical malpractice insurers sponsored by organized medicine have become important suppliers of coverage; in some states, they are dominant (Chapters 2 and 4). But the commercial insurers are not immune from such share-the-burden pressure either; after all, they must sell to physicians (and the medical society's attitude is important), and they also face potential entry from physician-sponsored plans.

Another complaint about experience rating by insurers was that surcharged physicians often left the company because they were able to secure insurance at lower premiums elsewhere. Sometimes the existing insurer included open claims in its experience rating, while a competitor used only closed claims. Thus, we heard that experience rating does not work when there is competition among insurers, whereas economic theory predicts that competition will force prices into line with accurately predictable losses. Apparently, either the competitors lacked access to a credible claims history, did not believe that an adverse record had any predictive value, or (in the interest of gaining market share) were willing to take their chances.

DISCUSSION

For the purpose of premium setting, insurers establish a number of rating classes. Major classifying variables are medical specialty, geography, and performance of certain operative procedures. Past experience of individual policyholders is used, but to a more limited extent.

How does practice rank in terms of the six desirable properties of a risk classification system? First, current classification practices appear to rank high in terms of admissability; classification is quite consistent with the norms of the medical profession. They also rank fairly high in terms of reliability; the risk classes typically are not subject to manipulation by policyholders. However, the current system does not perform as well in terms of providing regular incentives for loss prevention. Moreover, the system does not use available predictive information, and there is often heterogeneity within risk classes with respect to expected loss.

It is curious that heterogeneity within risk classes appears to persist, and we can only speculate as to the reasons. One possibility is that the statistical evidence suggesting considerable heterogeneity is simply wrong. However, this result is highly robust across studies using different data. Hence, this explanation probably does not have much merit. Second, physicians may not be aware of the heterogeneity. Even when variability in claims and losses among policyholders within risk classes is observed, it may be attributed to chance.

Third, many medical malpractice insurers are sponsored by medical societies, and such organizations and their active members may value solidarity against a supposedly unjust legal system above accuracy and equity in premium setting. Medical societies may oppose experience rating even if it is in the business interest of the insurer to offer it and in the personal interest of most physicians to buy it. One respondent suggested that, given their reliance on being able to refer patients to specialists, doctors value ready availability of physicians in high-risk specialties. For example, neurologists want neurosurgeons to handle some of their patients and are therefore willing to pay some-what higher premiums to subsidize the neurosurgeons.

Fourth, physician policyholders (and board members) may place a high weight on avoiding risk classification error. They may be willing to tolerate some inaccuracy or unfairness in average premiums in order to avoid a few cases in which a low-risk physician may be mistakenly classified as a high risk.

Fifth, physicians may be quite risk averse and unwilling to gamble on the possibil-ity of very large premiums for one to three years after a "big hit" for a small savings in any given year when they are free of a surcharge.

We suspect that the main reasons for the lack of experience rating reflect a combination of the third, fourth, and fifth reasons. Physicians and insurers must know that at least some of the adverse claims experience of physicians is not due to random error.

An alternative to implementing experience rating is for the insurer to refuse to renew coverage. To the extent that denial of coverage would force physicians to obtain coverage from surplus-line companies that charge premiums many times the standard rates, there would still be a deterrent based on price. But physicians have other options, including continuing practice without insurance ("going bare") and, in some cases, obtaining coverage from a JUA at standard rates (Schwartz and Mendelson 1989a).[17]

Very few physicians actually lose their coverage.[18] However, this does not happen frequently. A national survey of physician-sponsored insurers revealed that, in 1985, 0.66 percent of physicians had their insurance terminated or were forced to relinquish their coverage because of negligence-prone behavior. In 1983 and 1984, the percent-ages were even lower, 0.42 percent and 0.50 percent, respectively (Schwartz and Mendelson 1989b). It is very doubtful that the remaining 98 percent or so physicians within a risk class are homogeneous with respect to their anticipated loss experience (Sloan and Hassan 1990).

The theoretical and empirical underpinnings of the experience rating plans that have been implemented to date are not strong. Pertinent statistical theory exists (see, e.g., Hossack, et al. 1983), but it is not clear that it has been used in the development of experience rating plans for medical malpractice. Nor is it apparent that the plans are based on prior statistical analysis of the relationship between the prior and future claims experiences of their companies. Evaluations of the success or failure of experi-ence rating have not been in-depth statistical studies, but rather seem to be based on impressions of whether experience rating worked and avoided controversy. In the companies' defense, the success of such plans has depended in part on implementation barriers, which are not subject to formal statistical analysis.

The argument that experience rating does not apply to a low-frequency, high-severity field such as medical malpractice no longer applies as much as it once did, certainly not to all physicians. In 1986, new claims per exposure had risen to 0.163, up from 0.099 in 1980, and claims frequency was much worse in certain specialties and in some states (Schwartz and Mendelson 1989a; Sloan and Bovbjerg 1989).

There are some fundamental conceptual problems with experience rating for medical malpractice. If adverse experience is too severely penalized, physicians may not report some incidents, which, if not investigated soon after they occur, could eventually result in high-cost claims. Insurance is purchased to protect the insured against expenditure risk. But with experience rating, there is a welfare loss to policyholders from increased risk bearing. Although the past does predict the future, it obviously does not do so perfectly. Some high-quality physicians who experienced a number of random claims will be wrongly surcharged. Moreover, physicians' practice patterns and the environments in which they practice often change over time—a source of prediction error. However, a fully community-rated system is probably less fair on balance; many high-quality physicians are paying premiums well in excess of the actuarial value of their losses. Ultimately, one's judgment depends on the weight one gives the two types of insureds—the few who may be (significantly) overcharged because of invalid claims or the many who are routinely overcharged as the price of heterogeneity.

With regard to system design, although claims frequency is used almost exclusively in such lines as automobile liability, there is a strong case for using both frequency and severity in medical malpractice experience rating: Frequency and severity are positively correlated (Sloan and Hassan 1990). Because of the long tail in medical malpractice, it probably makes sense to consider open as well as closed claims in the experience base.

Experience-based classification should be combined with classification based on other nonexperience variables that accurately predict the individual physician's losses. If one relies totally, or almost totally, on the experience of the individual policyholder, actuarially sound calculations of premiums produce a very steep premium gradient with respect to experience (Sloan and Hassan 1990). The gradient is much flatter with more categories, as long as these categories are defined on the basis of factors other than the physician's own experience. Choosing appropriate classifying variables that satisfy the criteria for a good risk classification system is no trivial task (see the second section).

A retrospective plan, such as the one recently implemented in Tennessee, may not encounter the same degree of opposition from physicians as have many prospective plans. However, unless the credit or dividend is large, such a retrospective plan may provide insufficient incentive for loss prevention and preserve the appreciable premium cross-subsidies currently operative in most locations.

There is a good case for peer review for experience rating. Peer review is clearly necessary if information on open claims is to be used; claims often take a long time to close, and hence no input on the merit of the claim, such as from a judicial decision, is typically available for quite some time. Since there is no guarantee that the judicial system produces accurate results on liability, there is a strong case for peer review of closed claims as well.

Counting blatantly nonmeritorious claims may have several adverse effects. Physician defendants may become more reluctant to settle claims even when it makes sense to do so in terms of the expected values of fighting versus settling. Counting certain open claims against the physician when there has been no determination of physician fault will also often be unfair. Further, there is the possibility that peer review coupled with experience rating will lead to improved quality of care, which is a major goal of the tort system.

Where peers are involved, interventions other than premium changes will also be more defensible, such as restrictions on practice pending a refresher course. Yet peer reviewers, especially in small communities, may be too generous to their peers. Sometimes it is in their business interest to rule against their competitors. In this sense, it is surprising that companies seem never to use peer reviewers from other states.

Centralizing peer review is potentially harmful to competition. Although a case can be made for peer review, there is also a strong case for decentralized peer review. Such review may be conducted by the hospital, the HMO, or professional peer reviewers on contract with the insurer.

The vast majority of experience rating plans in medical malpractice use the individual physician as the experience rating unit. Yet groups are commonly used in other lines of insurance, such as Workers' Compensation and unemployment insurance. It is surprising that so few group plans seem to exist in medicine, apart from situations where a large group practice self-insures or obtains a special rate from an insurer. Some physician-owned companies have adopted or are considering programs where policies are written through hospitals as a possible first step toward hospital-based group plans.

The appropriate role of the public sector in the design and operation of experience rating plans needs to be defined. As noted above, several companies reported that surcharged physicians left them for competitors that charged them lower premiums. Although it is possible to offer several conjectures, it is puzzling why the competitors would disregard information bearing on policyholders' future losses if in fact they have access to it. These are some of the questions to be addressed: Should the public sector regulate or operate a pooled information-sharing mechanism? Should precise forms of experience rating be mandated, as is frequently the case in other lines in other countries (Lemaire 1988)? Or is the appropriate role of government more limited, that is, to approve experience rating programs proposed by companies under its jurisdiction?

NOTES

1. For an anecdotal account of one physician who had 200 claims in a five-year period, see Holoweiko (1989).
2. These points are made in greater detail by Shayer (1978, 2–6) and Abraham (1986, 68–76).
3. This property supports the existence of an underlying cause and not a mere spurious correlation of some underlying cause during the observation period. Plausibility may also increase social acceptability and facilitate marketing. Regardless of what actuarial correlations might imply, for example, an insurer would think hard before surcharging red-headed physicians.
4. A number of facts suggest this is so. Many settlement agreements of malpractice cases contain provisions for nondisclosure of settlement terms and other facts of the case. The Health Care Quality Improvement Act of 1986 requires that a data bank be established,

documenting all disciplinary actions against physicians and details of all medical malpractice settlements and verdicts. Organized medicine has vigorously opposed disclosure of such
data to the public, even when the information is a matter of public record.

5. This finding is consistent with the results of a national survey of physician-sponsored
   medical malpractice insurers conducted by Schwartz and Mendelson (1989b). They found
   that 90.3 percent of companies employed surcharges, but in 1985, only 1.6 percent of
   physician policyholders were subjected to surcharges and another 0.9 percent faced other
   sanctions, such as restrictions on the scope of their practices or requirements for further
   training or supervision.

6. Depending on the company, insurers may track experience by subcategory classes as well,
   with subclasses running into the hundreds of categories. One company interviewed keeps
   track of individual physicians by five-digit class codes within its 10 basic specialty rating
   categories. Periodically, different classes may be moved from one rating class to another
   based on this experience. Moreover, in addition to the basic geographic-specialty rate, there
   may be a discount available apart from the experience rating per se: for example, if all
   members of a group practice insure individually with the same carrier.

7. Report by James P. Corcoran, Superintendent of Insurance, *A Balanced Prescription for
   Change*, *Report of the New York State Insurance Department on Medical Malpractice*,
   1988, p. 2.

8. As of July 1989, these suits were unresolved. Telephone conversation between Penny
   Githens, Health Policy Center, Vanderbilt University, and Ann Kelley, Chief Actuary, New
   York Department of Insurance.

9. See source listed in footnote 7 at 46.

10. The source of our information on this plan is telephone conversations between Penny
    Githens and Mark Leymaster, Massachusetts Department of Insurance, October 3, 1988;
    Randall Bovbjerg and Mr. Leymaster, May 5, 1989; and Penny Githens and Amy Novick,
    November 1, 1989.

11. Telephone conversation between Penny Githens and Larry Smarr, PMSLIC, July 19, 1989.

12. Additional details on this program may be found in "Pennsylvania Medical Society Liability
    Insurance Company Three-Tier Rating Plan" (September 1987).

13. Further information on the Quality Rating Program was provided in written form by PIE
    Mutual. This was supplemented by a telephone conversation between Penny Githens and
    James Winterick, PIE Mutual, October 4, 1988.

14. Telephone conversation between Penny Githens and Steven Williams, State Volunteer Mu-
    tual Insurance Company, April 7, 1989, and letter to Ms. Githens from Mr. Williams dated
    July 17, 1989.

15. Conversation between Penny Githens and Robert Miller, Medical Protective, January 20,
    1988.

16. Telephone conversation between John Newmann, The Urban Institute, and John Kenny, The
    Doctors' Inter-Insurance Exchange, March 31, 1988.

17. According to Schwartz and Mendelson (1989a), about 900 physicians annually who lose
    coverage from standard-lines carriers have access to a JUA.

18. See the text above and note 5.

9

Profitability in Malpractice Coverage: Excessive or Normal?

ACCUSATIONS AND ASSESSMENTS

Perhaps the single most inflammatory accusation raised against malpractice and other property-liability insurers is that they have made excessive profits at the expense of consumers. Such charges have frequently surfaced in times of stress—notably after requests for substantial premium increases or withdrawal of insurers from some geographic areas or lines of coverage. Critics have insisted that crises of availability are trumped up by an industry seeking excessive profits and have often demanded investigations, pressured regulators to reject price rises, and even voted rate rollbacks, as under California's Proposition 103 in 1988. The belief in insurance "ripoffs" is widespread, but systematic, long-term evidence has been sparse. Policymakers and other interested observers need more.

How much profit is too much? The theoretical answer is straightforward. Excess, or monopoly, profits means higher rates of return than required by suppliers of capital. On the other hand, if prospective, risk-adjusted returns fall too low, short of the going rate, capital will flee the industry. If sufficiently severe, such capital flight may cause withdrawals from the market and a crisis of availability. In an idealized competitive market, suppliers of capital would routinely receive the market-determined, risk-adjusted rate (Chapter 2). Returns above this rate would elicit entry of lower-priced competitors and lower rates would prompt exit, allowing rates to rise. Either response would bring returns to investors into line with competitive investments.

Society, both here and abroad, however, has not trusted insurance markets to be sufficiently competitive. Rate regulation reflects the concern that consumer ignorance and other factors keep market forces from disciplining insurers' premium setting and hence their profits (Chapter 3). Another regulatory concern is that insurers seeking undue profits may undertake high-risk, high-return investments of funds held in reserve for future payments on claims, and then may later be unable to satisfy their obligations to policyholders. Both high premiums and risky investment strategies could result in excessive returns to suppliers of capital.

Regulators thus seek a "fair rate of return" to balance customers' desire to avoid overcharges, with the need to pay a sufficient return to attract the requisite capital. Few dispute this overarching objective, but considerable debate remains about how to measure profitability in practice.

CHAPTER OVERVIEW

How plausible is the familiar accusation of overcharging? How can it be resolved? This is the main question for this chapter. Anecdotally, one often hears that insurers collect more in a year than they pay out. Yet that is not unexpected where claims severity is rising over time, especially in a long-tail line like malpractice. Conversely, insurers object that they ultimately pay out much more on each year's policies than they collected—as shown by loss ratios. Individual years' rate hikes may seem extreme, as they did to many in the 1970s' and 1980s' crises years (Chapter 1). But a longer-term perspective is needed, for rates may fall as well as rise. For malpractice coverage, complaints of excessive rates and profits were less strident in the 1980s than they were in the 1970s. Physicians commonly complained about the predominant commercial insurers of the 1970s, but few of them remain significant participants in the market—if indeed they sell malpractice coverage at all. In the 1980s most carriers were physician-run companies, which understandably drew less fire from their policyholders. When physician insurers wrote coverage, it was much less plausible that physicians were systematically overcharged.

What empirical evidence supports or negates this intuition? This chapter addresses the following issues:

- By various measures, how profitable has malpractice insurance been, seen in historical perspective? What variation has existed over time?
- Does profitability vary by insurer ownership?
- What have the loss ratios been for malpractice insurance (claims expense relative to premiums)? What do various approaches for computing fair premium suggest that premiums should have been, in light of the risks taken?
- What do the results imply for public policy?

Good empirical analysis of profits is not easy for a number of reasons. First, there is no "gold standard" by which to measure profits. All measures have some deficiencies, as shown in this chapter's method-by-method presentation. Second, a given year's profits cannot be quickly assessed. Premiums are known immediately, but not return net of claims. The long tail of malpractice claims payment means that initial measures of claims costs are largely estimates, only as accurate as the underlying claims reserves. To use mainly final data, analysis needs to wait seven or eight years or more after a policy year (and even so, results are not 100 percent complete). Third, given the cycles expected in premiums and profits, one would like to observe many years' experience. But separate malpractice-specific data on premiums and claims losses became available only for policy year 1976. Even then, the early years' data seem less reliable, for physician companies were brand new at the time.

So, historical analysis must accept a late start, an early end, and a variety of measures. This chapter begins with two conventional insurance measures of profitability—rates of return on policyholders' surplus and on assets (second section). These indicators allow useful comparisons of profitability across ownership types, but reflect book values rather than market valuations, fail to discount losses, and ignore returns to owners. So, the second section continues by presenting returns to equityholders, which correct some of these deficiencies. However, annual rates of return on equity are by definition available only for publicly held companies, mainly major commercial stock insurers, for which malpractice is only one of many lines of coverage. We also review the major findings of a fourth approach—comparing a year's premiums with the current value of all subsequent claims on that year's policies. A recent U.S. GAO (1987b) study took this approach. This study had the major advantages of measuring profits specific to malpractice and of using discounted losses.[1] However, the GAO discount rates were somewhat arbitrary, ungrounded in any explicit financial theory. And its return-on-premiums measure lacked any point of comparison to the "right" rate of return.

Thus, in the third section, we go beyond the GAO, using theory-based discount rates to compute premiums yielding a theoretically fair rate of return, according to modern financial theory. Two main approaches are presented—the Capital Asset Pricing Model (CAPM) and the Discounted Cash Flow (DCF) method—with their predicted fair premiums compared with actual premium income. The fourth section sorts out the interrelated results of the various profitability measures and their relevance to policy.

PROFIT PERFORMANCE BY STANDARD MEASURES

Conventional insurance reporting often measures profit as return on surplus (net capital value) or on total assets, net of loss reserves, policyholder dividends, and other expenses as traditionally calculated. We discuss these two measures first.

Rates of Return on Policyholders' Surplus

Rates of return on surplus vary appreciably by year and by company. No one year provides a reliable indicator, either for a company or for a group of companies. Table 9.1 presents returns on policyholders' surplus for the five years 1982–86 as an illustrative period. Overall, malpractice insurers made positive accounting profits, even in the recent years, which include the 1980s' crisis.

From 1982 to 1986, the noncommercial companies (which specialize in malpractice coverage) were more profitable, regardless of category—mutual, exchange, and physician stock—than were commercial stock insurers (for which malpractice is a relatively small line).[2] It would seem that malpractice is not an unprofitable line relative to others on this measure—rather the reverse. Among the three types of physician-sponsored companies, the exchange insurers tended to be the most profitable. One exchange was an extreme outlier, at 92.6 percent for five years. Excluding this company, the mean rate of return on policyholders' surplus for exchange companies was 19.9 percent versus 11.9 percent for the mutuals.

The year 1984 was a relatively unprofitable one for both physician-sponsored and commercial companies by this measure. By contrast, 1986 was a relatively profitable year, far more profitable than 1984. Rates of return were also high in 1982, but lower than in 1986.

This year-by-year pattern in profitability for medical malpractice insurance was very similar to that for property-liability insurance more generally. One might expect this similarity, for the commercial stock companies that sell medical malpractice insurance are representative of the larger property-liability industry. Although property-

Table 9.1.   Trends in Rates of Return on Policyholders' Surplus, 1982–86

Company	1982	1983	1984	1985	1986	1982–86
Mutual						
Mutual Assurance Society of Alabama	−26.8	32.3	17.8	16.2	54.0	18.7
Mutual Insurance Company of Arizona	28.7	17.6	−1.4	15.1	27.6	17.5
Group Council Mutual Insurance	−0.3	−5.6	−36.5	65.7	42.1	13.1
Norcal Mutual Insurance Company	29.4	42.0	24.1	22.9	37.9	31.1
Louisiana Medical Mutual Insurance Company	18.7	17.4	−14.6	0.1	1.9	4.7
Medical Mutual Liability Insurance Company of Maryland	107.0	−37.0	24.2	19.3	31.9	29.1
Michigan Physicians Mutual Liability Company	1.7	−18.5	−9.1	−35.8	−0.1	−12.4
Medical Liability Mutual Insurance Company of New York	3.6	−15.3	−9.1	−1.1	18.6	−0.7
Medical Mutual Insurance Company of North Carolina	37.1	−14.5	−26.4	−12.2	34.0	3.6
P.I.E. Mutual Insurance Company	38.8	40.6	24.9	−46.6	−36.4	4.3
State Volunteer Mutual Insurance Company (TN)	27.0	9.0	27.5	24.6	22.4	22.1
Mean	24.1	6.2	1.9	6.2	21.3	11.9
Exchange						
Doctors Company	−4.6	14.1	−0.4	36.8	41.0	17.4
Medical Insurance Exchange of California	28.5	28.2	16.1	16.8	23.8	22.7
Southern California Physicians Insurance Exchange	14.8	25.5	14.6	18.8	36.0	21.9
Illinois State Medical Inter-Insurance Exchange	−25.2	−42.0	121.0	78.6	330.4	92.6
Minnesota Medical Insurance Exchange	−21.1	11.9	−1.1	38.4	14.5	8.5
Medical Inter-Insurance Exchange of New Jersey	4.5	−25.4	89.4	46.2	28.7	28.7
Utah Medical Insurance Association	9.5	−9.8	−4.1	−8.6	10.8	−0.4
Washington State Physicians Insurance Exchange	11.5	12.1	39.4	24.3	14.9	20.4
Mean	2.2	1.8	34.4	31.4	62.5	26.5
Physician Stock						
Kentucky Medical Insurance Company	5.5	6.8	8.9	5.5	−12.7	2.8
Physicians Insurance Company of Michigan	22.4	22.1	−53.1	0.0	0.0	−1.7
Missouri Medical Insurance Company	−7.7	1.1	−11.6	3.6	20.0	1.1
Physicians Insurance Company of Ohio	16.5	25.3	5.4	12.0	31.6	18.2
Pennsylvania Medical Society Liability Insurance Company	31.2	193.3	−43.2	25.4	14.2	44.2
Mean	13.6	49.7	−18.7	9.3	10.6	12.9
Mean—Mutual, exchange, and physician stock companies	14.6	13.8	8.4	15.2	32.8	17.0
Commercial Stock						
American International Group	17.0	3.3	8.1	10.0	23.0	12.3
Farmers Insurance Group	−3.5	−7.4	−3.4	3.5	9.8	−0.2
Fireman's Fund Insurance Companies	14.4	−3.8	−44.9	10.2	25.1	0.2
Hartford Insurance Group	17.7	8.7	−17.7	20.5	18.7	9.6
St. Paul Group	33.2	3.6	−34.2	20.7	22.2	9.1
Travelers Group	11.0	14.3	−5.2	15.8	9.3	9.0
Mean	15.0	3.1	−16.2	13.5	18.0	6.7

Source: A. M. Best Co., *Best's Insurance Reports—Property/Casualty*, 1983–87 editions.

Box 9.1. Computing Return on Surplus

Rates of return on insurers' surplus are simple accounting ratios based on standard insurance practice. Surplus is capital (at book value) net of obligations on a companywide basis. Calculations are not malpractice specific.

Rates of return are calculated as total income (i.e., the sum of underwriting income, income from investments, and realized and unrealized capital gains in a calendar year after payment of income taxes) divided by policyholders' surplus (as of the last day of the preceding year). The companies incurred no income tax obligations during some of these years, so after-tax rates of return do not differ substantially from their pretax counterparts. Computing income after taxes does smooth out fluctuations in earnings, since taxes are highest in years with the highest profits and conversely. Income, taxes, and surplus come from insurers' annual Convention Statements, as summarized in annual volumes of *Best's Insurance Reports—Property/Casualty*. The companies report income and surplus using statutory accounting rules developed for the industry and required by state insurance departments.

---

liability insurers overall had sizable positive realized capital gains in each year between 1984 and 1986, the total return was negative in 1984. Between 1984 and 1986, the rate of return went from below zero to almost 20 percent, largely because of substantial rises in operating income accompanying premiums increases (Harrington and Litan 1988).

Very few companies in Table 9.1 consistently had positive net income. Only 6 of the 24 physician companies had positive net income in all five years, only 1 of 6 for the commercials. Five of the physician companies lost money in three of the five years. The St. Paul, the largest single malpractice carrier, had a −34 percent return on surplus in 1984 but was profitable in the other years.

Rates of return on policyholders' surplus for a few companies fluctuated tremendously between 1982 and 1986. Most notable was the Illinois State Medical Inter-Insurance Exchange, whose returns ranged from −42 to 330 percent per year. One reason for fluctuations in this profitability indicator may be a small surplus—that is, the denominator in the return ratio. This was true for the Illinois company's 330.4 percent in 1986.[3] The measure is more volatile for physician companies (smaller, single-line) than for commercials (much larger, multiple-line). Across companies within a given year, physician firms varied considerably (at the extreme, from −36.4 percent to +330.4 percent for 1986), commercials, much less so (extreme of −44.9 percent to +8.1 percent in 1984). The same holds true for any one company across years; the commercials' performances in any year varied much less from their five-year average than did the physician companies. Some additional volatility in returns may be expected in the start-up years of rapid company expansion. The physician-sponsored companies were still new during this time period.

The potential distortion due to an abnormally low surplus is one reason for seeking out other measures of profitability. Return on assets, discussed next, has much less year-to-year fluctuation because its denominator is so much more stable.

Rates of Return on Assets

This measure of profitability is a ratio whose numerator is also net income (defined as for return on surplus). But the denominator differs; here it is total assets on the last day of the preceding year (instead of surplus). Rates of return on total assets, unlike return on surplus, are not sensitive to the nature of the firm's capital structure. All assets, even those offset by obligations, are in the denominator. The rationale for this measure is that total assets provide the base on which returns are realized.

Table 9.2 shows a summary of one illustrative year of returns, 1986. Overall, the noncommercial, single-line insurers earned a 3.1 percent return on assets (below the corresponding return on surplus shown in Table 9.1 because the denominator, assets, is larger). The corresponding rate for the commercial stock companies was 3.3 percent (versus 18.0 percent for the rate of return on surplus, the latter percentage shown in Table 9.1). As before, the exchanges had the highest returns (4.2 percent). Physician companies, at 3.1 percent total return on assets, were much closer to commercials, at 3.3 percent for return on assets than for surplus, so the difference in return on surplus seems due to the varying capital structures of the firms.

The total return on assets was substantially reduced on average by negative underwriting income. Eliminating underwriting income from the calculation yields the investment return on assets (including realized and unrealized capital gains) (Table 9.2). The investment return on total assets was 11.2 percent for the noncommercial stock companies and 7.4 percent for the commercial stock companies in 1986. Five physician mutuals and 1 physician stock company (of 24 physician companies) had investment rates of return in excess of 15 percent; only 1 commercial (of 6) did so well (not shown). The higher return for the single-line companies may reflect a different investment strategy, given the longer tail on claims and their ability to make longer-run, higher-yield investments.

Asset Composition

The investment return on assets is highly dependent on the insurer's asset composition because asset returns tend to vary greatly by asset type. To some extent, asset composition is regulated. The mutuals and exchanges on average have put the major part of

Table 9.2. Investment and Total Returns on Assets, 1986 (Mean Values)

	Total Return on Assets	Investment Return on Assets
Mutual	3.0	12.2
Exchange	4.2	10.2
Physician stock	1.7	10.5
Mutual, exchange, physician stock	3.1	11.2
Commercial stock	3.3	7.4

Source: A. M. Best Co., *Best's Insurance Reports—Property/Casualty,* 1987 edition.

Note: The means are based on the companies listed in Table 9.1.

their assets, 73 and 75 percent, respectively in 1986, in intermediate and long-term bonds and very little in common and preferred stock (Table 9.3). The physician stock companies have also invested virtually nothing in traded stock, but one of the five companies had substantial investments in affiliate companies (included in "Other"). The commercial stock companies also held a smaller share in intermediate and long-term bonds, but held more in real estate and mortgages (also in "Other") and slightly more in common and preferred stock. Based on asset composition alone, the commercial stock companies should have had a higher rather than a lower rate of return on assets. Clearly, then, the commercial stock companies realized lower yields on their investments.[4]

Critiques of Returns Based on Surplus and Assets

Critics cite several weaknesses in these measures, with the same arguments applying to malpractice as to property-liability more generally.[5] First, they reflect conventions of insurance accounting that deviate from methods used in other sectors, although this does not seem to be an important deficiency. For example, expense deductions are not generally consistent with generally accepted accounting principles (GAAP). As another example, income in the insurance industry is computed after payments of dividends to policyholders. Harrington and Litan (1988) assessed the impact of insurers' expense accounting conventions and concluded that the results for insurers would be quite similar to those reported if GAAP expensing procedures were used. This conclusion is supported by a comparison of rates of return on property-liability insurance companies' net worth published by the Insurance Information Institute (1987, 25). According to the institute, the mean annual rate of return for the years 1977–86 was 12.4 percent, as calculated using accounting principles required by insurance statutes. The rate of return based on GAAP accounting rules was 11.3 percent.

Second, critics charge that insurers also understate profitability by not discounting future claims at present value before subtracting them from premium income. Federal tax law since 1986 has required discounting for computations of taxable income, but traditional, conservative insurance practice has called for the creation of a full dollar reserve now for every dollar of future claims expected without discounting.

Failure to discount loss reserves does lead to an understatement of income and surplus. Rates of return on surplus are biased downward because of the understatement of income but biased upward because the surplus is understated. Rates of return on assets are unambiguously biased downward because only the numerator is affected by accounting practices in the insurance industry.

Third, critics note that insurers can change earnings by manipulating their loss reserves. Systematic overreserving would cut profits (and, in the short run, may be used to justify premium rises or to postpone income taxes), whereas underreserving would raise profits and, presumably, attractiveness to investors. We found some evidence of overreserving in the late 1970s, but the tendency to overreserve diminished over time (Chapter 6).

Fourth, bonds are typically recorded on insurance company balance sheets in book values; common stocks are, by statutory requirement, recorded in market value (Troxel and Breslin 1983). Thus, since much of the insurers' assets are in intermediate and long-term bonds, the market value of assets and surplus is understated during periods

Table 9.3. Asset Composition of Insurers, 1986 (Percent Distribution)

	Common Stock	Preferred Stock	Bonds	Cash and Short-Term Investments	Premium Balances	Reinsurance Funds	Other	Total
Mutual	4.1	0.8	72.5	14.0	4.1	0.6	3.9	100.0
Exchange	1.9	2.2	74.7	10.0	4.5	1.7	5.0	100.0
Physician stock	0.3	0.0	56.4	12.8	11.5	1.4	17.6	100.0
Mutual, exchange, physician stock	2.6	1.1	69.9	12.4	5.8	1.2	7.1	100.0
Commercial stock	7.6	1.4	50.1	6.8	8.2	3.4	22.5	100.0

Source: A. M. Best Co., *Best's Insurance Reports—Property/Casualty,* 1987 edition.
Note: The percentage distributions are based on the companies listed in Table 9.1.

of falling interest rates and overstated when interest rates rise. In sum, these various objections are not weighty.

Fifth, a more serious point is that the returns presented to this point are those accruing to the companies themselves; the "proof of the pudding" of adequacy is returns to investors. We turn to this next.

Rates of Return on Equity

Returns to investors consist of the sum of dividends and capital gains in the company's share price (see, e.g., Kolbe et al. 1984). Such returns are readily calculated for commercial stock companies that sell equity in public markets, although not for most physician companies. In addition to representing returns to investors, they have the advantage of being expressed fully in market rather than in hybrid book-market terms.

This section investigates returns to investors from commercial companies, which are easily computed. The returns of large insurance companies that sell malpractice coverage give some indication of the likely returns among physician companies. For one, investments in single-line companies limited to a single geographic area (physician insurers) should be as risky as, if not more risky than, investments in multiple-line, national insurance companies (commercial). (See Chapter 6.) If returns to investors in the commercial companies are inadequate, they are likely to be inadequate for malpractice insurance companies as well. In other words, the long-run required return on equity should be at least as high for single-line companies with limited geographic scope as for the commercial stock companies. Also, short-run fluctuations in reported profitability (as return on surplus) appear to be about the same for single-line and multiple-line companies (Table 9.1).

Hence the data in Table 9.4 are useful beyond the particular insurers listed. They derive from Compustat data, a compilation of company-provided information from 10-K reports filed with the Securities and Exchange Commission. We analyzed returns from a different set of commercial insurance companies than in previous tables because many of the companies previously analyzed were not included in the Compustat file. Only American International Group and the St. Paul are common to both lists. As above, only the St. Paul had an appreciable share of its business in medical malpractice insurance.

As comparisons to insurers' returns on equity, Table 9.4 presents the average return on the stock market (from the monthly returns file compiled by the University of Chicago's Center for Research in Security Prices). Judging from the companies' beta, which is generally reported by *Value Line* and our computations to be around 1.0 (i.e., of average riskiness), investors in property-liability companies' stock expect to receive the same average return provided by the stock market as a whole (Chapter 2). In fact, the mean rate for the seven insurers listed in Table 9.4 was slightly less than for the market as a whole—18.1 percent for 1982–86, 15.8 percent for the longer period 1976–86—compared to stock market returns of 19.8 and 16.4 percent, respectively. The St. Paul, the only commercial insurer with an appreciable share of its business in the medical malpractice line, yielded returns of 16.6 percent for 1982–86 and 14.6 percent for 1976–86, slightly below the averages for the seven insurers. Returns from equity investments in the 1982–86 period were 8 to 9 percent higher than the risk-free yields on 90-day U.S. Treasury bills. Rates of return to investors typically led rates of

Table 9.4. Annual Returns on Equity (Percent)

Company	1976	1977	1978	1979	1980	1981	1982	1983	1984	1985	1986	Mean 1976–86	Mean 1982–86
Aetna Life & Casualty	53.9	6.9	11.5	-8.8	12.3	29.7	-10.4	6.3	8.6	50.3	10.1	15.5	13.0
American International Group	-4.4	11.5	22.2	17.9	26.7	-13.1	22.6	-18.0	6.7	56.0	-42.0	7.8	5.1
CNA	29.2	3.2	25.0	60.0	0.0	-6.3	15.8	21.6	51.5	101.6	-16.6	25.9	34.8
CIGNA	33.2	-10.3	-28.5	2.6	38.3	11.1	-6.5	4.5	7.3	48.8	-9.6	8.3	8.9
Continental	30.3	3.2	-47.3	16.2	0.3	18.4	21.1	2.3	40.7	33.4	1.0	10.9	19.7
St. Paul Group	18.7	-9.6	10.1	27.1	0.5	30.9	29.3	3.6	-5.8	52.2	3.8	14.6	16.6
U.S. Fidelity and Guarantee	69.3	34.3	0.0	32.5	16.7	5.4	17.6	28.9	42.8	47.7	7.8	27.5	29.0
Mean	32.9	5.6	-1.0	21.1	13.6	10.9	12.8	7.0	21.7	55.7	-6.5	15.8	18.1
Market[1]	24.5	-4.3	10.0	21.7	32.6	-2.8	23.9	20.9	7.2	28.9	17.9	16.4	19.8
1-year Treasury bill[2]	5.5	5.7	7.7	9.8	10.9	13.1	11.1	8.8	9.9	7.8	6.0[3]	8.8	11.3
90-day Treasury bill[2]	5.0	5.3	7.2	10.1	11.4	14.0	10.8	8.6	9.5	7.5	6.0[3]	8.6	11.3

Sources: Unless otherwise noted, the calculations are based on data from Industrial Compustat, 1987; [1]Center for Research in Security Prices, University of Chicago; [2]U.S. Department of Commerce, *Statistical Abstract,* 1987, p. 492; and [3]*Survey of Current Business,* Vol. 68, No. 3, March 1988, pp. 5–14.

return on policyholders' surplus by a year or so (compare the cyclical fluctuations in Table 9.1 to those in Table 9.4).

The results from Table 9.4 suggest that returns to equity investors in the insurance industry have been adequate or perhaps slightly inadequate in recent years, for they fall a little below returns on the stock market as a whole. If returns to equity holders in malpractice-specific insurance companies were as low, one could conclude that their returns were inadequate as well. However, judging from the comparative profitability performance of physician-owned and commercial insurers in Tables 9.1 and 9.2, one could infer that returns on equity in malpractice insurance may have been somewhat higher than for other property-liability insurance lines, but probably well short of evidence that returns to equity investments in malpractice insurance were excessive during the 1980s. A more malpractice-specific measure would be preferable.

Using Discounted Cash Flow to Estimate Profitability

One good measure of earnings specifically in medical malpractice insurance is how much insurers pay out over time for each policy year, compared with premiums collected in that year. The U.S. GAO (1987) recently performed such an analysis of profitability of medical malpractice and general liability lines for the 11-year period

---

Box 9.2. Discounting Reserves: The GAO Approach

Discounting has a greater effect on loss reserves when (1) the discount rate is high and (2) much of the loss payment comes many years after the premiums are collected. To properly compute the discounted value of future loss payments, the discounted loss reserve, it is important to assume a realistic time stream of payments rather than use an arbitrary assumption, such as that payments are made equally over a decade or another fixed time period.

The GAO selected the yield on ten-year U.S. Treasury bonds as the discount rate—from a low of 7.4 percent (in 1977) to a high of 13.9 percent (in 1981). Rather than simply discount loss reserves, the GAO used a "cash flow" model, which amounts to the same thing. (For insurance, the cash flows out over time, not in, as for the more familiar cash flow case in other industries.) All loss payments associated with a single policy year were discounted at the same rate. For example, assume that $100 in premiums were collected in 1975. Suppose that $5 was paid out immediately in loss payments, leaving $95 to be invested at the interest rate earned on bonds in 1976. Similar calculations are performed for future years; as claims are made against the amount invested, such as expenses, losses, and taxes, they are subtracted from the principal and accumulated interest earned on the dwindling investment. The losses used by the GAO for discounting were the loss reserves apportioned so as to reflect the historical time pattern of loss payouts.

To determine the possible effects of underreserving on profitability, the GAO reestimated profits under assumptions of 10 and 20 percent underreserving. Given discounting, underreserving by 20 percent cuts profits by a third.

1975–85. This study has three noteworthy features: First, the GAO used premiums and claims data specific to the malpractice line. Second, the profitability estimates discounted loss reserves. Third, the GAO performed sensitivity analysis to gauge the consequences of varying amounts of underreserving on profitability. As seen in Chapter 6, we found no evidence that medical malpractice insurers as a group have underreserved in recent years. The GAO used data from A.M. Best's, the same data set we have used.

Without discounting, the GAO estimated that insurers lost $653 million (undeflated or current dollars) on medical malpractice insurance during 1975–85 (Table 9.5). However, discounting by the rate on ten-year U.S. Treasury bonds, estimated profits rose to $2.2 billion, or a return on premiums of 15.3 percent. The GAO expressed the return as a percentage of premiums earned rather than as a percentage of net worth or assets because net worth and assets cannot be reliably apportioned by line. Even with an assumption of 20 percent underreserving, the rate of return on earned premiums was 10.9 percent. The GAO found that insurers incurred no income tax obligations on the medical malpractice insurance line, since such insurance generated accounting losses.

The Insurance Information Institute, representing the industry, criticized several aspects of the GAO report. First, the institute stated that averages for over a decade obscure the relatively poor profit performance of some recent years, although 1986 saw better returns than earlier years in the decade. The price increases of 1986 were necessary to return the industry to an operating gain and to the required rate of return (p. 1). The upturn in profitability is evident from the return on surplus (Table 9.1). Second, the after-tax gain may look large in absolute terms, but when standard industry accounting methods are used, the after-tax profit margin per premium dollar earned was only 6 cents. Returns on net worth, presumably for the property-liability insurance industry as a whole (similar to those in Table 9.4), were less than for Fortune 500 companies. Third, the GAO added unrealized capital gains and excluded dividends to policyholders, both contrary to required industry practice. The GAO, in our view, correctly defended its inclusion of unrealized capital gains. Realization of such gains is at the discretion of the asset owner. Although policyholder dividends are considered a legitimate expense in the insurance industry, this is not standard practice in other sectors. In any case, the GAO found that after-tax earnings were almost as great when unrealized capital gains were excluded from income and dividends were included as an expense.

Table 9.5. Earnings from the Medical Malpractice Line, 1975–85, as Computed by the GAO

Reserves	Not Discounted by GAO		Discounted by GAO	
	Earnings (Mil.)	Percent Rate of Return	Earnings (Mil.)	Percent Rate of Return[1]
Adequate	($653)	(4.6)	$2,171	15.3
10% inadequate	(1,245)	(8.8)	1,861	13.1
20% inadequate	(1,838)	(13.0)	1,551	10.9

Source: U.S. General Accounting Office (1987b), p. 26.

[1] The rate of return was calculated as a percentage of the premiums earned.

Perhaps the most telling complaints with the GAO methods are (1) that it took as given the state of a company's reserves for a particular year, (2) that its discount rates arbitrarily assumed that reserves could be invested for fully ten years, and (3) that its measure of return on premiums gives little policy guidance. Is a 15 or 10 percent return a year fair, excessive, or inadequate? Both the GAO (1987b, 6–7) and the industry drew limited comparisons to allegedly comparable businesses. But neither systematically assessed comparability. We turn next to more formal assessments, based on modern financial theory, that address these weaknesses.

FAIR MALPRACTICE INSURANCE PREMIUMS

Like the GAO, regulators generally consider insurer profit relative to premiums. Specifically, in rate-making calculations, they allow a stated percentage markup over anticipated losses and expenses as fair (Chapter 3). A major deficiency of this approach is that the markup allowed by this method bears no necessary relationship to the risk-adjusted rates of return that investors require to supply equity capital to insurers in competition with similarly risky companies. Such arbitrary calculations of premium may be unfair to premium payers, by generating more profit than investors require, or unfair to investors, by generating less than the required rate of return.

In our analysis, we used two methods to derive fair medical malpractice premiums. The first is the capital asset pricing model (CAPM), as applied by Fairley (1979), Hill (1979), and Biger and Kahane (1978). The second is the discounted cash flow method (DCF), as developed for insurance regulation by Myers and Cohn (1987). These methods rigorously derive discount rates and required risk-adjusted rates of return, which we use in conjunction with actual premiums and claims losses to consider the adequacy of returns. Next, we formally develop the two methods used and describe their empirical application.

Two Methods for Computing Fair Premiums

Capital Asset Pricing Model (CAPM)
The return an insurer expects to deliver to its equity holders, $E(r)$, is a weighted average of profit from investments and underwriting. Underwriting profit is the product of premiums (P) and the expected underwriting profit rate, $E(r_u)$.

Expected investment income is the expected rate of return on the insurer's investment ($E(r_i)$) times the amount invested. The amount invested is premium income not yet used to pay losses and therefore available for investment purposes. Let k be a constant reflecting the average time a dollar of premium income is available for investment. If, for example, it takes a year on average between the date the premium is collected and the loss payout date, k equals 1.0. Let x be the fraction of a dollar premium used for expense. This expense includes production, marketing, and other costs excluding the cost of capital. Then the amount available for investment is the equity at the beginning of the period plus k times the premium times $(1 - x)$, the fraction of premium income not allocated to expense.[6] Then the following relationship holds for $E(r)$:

$$E(r) = \left[1 + k\left(\frac{P}{S}\right)(1 - x) \right] E(r_i) + \left(\frac{P}{S}\right)(E(r_u)) \qquad (9.1)$$

where S = value of equity in the insurance company. For $E(r)$ to be expressed as a rate of return, we divided both sides of the profit equation by S.

CAPM theory states that the rate of return on the insurer's investment is given by

$$E(r_i) = r_f + \beta_i[E(r_m) - r_f] \qquad (9.2)$$

where

$E(r_i)$ = rate of return on insurer i's investments
r_f = risk-free rate of return
β_i = the beta on the insurer's investment portfolio
$E(r_m)$ = expected rate of return for the market as a whole

Substituting equation (9.2) for $E(r_i)$ in equation (9.1),

$$\left[1 + k\left(\frac{P}{S}\right)(1 - x) \right] [r_f + \beta_i(E(r_m) - r_f)] + \left(\frac{P}{S}\right)(E(r_u))$$

$$= r_f + \beta[E(r_m) - r_f] \qquad (9.3)$$

From CAPM, the beta for an insurer's stock, β, is

$$\beta = \frac{\text{Cov}(r, r_m)}{\sigma_m^2} \qquad (9.4)$$

where

r = rate of return to investors in stock of the insurer
σ_m^2 = variance of the return on the market portfolio

It can be easily shown that β is a weighted average of β_i, the beta on the insurer's investment portfolio and an "underwriting beta," β_u.

$$\beta = \left[1 + k\left(\frac{P}{S}\right)(1 - x) \right] \beta_i + \left(\frac{P}{S}\right) \beta_u \qquad (9.5)$$

While a high β from equation (9.4) implies that returns to investors in the insurance company are strongly and positively related to returns on a diversified market portfolio, m, a high β_i implies that returns on the insurer's investments are strongly and positively related to r_m. As indicated above, β for insurance companies is estimated to be around 1.0. The underwriting beta (β_u) may be positive or negative. A negative beta would imply that insurers make substantial loss payments when the economy as a whole is booming, and a positive underwriting beta would imply the reverse. Substituting equation (9.5) into equation (9.3) and simplifying yields an equation for the expected underwriting profit, $E(r_u)$:

$$E(r_u) = -k(1 - x)r_f + \beta_u[E(r_m) - r_f] \qquad (9.6)$$

Equation (9.6) gives the underwriting profit rate for the insurer in competitive equilibrium. When this profit is added to the sum of expected loss and expense, one obtains the fair premium.

According to equation (9.6), this margin depends on four factors. The first is $[-k(1 - x)]$, the fraction of a premium dollar available to the insurer for investment purposes. For long-tail lines such as medical malpractice, k is large. Thus, holding other factors constant, the underwriting profit should be lower (underwriting loss higher) for medical malpractice than for lines with a shorter claims tail. Second, when the yield on a risk-free security such as a 90-day Treasury bill, or other short-term government security such as a one-year Treasury bill, is high, the effect of k is greater because of compounding. Thus, an insurer should be willing to take a lower underwriting profit when investment yields are high; the effect of r_f is comparatively great for lines with a high k, that is, those that yield higher proportions of investable funds. Third, a high underwriting beta (relatively nondiversifiable riskiness of the line) implies a higher underwriting profit, other factors equal. Because such a liability does not help reduce fluctuations in the value of the insurer's overall portfolio, a higher expected return is required. Conversely, if the underwriting beta is negative, issuing insurance policies does increase overall diversification, and investors demand a lower expected underwriting profit margin. Fourth, the effect of a given underwriting beta is higher when the difference between the expected return on the market and the yield on risk-free securities is large. This "market risk premium" has been comparatively stable over time.[7] To add realism to equation (9.6), one should consider the effect of taxes. We shall deal with this issue below.

Empirical Implementation of the CAPM

Empirical implementation of equation (9.6) requires knowledge of k, the risk-free rate of return, the expense ratio, the underwriting beta, and the market risk premium. Empirically, k has been measured as the ratio of loss reserves to earned premiums for a policy year (Fairley 1979). We estimated k for several lines, including medical malpractice, from a sample of 11 multiple-line insurers, using data from each insurer's Convention Statements for 1978–86 (Table 9.6). As anticipated, k was comparatively

Table 9.6.   Values of k by Line

Line	k
Medical malpractice	4.12
Auto	1.12
Multiple peril	0.91
Other liability	2.67
Workers' Compensation	2.10
All five lines (weighted by premiums)	1.60

Source: Convention Statements from 11 multiple-line insurers, 1978–87.

high for medical malpractice (4.12) and small for auto (1.12) and multiple peril (0.91). The risk-free rate of return was represented by a one-year Treasury bill. Following Hill and Modigliani (1987), we used a one-year bond for r_f to better match the payment period for short-tail lines. The one-year Treasury bill tends to be about half a percentage point higher than the 90-day Treasury bill. Information on Treasury bill yields is available from several sources. Data on the fraction of loss expense to earned premiums came from *Best's Casualty Loss Reserve Development*. Data on the stock market returns came from the University of Chicago's Center for Research in Security Prices (CRSP).

We estimated the underwriting beta for medical malpractice insurance in several ways. Equation (9.5) shows that the firm's beta is a weighted average of its investment beta, β_i, and its underwriting beta, β_u. β_u, which is defined for underwriting profit, can be converted into a beta for underwriting losses (β_L) by noting that

$$\beta_u = -k\beta_L \tag{9.7}$$

Once the first two betas are known, the underwriting beta can be obtained by subtraction (see equation 9.5).

We estimated β with monthly data for 1976–86 on the four insurers (Aetna, CNA, Continental, and U.S.F.& G.) available from CRSP. We obtained a β of 1.0, which agrees with the values presented in *Value Line*. We had to assume that insurers with nontraded stock have the same beta.

We estimated the beta on insurers' investment portfolios (β_i) in two ways. The first approach involved estimating β_i directly by regressing rates of return on company investment portfolios on the market risk premium (as in Fairley 1979). We used data for the same four companies. Returns came from CRSP for 1976–86 and asset values from *Best's Insurance Reports—Property/Casualty* for the same years. We took an average of assets as of the last day of the preceding year and the last day of the current year. The resulting estimate for β_i was 0.151. However, this estimate was derived from annual data. To convert to a monthly equivalent value, we estimated β using monthly and annual data. We computed the ratio of β from monthly data to the β from annual data. We multiplied this ratio by 0.151, and the resulting value for β_i was 0.237.

While this is a direct method, it has two important deficiencies. First, assets (which form the denominator of the rate of return on the investment portfolio) are closer to a book value than to a market value. The underlying CAPM theory clearly requires a market value. Second, the asset portfolio mix of commercial stock insurers differs from that of the physician-owned companies (Table 9.3). Therefore, following Hill and Modigliani (1987), we derived an alternative β_i based on the asset mix of the insurers' portfolios. For common stock we assumed a beta of 1.0, for bonds and preferred stock 0.125, and for other assets 0.063. The other assets include cash and other short-term investments, premium balances, and reinsurance funds, all of which plausibly have a beta of zero; some firms have investments in affiliates. Unfortunately, there is no information on the composition of such investments.

An alternative way we used to derive a value for the underwriting beta is the residual approach suggested by Hill (1979). Hill started with an identity expressing the market value of the firm's equity that equals the sum of the value of the firm's (noninsurance) investment and the value of the firm's underwriting business. Subtracting investment from equity value, he obtained the value of the underwriting business (V_u). V_u for one year divided into V_u for the next year yields the return to underwriting (R_u). R_u was then regressed against the value of the market portfolio to obtain an underwriting beta by company. As Myers and Cohn (1987) noted, however, this method assumes that all of the insurer's investments are in the form of securities that have a current market value and no liabilities except from the sale of policies.

Assuming that a single corporate income tax rate (t) applies to profits from underwriting and investment income, equation (9.6) becomes (Fairley 1979):

$$E(r_u') = -k(1 - x)r_f + \beta_u[E(r_m) - r_f] + \frac{r_f t}{[(1 - t)(P/S)]} \tag{9.8}$$

We assumed two values for the tax rate (t): zero and 0.22. The rationale for a zero tax rate is that medical malpractice and other property-liability insurers have paid little or no income taxes in recent years (U.S. GAO 1987b; our own calculations for several large commercial stock companies). The value 0.22 is the midpoint of values for the tax rate derived by Hill and Modigliani (1987).[8]

Discounted Cash Flow (DCF) Model

The DCF model, as developed for fair premium regulation by Myers and Cohn (1987), is similar to the CAPM but gives a better account of time phasing of cash flows. The DCF starts with the premise that a fair premium must allow insurers to recover the present value of losses and expenses on policies sold, as well as the present value of the tax obligations on underwriting and investment income. The authors argued that policyholders should pay the tax on investment income, since if equity holders paid such a tax, they would be subject to double taxation. The CAPM is a single-period model adapted to a multiperiod problem. The pattern of underwriting and investment cash flows is roughly captured in the CAPM approach by the parameter k. In the DCF, by contrast, one needs to estimate cash flows by year. This is an empirical task. The primary conceptual problem is to determine the rate to be used for discounting.

The DCF model offers more precision than the CAPM with respect to the timing of cash flows. However, observed cash flows are taken as givens. The CAPM is more realistic in the sense that it recognizes the stochastic (random) nature of cash flow.

With the DCF, one computes the present value of premiums (PVr_f) as the sum of three cash flows: the present value of loss and loss expense payments ($PVr_L(L)$); taxes on the investment income ($PVr_f(IBT)$); and taxes on underwriting profit ($PVr_f, r_L(UWPT)$).

Unlike the GAO (1987b), which discounted uniformly by the yield on ten-year U.S. Treasury bonds, Myers and Cohn (1987) recommended discounting different types of cash flows with different discount rates. For losses and expenses, they discounted by r_L, where $r_L = r_f + \beta_L(r_m - r_f)$. This payment stream is uncertain; r_L may exceed or be less than r_f, depending on the sign of β_L. This beta applies to losses, in contrast to the underwriting beta, which applies to underwriting profits. For investment income and the premium component of underwriting profit, Myers and Cohn discounted by r_f.

Implementing the DCF requires knowledge of cash flows for future periods. In our case, several years of actual claims experience were known, and to project remaining future losses, we used the chain ladder method (Chapter 7; Hossack, et al. 1983). We forecasted losses out to ten years after the policy year to which they corresponded. With this method, we added all first-year losses for nine policy years. We then added all second years for eight policy years, plus the projected second-year loss for the most recent policy year. Third, we added all third-year losses in all but the two most recent policy years to the projected loss for the year preceding the most recent policy year. We continued summing in this manner, adding fourth-year and successive-year losses. For each successive year, there was less information on the actual losses incurred. The next step was to compute growth factors. The first growth factor was the sum of the first-year losses for policy years 1978 through 1986, our most recent year, divided into the sum of the second-year losses for policy years 1978 through 1986. This factor reflects the pattern of loss development in the year after the policy was sold relative to the losses in the year the policy was sold. Similarly, we computed growth factors for each adjacent year. Thus, for example, the ratio of losses in the seventh to the sixth year was 1.38. The corresponding ratio in the fourth to the third year was 2.32. For a number of years, data on loss reserves were not available from Best's *Casualty Loss Reserve Development*. In those cases, it was not possible to compute a ratio. Even considering the volatility due to discrepancies between net premiums earned as originally reported and the revised estimates, there was considerable year-to-year and intercompany variation in the ratios.

We computed discount rates based on methods proposed by Fairley, Hill, and Hill-Modigliani. These approaches yielded estimates of β_L using Fairley's method of 0.04 without taxes and -0.03 with taxes; of -0.40 with Hill's method with taxes; and of 0.05 and 0.003 with the Hill-Modigliani method without and with taxes, respectively. A negative β_L implies that losses rise when the market return on a well-diversified portfolio falls, meaning that in a recession the insurer is likely to take a beating on both the underwriting and investment sides of its business, and conversely for a positive β_L. For this reason, r_L exceeds (falls short of) the risk-free rate when β_L is positive (negative) as long as the market return exceeds the risk-free rate of return, the usual case. A higher r_L means a lower fair premium. If the market return falls short of the risk-free rate and β_L is positive, r_L is smaller than r_f. Estimates of 0.04 and 0.05 suggest that losses in the medical malpractice line are reasonably independent of returns on a well-diversified portfolio of securities. In implementing the DCF model, we alternatively assumed zero tax rates and the rates of 0.21 and 0.24 reported by Hill and Modigliani.[9]

Results: Comparing Fair Premiums with Actual Premiums

The discount rates applied are key factors in both the CAPM and the DCF. Alternative discount rates for the period 1976–86 are shown in Table 9.7. The CAPM discount rates using the Fairley method and the DCF discount rates based on Hill-Modigliani's approach are quite similar to the rates for the one-year Treasury bill. Over the entire period, and for almost every year, the ten-year Treasury bond yields were higher by one to two percentage points. The CAPM estimates of r_L using the Hill method yield the lowest discount rates, but the year-to-year variation is also much higher. In fact, in one year, 1985, the Hill-based discount rate is negative. On balance, given that insurers could have expected to have tax obligations at around the 22 percent rate, and given

Table 9.7. Discount Rates

Year	One-Year[2] Treasury Bill	Ten-Year[2] Treasury Bond	CAPM (Fairley)		CAPM (Hill)	DCF (Hill-Modigliani)	
			$t = 0.00$	$t = 0.22$[3]	$t = 0.00$	$t = 0.00$	$t = 0.21, 0.24$[4]
1976	5.52	7.61	6.28	4.95	−2.06	6.47	5.58
1977	5.71	7.42	5.31	6.01	9.72	5.21	5.68
1978	7.74	8.41	7.83	7.67	6.85	7.85	7.75
1979	9.75	9.44	10.23	9.39	4.95	10.35	9.79
1980	10.89	11.46	11.76	10.24	2.19	11.98	10.96
1981	13.14	13.91	12.52	13.60	19.30	12.37	13.09
1982	11.07	13.00	11.58	10.69	5.95	11.71	11.11
1983	8.80	11.11	9.28	8.44	3.97	9.40	8.84
1984	9.92	12.44	9.81	10.00	11.01	9.78	9.91
1985	7.81	10.62	8.65	7.18	−0.63	8.87	7.81
1986	6.08	7.68	6.46	5.63	1.23	6.58	6.03
Mean, 1976–86	8.77	10.28	9.06	8.53	5.68	9.14	8.77

[1]Based on an estimated equity beta of 1.01, asset beta of 0.24, and underwriting beta of 0.04 (source: Industrial Compustat, 1982, and the CRSP file).

[2]U.S. Department of Commerce, *Statistical Abstract of the United States*, 1988, pp. 484–85.

[3]Based on an effective tax rate of 22 percent in *The Wall Street Journal*, September 23, 1988, p. 2.

[4]Based on an investment tax rate of 0.21 and an underwriting tax rate of 0.24 from Hill and Modigliani (1987).

the instability of the Hill-based estimates, the CAPM-Fairley ($t = 0.22$) and the DCF-Hill-Modigliani estimates ($t = 0.21, 0.24$) are probably the most reliable, and these estimates are virtually identical to the one-year Treasury bill rates that would be expected with a low r_L. The assumed rate of taxation has very little effect on the computed discount rate.

We computed fair medical malpractice premiums by policy years 1978, 1979, and 1982 for a sample of companies (Table 9.8). The table shows that total premiums changed little (in real dollars) for 1978–82 but that losses rose slightly (undiscounted) in 1979 and substantially in 1982. Fair premiums based on the more plausible CAPM and DCF discount rates are shown to the right, with two tax rates (0 and 22 percent). The different DCF rates were rather similar to one another; the CAPM yielded considsiderably lower fair premiums. Actual premiums substantially exceeded fair premiums for medical malpractice insurance policies issued during 1978 and 1979. By 1982, however, with the exception of mutual insurers, actual and fair premiums computed using DCF were approximately equal. Actual premiums for the mutuals were still higher than corresponding fair premiums. Part of this difference may be explained by the physician-owned companies' desire to build up a surplus in their initial years. Using the CAPM, actual premiums were still appreciably more than their fair premium counterparts. Thus, the trend between 1978–79 and 1982 was toward decreased profitability. It is possible that malpractice insurance was no longer generating excess returns by 1982.

In computing the fair premium for 1982, we used the chain ladder method to

Table 9.8. Actual vs. Fair Premiums in Medical Malpractice (Mils. $)

Company Type	Actual Premium	Actual Undiscounted Loss	Fair Premiums[1]		
			CAPM (Fairley) $t = 0.22$	DCF (Fairley) $t = 0.22$	DCF (Hill-Modigliani) $t = 0.21, 0.24$
1978					
Mutual	29.3	21.3	14.6	16.2	16.2
Exchange	18.2	14.5	10.0	10.9	10.9
Physician stock	—	—	—	—	—
Commercial stock	93.8	43.5	29.7	33.1	33.0
Mean	37.0	22.9	15.6	17.3	17.3
1979					
Mutual	24.1	18.7	11.4	13.3	13.1
Exchange	24.0	20.8	12.7	14.6	14.4
Physician stock	20.8	13.6	8.4	9.0	8.9
Commercial stock	70.2	37.1	22.7	27.5	27.1
Mean	34.7	23.3	14.3	16.7	16.4
1982					
Mutual	29.8	29.3	16.4	18.6	18.3
Exchange	30.4	48.8	27.3	31.3	30.8
Physician stock	18.2	30.0	16.8	19.6	19.3
Commercial stock	81.3	134.9	75.0	85.2	83.8
Mean	35.0	51.6	28.9	33.0	34.1

Source: Actual premium, indemnity, and loss expense data were taken from *Best's Casualty Loss Reserve Development*, 1986 and 1987. All values are expressed in 1987 dollars. Means are weighted.

[1]Based on the computed underwriting profit rate for the respective method.

project losses in the outlying years. Company estimates of losses by policy year were not available. Thus, we had to generate our own estimates. We also computed fair premiums for years later than 1982. However, these estimates relied extensively on losses projected by the chain ladder method. The estimates were quite unstable and implausible.

Particularly in view of the change in profitability of medical malpractice insurance between 1978–79 and 1982, we cannot rule out the possibility that such insurance was underpriced at the height of the malpractice insurance crisis around 1983–85.

FURTHER DISCUSSION AND CONCLUSION

Gauging profitability is a complex undertaking. The numerous indicators do not always point in the same direction, and they all vary markedly over time. Our most rigorous measures of profitability (CAPM and DCF) can be applied only with considerable hindsight once the large tail of claims payment is mostly played out. And data before the late 1970s were unreliable or unavailable. So, we have not been able to examine as large a run of profits as we would have liked with the better measures. Despite these limitations, our empirical analysis permits some conclusions.

At least in some years, notably for policy years 1978 and 1979, medical malpractice insurance yielded returns in excess of those that would prevail for long in a competitive market. However, our analysis suggests fluctuations in rates of return rather than persistent excess returns, and even in a competitive market, sellers may realize excess returns in the short run.

Single-line medical malpractice insurers on the whole appear to be as profitable as, if not more profitable than, multiple-line commercial stock companies. And physician policyholders control the higher-profit single-line companies, so they can assure that excessive profits are not accumulated. Rates of return to owners of the multiple-line commercial stock companies have, if anything, been slightly inadequate in recent years. We are unable to explain why one type of physician insurer (the exchanges) seem to have done better than others or how physician companies have earned better investment returns than the commercials despite an apparently more conservative mix of investments (less stock, more bonds).

The recent U.S. GAO (1987b) study of this issue has been used to suggest that profitability from the medical malpractice line have been excessive—some 15 percent a year on sales or premiums earned when claims reserves are discounted. Discounting is appropriate. The GAO used a somewhat higher discount rate than we, and our rates were selected on a more rigorous basis. To this extent, the GAO slightly overstated profitability. But, more important, the insurance industry was correct in criticizing the GAO for basing conclusions about profitability on average profitability measured over a decade, especially without looking for trends in profitability. Realized rates of return vary markedly over time, and the average computed over a past decade will not generally provide a useful guide for future policy. The majority of the medical malpractice insurance companies were brand new in the first years of the decade included in the GAO's calculations.

It is appropriate to account for the amount of risk involved in issuing insurance policies when calculating fair premiums and competitive profit levels. However, there is substantial disagreement among the experts about the appropriate measure of under-writing risk to use. Some argue that only diversifiable risk should be considered, and this assumption underlies the CAPM and DCF calculations presented in this chapter. Others who question whether the complete diversification of certain types of risk is reasonable favor a more inclusive measure of risk that incorporates at least part of what CAPM theory would call "diversifiable" risk (see, e.g., Cox and Griepentrog 1988). Even among those who may accept diversifiable risk as the appropriate concept for gauging insurance premiums and profits, there is a sense of unease about how accurate CAPM-generated premiums and profits are in practice (e.g., Cummins and Harrington 1988). In particular, a wide range of estimated underwriting betas have been obtained. We have seen this in our work as well. There is no generally accepted method for estimating underwriting betas. Restrictive assumptions are needed to estimate betas for particular lines of insurance.

When there is uncertainty about the appropriate methodological technique, it is appropriate to conduct sensitivity analysis—that is, to try several alternative methods and compare the results. Fortunately, in this application, alternative techniques gener-ally yield fairly similar findings about profitability.

The increase in real interest rates in the early 1980s should, holding other factors constant, have reduced fair premiums; in fact during the 1980s' crisis, premiums rose rapidly. But other factors were not constant. In particular, losses were increasing rapidly. The chain ladder projection method, for one, makes much of such changes in developing forecasts of future losses. It is therefore easy to over- or undershoot true losses using this extrapolation method. With losses growing in the early 1980s, the tendency would probably have been to overshoot. The methods we have used may exaggerate the fluctuation in profitability. Unfortunately, regulators trying to set pre-miums to achieve normal profits in the industry face the same problem.

We have been able to observe profits from only part of the insurance cycle. The seeming peaks observed with our best measures in 1978 and 1979 do show above-normal profits, but by 1982 profits were normal. The deeper valley centered on 1984 is unobservable with our best measures but seems, from other measures, to be there. On balance, the empirical results seem consistent with common sense. Neither the case for systematic, long-term relief for insurers nor the case for rate rollbacks for insureds has been made. The intuition that the dominant role played by physician companies should discipline the market seems even more appealing after this examination of empirical measures. The most rigorous conclusions could be drawn only after more years of claims development, examining a full cycle of profitability, based on actual results.

NOTES

1. Part IV of subchapter L of Chapter 1 (Section 846) of the U.S. Tax Code was amended in 1986 to require discounting of unpaid loss reserves in computing the federal income tax.
2. Of the commercial insurers listed, only the St. Paul had more than 5 percent of its business in malpractice insurance (malpractice net premiums as a percentage of total net premiums written). All of the companies sold some medical malpractice insurance.
3. An employee of another insurer told us that the Illinois State Medical Inter-Insurance Ex-

change switched from occurrence to claims-made coverage in the year it earned the 330 percent return without reducing premiums.

4. This was confirmed by a reviewer of a draft of this chapter who worked for a commercial stock company. He cautioned that this pattern applied to the period we analyzed and may not generalize.

5. For an evaluation of these criticisms, see Harrington and Litan (1988).

6. D'Arcy and Doherty (1987) suggested including x. We shall use their notation. The theory is standard.

7. See, for example, Fama and MacBeth (1973).

8. To determine effective corporate income tax rates, Hill and Modigliani (1987) regressed total taxes paid, by property-casualty insurance company and year, on explanatory variables for before-tax investment income and for underwriting income. They obtained marginal tax rates of 0.21 for investment income and 0.24 for underwriting income. These values were substantially less than the statutory tax rates of 0.46 applicable at the time.

9. See note 7 for additional details.

10

Conclusion: Summing Up and Looking Forward

SALIENT FINDINGS ABOUT PHYSICIANS' MALPRACTICE INSURANCE

This book has reviewed many features of physicians' malpractice insurance, the insurers that sell it, and the markets in which it is bought and sold. Our final chapter emphasizes the main policy-relevant findings, somewhat at the expense of information of purely descriptive or abstract analytical interest. Each of the foregoing chapters has its own summary.

Competitiveness of the "Industry"

A fundamental finding is that the market for malpractice insurance appears to be reasonably competitive, rather than monopolistic, a finding in accord with other analyses of property-liability insurance (Chapter 4). In the popular mind, insurers may be seen as a monolithic "they," prone to uniform exploitation of consumers, but things are not as bad as many think. By "competitive," we do not mean to imply that the market fits the paradigm of perfect competition as well as the markets for wheat and soybeans. Rather, we argue that insurers are at least ultimately subject to the discipline of competitive pressures.

Nationally, there are numerous sellers and buyers. Within any given state (the natural market area for liability coverage), one or a few carriers often dominate the market, but the threat of entry by a newly licensed company is ever-present. Insurers incur costs associated with entry, but these are hardly insurmountable, particularly for well-capitalized, multistate, multiple-line companies but also for medical malpractice insurers from other states. Regulation is not a large barrier to entry, and few entry barriers of any kind were reported to us in our Survey of Medical Malpractice Insurers. Moreover, other competition now comes from more exotic sources of coverage such as physician trusts and risk retention groups, as well as from self-insured groups at teaching hospitals and elsewhere. One potential barrier to competition is that physician mobility across companies is to some extent impaired under claims-made policies. A mover may need to buy a tail policy at the price of up to a year's annual mature premium, a penalty for changing suppliers. We have no direct evidence on the extent to which doctors' changing insurers may be hampered, although conventional wisdom is that insurance persistence rates are very high.[1] In fact, we found persistence rates to be high for the three years prior to our Survey of Medical Malpractice Insurers, but there was a substantial decline in rates for longer periods (Chapter 4).

Another noncompetitive portent is that, historically, physician-sponsored companies have been reluctant to compete with one another. Today this attitude is changing somewhat. At least a few physician insurers operate across state lines in competition with their sister companies.

The use of quotation marks around "industry" in the heading above reflects our ambivalence about whether malpractice is a separate industry or merely a line of property-liability coverage like many others. As just noted, many property-liability insurers sell malpractice coverage, and most regulation and other insurance practices treat it as a line. Still, the field is quite specialized; it is notable that single-line, physician-sponsored companies sell most of the coverage. Among the multiple-line companies that do so, the most successful tend to be the larger firms, those that specialize in the area. The era of many sellers with tiny market shares appears to be over. Consumers of medical malpractice insurance obviously do not regard other types of insurance (automobile casualty, product liability, etc.) as substitutes. Thus, a case can be made that medical malpractice is a separate product (Chapter 4).

Availability of Coverage

Physicians' problems in obtaining coverage, which is virtually essential to practice medicine even where not required by law, has been the central reason for recent policy concern about medical malpractice insurance (Chapter 1). It appears that the physician-sponsored companies have almost completely solved this problem for physicians in most states since their first appearance in the mid-1970s. JUAs, creations of the crisis of the mid-1970s, also contribute capacity in several states, occasionally dominating the market, and provide standby capacity in others. Even at the height of the 1980s liability "crisis,"[2] when many carriers were refusing to extend coverage to new policy-holders, it appears that physicians could generally get coverage. Indeed, most standby JUAs were not activated. Similarly, few physicians in the late 1980s and early 1990s seemed unable to find coverage through licensed insurers and needed to deal with so-called excess limits firms that specialize in hard-to-insure physicians. By one account, the two principal excess limits firms accept only a few hundred physicians a year (Schwartz and Mendelson, 1989a). Whether physicians typically have choices among multiple companies is another matter, as is the affordability of available coverage—which we address in a later section on prices and profits.

Insurer Solvency

Continuing availability depends in part on insurer solvency, for an undercapitalized or underreserved company may prove unable to meet its long-term obligations. Assuring solvency is, of course, the bedrock justification for regulation of insurance (Chapter 3). We found no particular evidence that solvency regulation plays a large role in influencing malpractice insurers' behavior; our Survey of Medical Malpractice Insurers' respondents denied that regulators were as hard on them as they were on themselves. Still, the premium-to-surplus ratios of some malpractice companies are not strong (Chapter 6), and a few have very low ratings from A.M. Best (other, unrated com-

panies would get low ratings if rated). Insolvencies have been rare in medical malpractice (Rosenberg, 1984) and in the property-liability insurance industry more generally.
Several other malpractice insurers have experienced financial difficulty (Rosenberg
1984; Chapter 6).

It would appear that state regulators have ample powers to intervene where warranted with regard to licensed insurers and, to a lesser degree, with regard to risk
retention groups (Chapter 3). Moreover, state guaranty funds stand behind licensed
carriers, though again, not behind risk retention groups. Primary insurers purchase
reinsurance to protect themselves against large fluctuations in losses (Chapter 5).
Without reinsurance, it is doubtful that many, if not most, of the single-line insurers
that now provide a substantial portion of the medical malpractice insurance coverage
(Chapter 1) would exist. In at least one state, observers blame regulatory zeal for
keeping rates low and impairing the long-run solvency of insurers, but we reiterate that
no insolvencies have been declared, even the during the 1980s crisis of affordability.

Prices and Profits

After availability, high prices are the major reason that malpractice insurance (and
other liability coverages) receives public attention. With the notable exception of
automobile liability insurance, the customers of third-party (liability) insurance tend to
be firms. Hence the direct effects of premium increases are of little political concern.
However, there is considerable concern over the possible downstream effects on physicians' fees and practice patterns (see Sloan and Bovbjerg [1989], for discussion of the
literature on the impact of premium increases on physicians' fees and practice patterns)
and on availability of care (see, e.g., Institute of Medicine 1989a, 1989b). Here our
findings over more than a decade are at variance with popular images of out-of-control
price hikes. The common popular impression seems to be a reaction to double-digit
rate increases, especially over more than one year, as in the 1980s' crisis. Forgotten are
the slower increases or actual drops of an earlier period, which we documented in
Figure 1.1.

Of course, price hikes are blameworthy only in relation to underlying costs—
losses and associated expense. A more sophisticated charge is that insurers collect far
more in premiums each year than they pay out in claims (e.g., Goddard 1985). The
observation is true, but the implication does not necessarily follow. Because of the long
tail of malpractice claims settlement and the relentlessly upward climb of claims
severity, companies must collect more each year than they pay out on a current basis
(Chapter 6). The reason is that their claims reserves must be sufficient to pay all
pending claims—which would take almost a decade—with no new premium income.[3]
Industry detractors may overlook this need, but private insurers ignore it at their peril.
Only public entities backed by taxing power can safely fund future obligations on a
pay-as-you-go basis.

The accuracy of claims reserving is a distinct issue. Our multiyear analysis indeed
found some errors in companies' reserving over periods ranging up to eight years after
the base year of 1979 (Chapter 6). Naturally, viewed after the fact, insurers' informed
guesses about future liabilities are bound to have been either too high or too low. That
is not a policy issue. Only systematic over-or underreserving is a concern. Here we also
found evidence that companies do vary reserves so as to lower the year-to-year vol-

atility of reported earnings. This practice, of course, has no net long-term effect on the adequacy of reserves, although it may lower the cost of capital to the firms.

Physician-sponsored companies have no incentive to overcharge physicians as a class, who are both customers and residual claimants. Such insurers may wish to build a comfortable amount of surplus, perhaps sometimes seemingly too comfortable. But the surplus generated by any overcharges ultimately belongs to the physician policy-holders, who are well motivated to assure reasonable operations. (The class interest of the physician remains constant, although the individuals may change. Depending on the precise organizational form of the firm, the physicians who originally paid the extra premiums may not be the ones who ultimately benefit.) Empirically, our study found that physician-sponsored insurers charged premiums that were the same as or lower than those of commercial stock insurers, holding other factors constant (Chapter 7). Perhaps this should not be surprising, given that the physician companies generally do not need to pay agents' commissions and that the physician "shareholders" do not expect the same cash dividend on their "investment."

One empirical finding on pricing was surprising: In our multivariate analysis of premiums, we found that competition (as measured by an index of market concentration) had no statistically significant effect on rates. On the other hand, the strength of insurance regulation of prices had a very strong and negative impact—lower rates with stronger regulation.

If premiums are excessive, then profits should also be, and complaints are commonly heard that insurers are overly profitable.[4] With regard to the fairness of profits, we could make independent assessments using statistical models of fair market return (the CAPM and variants on it; Chapters 2 and 9). We were able to analyze profits for only a limited number of years. If we tried to go back very far in time, the data were unavailable (medical malpractice insurance data began to be reported as a separate line only in 1975) or unreliable (during the new physician insurers' initial years). If we focused on data from recent years, the long claims run-off tail made experience incomplete—hence our focus on policy years 1978, 1979, and 1982. For those years, profits exceeded fair premiums or bordered on excess. But we observed only a time in the cycle before the major underwriting losses and premium increases of the mid-1980s. Moreover, profitability dropped over time, a trend that may have continued up to the time of the major premium increases.

On balance, our analysis suggests fluctuations in rates of return rather than persistent excessive returns. Further, it is obvious that there has not been the glut of entry one would expect to see if there were persistent excessive profits.

The rate of return required by suppliers of capital to insurers depends on the perceived riskiness of such investments. There is presently no consensus among the experts about appropriate measures of risk in this context. The debate centers on the extent to which it is possible to diversify away risk through a combination of underwriting and investment portfolio decisions. To the extent that insurers cannot do this, premiums must be commensurately higher.

To gauge insurer profitability, we relied on the CAPM and a related approach. Critics of the CAPM as applied to the insurance industry maintain that it assumes a degree of risk diversification impossible to achieve in practice (Chapters 2 and 9). Although we encourage further research on this issue, we doubt that other approaches would have yielded appreciably different estimates of insurer profitability. A more serious problem has been our inability to observe profitability over an entire insurance cycle. Evidence on profitability from part of the cycle must be interpreted with caution.

Again here, common sense indicates that physician-sponsored insurers are not likely to wring excess profits from their physician policyholders. Judging from available evidence, these insurers have been as profitable as or more profitable than their commercial stock counterparts. Notably, during the 1970s' malpractice crisis, physicians were quick to blame insurers at least in part for their troubles, typically seeking insurance reforms as well as tort reforms. By the 1980s, when physicians had to a great extent become the insurers, they (and their sponsored insurers) focused much more of their attention on (prodefendant) tort reform. In this they were joined by other defendants and insurers, and most tort reforms enacted during the 1980s applied not merely to medical malpractice but also to injuries more generally (Bovbjerg 1989).

Claims Settlement and Other Expense Levels

Insurers' expenses (other than losses) are an important component of insurance pricing. Indeed, from a social perspective, these insurance loadings are the true cost of insurance, not the asset transfer of loss payments. Here malpractice insurance is substantially more costly than other lines of coverage. Its cost of claims settlement is more than double the percentage for automobile passenger liability and Workers' Compensation (Blumstein et al. 1991).

Why loss adjustment expense should be higher in malpractice is not known with certainty. A reasonable working hypothesis is that issues of fact and law are both generally more complex in malpractice than in other lines, requiring more investigation and higher litigation costs should the case go to trial. Moreover, higher severity and high uncertainty with regard to case outcome prompts higher spending on litigation. Potentially, legal reforms to clarify or simplify the law and the process of determining liability and damages could yield a savings here. Most tort reforms to date, however, have instead sought to cut back on remedies rather than to make the exercise of those remedies more certain or cheaper (Bovbjerg 1989).

Insurance Management of Investable Funds

Insurers engage in two interrelated businesses: On the one hand, they predict, assume, and manage risks; on the other, they manage investments—the float of cash received in premiums but not yet paid out in claims or expenses. What can be said of the money-management side of the business? Here we conducted no focused analysis. Trying to draw meaningful comparisons with other money managers would have required still more micro-data and would have greatly expanded the scope of this insurance-focused inquiry. It is also hard to assess the rate of return earned without a benchmark for acceptable levels of risk. Insurers have to set more conservative standards than the typical mutual fund. Our analysis of reserves and investment income (Chapter 9) did reveal that earnings on assets were not out of line with the interest rate on government bonds. Interestingly, the rates for physician-sponsored companies were higher than for commercial stock companies. Perhaps the physician companies were less risk averse. Or perhaps the physician companies, newly incorporated in the high-interest late

1970s, simply obtained a higher-yield portfolio because they had no assets locked in to earlier investments at a lower rate.

Insurance Cycles

As in other lines of property-liability insurance, and to a greater extent than some, there have been cycles in malpractice losses, premiums, and availability. Most emphasis is placed on the underwriting cycle—years of good underwriting experience followed by bad ones. The most persuasive explanation (Chapter 2) is that in good times, perhaps prompted by high rates of return on investments, existing insurers relax their underwriting standards, and more capacity flows into the system from existing insurers and new entrants. Then some unexpected shock, perhaps an increase in claims frequency or severity, leads to an unanticipated major decrease in surplus, followed by rising premiums. Accompanying the increase in premiums is pressure on availability, especially in volatile lines such as medical malpractice insurance. Although several articles have developed theoretical explanations for cycles (Chapter 2), empirical research on this issue is in its infancy. Our own analysis established only that the real interest rate in a year was a statistically significant determinant of the level of premiums in the same year (Chapter 7). Part of the analytical problem is the very long time frame needed for a researcher to observe both the up side and the down side of the same cycle. The topic of insurance cycles is a fertile field for further investigation.

Claims frequency and severity are to a considerable extent beyond insurers' control. Although there is an upward secular trend, there appears to be a claims frequency cycle as well. There was a rise in the early 1970s and again in the 1980s, followed by leveling or actual falling off in the latter parts of the two decades (Chapter 1). It has been hypothesized that cyclical recessions cause rises in claims frequency as out-of-work people make more claims, given their loss of job-related medical insurance and disability coverage as well as their lower time costs. However, in this study's multivariate analysis of claims frequency, done in a parallel fashion to that of premiums (Chapter 7), we were unable to explain such patterns. Most variables did not yield statistically significant results, including the unemployment rate.

Risk Spreading versus Deterrence

On the basis of reasonable availability and not unreasonable profits, and with a low risk of insolvency, medical malpractice insurers are performing reasonably well in their function of assuming and spreading risk. Physicians are thus able to engage in their risky profession without excessively costly coverage. But there is another important and distinct social function that is also meant to be served by malpractice law and arguably by malpractice insurance (and other liability coverage), namely, deterring medical injury. Here the current picture is far less favorable.

In research reported elsewhere (Sloan et al. 1989b), we found that a small percentage of physicians within particular specialties accounted for the majority of medical malpractice losses, as others have reported (e.g., Rolph 1981). Further, the past adverse loss experience of a physician was highly predictive of future adverse experience, a new finding.

There are several nonmutually exclusive explanations of such persistent adverse experience. First, patients of such physicians may be prone to have bad outcomes or to sue their physicians following a bad outcome. Second, such physicians (or their staffs) may have poor interpersonal skills or other predispositions to suit. Third, such physicians may be technically incompetent or accident prone. Although the medical community has emphasized the first factor and plaintiffs' attorneys the latter two, there is insufficient empirical evidence with which to settle this rather fierce debate. The truth probably involves a combination of these factors.

There is some reason for concern that medical malpractice insurers may not be sufficiently vigorous in getting the medical house in order. After all, physician-sponsored insurers by and large arose out of initiatives of organized medicine and represent their physician policyholders, and even commercial insurers to a considerable extent rely on medical society endorsement for marketing. Of course, with regard to truly substandard providers (as opposed to occasional infortuitous accidents), society has delegated primary responsibility to state boards of medical discipline. Judging from the patterns of enforcement of one state licensure board, which had not investigated the records of most of the physicians with appreciable medical malpractice losses, it would appear inadvisable to rely solely on these public agencies to police the profession (Sloan et al. 1989b). Another study reported that the percentage of physicians disciplined by state licensure boards was even less than the percentage of physician policyholders surcharged or dropped by medical malpractice insurers (Schwartz and Mendelson, 1989b).

Yet, our investigation found that malpractice insurers do less than they might to classify risks or to use experience rating to differentiate individual risks within broad classes.[5] It is also notable that the industry has created no institutional mechanism to share information on experience analogous to the Medical Information Bureau of Life Insurance (Mehr and Cammack 1980, 611), although insurers often request information on a new applicant from a former carrier. The new federal data base on malpractice and disciplinary history may change this situation, but it has only just begun.[6] It seems a fair conclusion that, in the main, the industry currently emphasizes risk spreading over risk classification and experience rating (Chapter 8). One may hope that this situation will change as knowledge of risk factors improves and acceptance of insurers' intervention increases.

POLICY IMPLICATIONS

Numerous policy interventions are available to address real or imagined flaws in insurance (and other) markets. But the first question for would-be interventionists should always be: What market or other defect calls for redress? After all, in the words of the sage, "If it ain't broke, don't fix it." From the prior review of our findings, it should be clear that nothing much seems "broke." We find little wrong with the performance of malpractice insurers as insurers; in their actions as physician collectives or managers of injury risks, there is potentially more to complain about. Three types of intervention deserve discussion: insurance regulation, antitrust law, and tort reform.

Insurance Regulation

In view of the current importance of the physician-sponsored insurers, and the possibility of entry of national multiple-line insurers if the physician-sponsored insurers were to raise their premiums above competitive levels for any length of time, the role of insurance regulation as a method of combating monopolistic pricing practices seems to be largely superfluous. But insurance regulation remains widespread, mainly as an aspect of general property-liability insurance regulation, not usually aimed specifically at malpractice. And, as far as medical malpractice is concerned, stronger forms of rate regulation are just as effective in lowering premiums (Chapter 7), although with unknown side effects on insurance availability or insurer solvency.

Since insurer bankruptcy is a possibility, the case for solvency regulation in malpractice is somewhat stronger. Although the insurers maintain that their precautions against insolvency are often greater than those demanded by state regulators, possibly the presence of some state oversight provides a useful reminder. Moreover, ratios of premiums to surpluses are not always the most robust (Chapter 6). Reinsurance, a private mechanism, also helps prevent insolvency. Reinsurance markets are not now regulated; the down side of doing this would probably outweigh any potential benefit. In any event, it would be difficult to regulate a market that is international in scope.

Antitrust Law

At least in a narrow sense, the market for medical malpractice insurance seems to be reasonably competitive. Thus, to this extent, it is probably of little consequence that the McCarran-Ferguson Act exempts the business of medical malpractice insurance, like that of other insurance, from federal antitrust law (the Sherman, Clayton, and Federal Trade Commission Acts). If there is a policy problem for antitrust scrutiny, it lies with a larger set of issues. The latter include the threat of withdrawal of medical malpractice coverage as a tool of organized medicine to discipline maverick physicians or to discipline physicians who work with nonphysician health professionals, such as optometrists, chiropractors, or nurse midwives. Although such potentially anticompetitive practices are sometimes alleged, no one really knows how often they actually occur.

McCarran-Ferguson provides an exception to the antitrust laws for practices that are properly considered to be the business of insurance, which is regulated by state law. The "business of insurance" includes underwriting or spreading of risk (Posner and Easterbrook, 1981, 1042), not broader activities in which insurers might engage (*Group Life and Health Insurance Company* v. *Royal Drug Company* 1979). Thus, denial of coverage to a policyholder who has demonstrated poor technical proficiency may be legitimately considered to be good underwriting practice and hence beyond antitrust scrutiny. In contrast, denial of coverage to a category of physicians who deal with chiropractors would probably not and should not be exempt unless it could be demonstrated statistically that physicians with professional links to chiropractors generate more losses on average. Even then, it should be possible to insure such physicians by assigning them to higher-paying risk categories. Thus, risk classification approaches, where rooted in statistical analysis, should be exempt. In fact, insurers should be encouraged to develop more sophisticated risk classification schemes. Antitrust concern should not be an impediment. Expert regulators might be deemed better able to weigh the adequacy of such statistical evidence than the courts in any event, and they should be concerned that professional goals not be confused with sound insurance practice.

Another potential antitrust concern is market segmentation agreements, such as understandings between adjacent physician companies not to cross territorial boundaries. We have found no evidence of such overt agreements, and border crossing appears to be on the rise.

Tort Reform

Insurers earn their living from risk pooling, and the demand for insurance rises with the amount of expenditure risk. This gives insurers reason to oppose the types of prodefendant tort reforms that state legislatures have enacted since the mid1970s. In another sense, however, since insurers value predictability of losses, they should be expected to favor legislation likely to make losses more predictable.

In practice, physician-sponsored insurers seem to prefer prodefendant tort reforms. Indeed, the PIAA (1989) has developed its own more thorough reform plan, as has the AMA (AMA 1988; Bovbjerg 1990). In contrast, commercial stock companies have tended to take a more agnostic or even a slightly negative position toward such legislation. One reason for the stock companies' moderate opposition appears to be that they fear pressure for premium reductions following enactment of such laws.

On the other hand, the physician-sponsored insurers' position appears to reflect largely their medical organization sponsorship rather than their views as insurers. Such involvement in the political process serves a broader view of policyholder interest than many would prefer.

Insurers indeed have been reluctant to reduce premiums in the face of tort reforms (Chapter 7) even though some reforms can be shown to reduce claims frequency and severity (Danzon 1986; Sloan et al. 1989a). Whether or not there is reason to be concerned about this depends on the extent to which competition (and, in many states, regulation) is sufficient to reduce excess returns in the long run. This appears to us to be the case; yet, any discrepancy between the effects of tort reforms on premiums and losses is certainly worth noting and monitoring.

One's view of the desirability of specific tort reforms should depend on concerns that extend well beyond the medical malpractice insurance industry. Such reforms potentially affect deterrence (some argue that the current system overdeters, while others contend the opposite) as well as victim compensation (the relationship between cost and compensation of injuries is not at all well documented) and larger conceptions of social justice.[7]

THE FUTURE OF THE INDUSTRY

Having described the past organization and performance of the industry, what of the future? We offer three possible scenarios.

Incremental Change

Given current conditions, the recent trends of the malpractice insurance industry look set to continue. The physician-sponsored insurers seem well established, after a rocky start for some. At least in the postcrisis years of the late 1980s, the market was moving to expand capacity rather than contract it, with some signs of more entry of commercial insurers rather than the departures characteristic of earlier years. One open question is whether physician-sponsored malpractice insurers will act more like traditional carriers, expanding beyond their home states and perhaps into other lines as a means of diversifying risk beyond the volatile malpractice line. Our Survey of Medical Malpractice Insurers, however, found that most physician insurer respondents had little or no interest in geographic expansion, especially into states where a sister physician company was located.

Another open question about the players in the market is to what extent other insurance vehicles may supplant traditional individual coverage of physicians, as physician companies have supplanted many former commercial writers. Three possible new contenders have already appeared. One is the physician trust, which in some ways resembles the cooperative coverage of the more elaborate forms of physician-sponsored mutual insurers or reciprocals. A trust's major natural advantages seem to lie in freedom from regulation, strong mutual incentives for controlling claims, and the ability to be very selective about membership. However, trusts also have the defects of their virtues. They may be too narrowly based for long-run actuarial credibility or for spreading risk well, and they may be vulnerable to rate-making errors or other shocks, whose consequences would not be mitigated by high capital reserves or their states' guaranty funds. As yet, trusts have not become major players except in the very-high-claim states of Florida and California.[8] In the mid- to late 1980s, existing trusts seem to have been able to undercut the rates of established insurers at least in those states, although their long-run viability remains untested (Crane 1989b). A very similar quasi-insurance vehicle is the "captive" insurance company, often organized offshore, outside any U.S. jurisdiction (Bawcutt 1982; Tillinghast 1990).

Another contender is the set of little-regulated risk retention groups, encouraged by federal enabling legislation. They, too, seem advantaged by lower regulatory requirements (needing mainly to achieve licensure in a single state to operate nationwide). Early groups seem to be trying to operate in numerous states, focusing on specialty groupings across states and undercutting established companies' rates in some instances (Crane 1990). Risk retention groups seem disadvantaged by their small scale in any one state and by their lack of the financial backstop of strong capitalization or guaranty funds. Given the state-specific nature of litigation, it is also not yet clear how well they are able to defend claims, especially the largest claims, which mature rather slowly.

A third form of organization is the hospital-based physician group. Hospitals (or HMOs or other large existing groupings) have natural advantages of scale and a preexisting community of interest, as well as the ability to monitor the performance of individual practitioners on an ongoing basis. These characteristics make them natural vehicles for insurance grouping. Many teaching hospital centers already insure their own staff physicians (provided that the bulk of their inpatient care is in the institution), and some hospital chains have insured affiliated physicians. No data exist to quantify this development, but in Massachusetts, for example, such plans are the major competitors with the state's JUA for physician coverage. Enhancing intragroup incentives for self-monitoring and avoidance of patient injury would be a benefit of more such plans (Steves 1975). Based on simulations, Sloan and Hassan concluded that, given a sufficient claims history, medical staffs of even some moderately sized hospitals should be able to form their own insuring groups.

Another question about future development is the market shares of physician versus commercial insurers. It would appear that many or most physicians greatly value the stability of a strong physician-sponsored company. Which form of physician sponsorship will prove most appealing in the long run and the extent to which commercial carriers maintain their market share remains to be seen. Several commercial insurers left the medical malpractice insurance market when ex ante returns dipped. A reasonable expectation is that externally imposed constraints on profitability would drive the commercials out. As a parallel, Wedig, et al. (1989) found that not-for-profit hospitals were dominant in states that limited hospital profits.

There is considerable heterogeneity among physicians within existing risk classes with respect to expected loss (Chapter 8; review of studies in Sloan 1990). It is therefore somewhat surprising that many more physicians with favorable anticipated losses have not dropped out of the common pool to form their own insuring groups, especially in the high-premium specialties. Such unraveling of insurance markets has been predicted on the basis of theoretical argument (see, e.g., Rothschild and Stiglitz 1976), and there is some empirical evidence that this has occurred in some other lines of insurance (Priest 1987). The emergence of trusts, risk retention groups, and hospital-based or HMO-based insuring groups of physicians suggests an incipient trend toward unraveling.

Systemic Change Eliminating the Industry

In a larger sense, the medical malpractice insurance industry faces issues not of its own making, and its future is subject to social decisions well beyond the current parameters within which the industry operates. That is, liability insurance is by definition a creature of the liability system; without modern tort law, today's insurance industry would not exist. (A respectable argument can be made that causation also runs the opposite way; that is, that only modern insurers' ability to raise collective funds makes the scope of today's tort law feasible. Certainly, insurance has brought new meaning to the compensatory concern that "deep pockets" bear costs of injury.) And today's approach to liability is by no means immutable. Many are questioning the validity and value of its fault-finding and compensatory approach. Indeed, the existing system of tort law and liability insurance is under attack on many fronts (U.S. Department of Justice 1986; Huber 1988). Tort reform, as prodefendant changes in current legal practice, has become widespread at the state level (Priest 1987; Bovbjerg 1989) and stirs serious federal interest as well, both within the executive branch (e.g., U.S. DHHS 1987) and in Congress, where reform bills are regularly introduced in each session (e.g., Moore and Hoff 1986).

Increasingly, there are proposals to replace tort law completely with another system for allocating responsibility for injury and computing appropriate damages.

Broadly speaking, there are three such possibilities: First is a move to social insurance on a no-fault basis, with public financing (and risk bearing) and administrative decision making. One model is the New Zealand approach, which compensates for all injuries, albeit at far lower levels of damages than are now available in tort (e.g., Litan and Winston 1988, 238–39). The New York Commissioner of Health seems to be advocating such a no-fault system, presumably financed through mandated premiums paid by medical providers rather than through conventional taxation (Harvard Medical Malpractice Study 1990; Winslow 1990). Such a system would almost certainly render the medical malpractice insurance industry, as it exists currently, obsolete, although private entities might play a limited role if certain normally governmental operations were privatized.

Systemic Change with a Role for the Industry

Alternatively, the replacement system could feature public administration but private financing (and risk bearing). The classic model here is Workers' Compensation (e.g., Larson 1988), but any scheme of public, alternative dispute resolution might qualify. The AMA has promoted an administrative alternative to conventional tort litigation (AMA, 1988), as has the PIAA (1989). Under such a public-private system, the private insurance industry would play a significant role in setting and collecting privately determined premiums to support the public awards of compensation.

Moreover, privately funded and run alternatives exist. For example, court-based litigation might be completely replaced by private contracts for different substantive rules and alternative decision-making mechanisms (e.g., Bovbjerg and Havighurst 1986). Different ways of determining responsibility, including various forms of "neo-no-fault" insurance, could play a role here (e.g., O'Connell 1986; Tancredi 1986). In such a system, the expertise and institutional knowledge of today's insurers would remain extremely valuable, although new operating methods would be needed.

Thus, what one expects the malpractice insurance industry to look like is in great measure a function of one's expectations about changing social conceptions of medical (and other) responsibility for injury. Liability insurance in particular is uniquely a creature of social policy—much more so than other forms of casualty coverage, like fire or disaster insurance.

Final Word

The highest calling of the tort system is to deter injury and mitigate its consequences. An efficiently functioning tort system would minimize the sum of three costs: accident, prevention, and administration (Calabresi 1970; Shavell 1987). In contrast, the principal function of insurance is risk pooling. Claims and litigation management are secondary. Insurance can create moral hazard; insured physicians may take fewer precautions. To the extent that they do, imperfectly checked by loss prevention, insurance works at cross purposes with the deterrence objective of the tort system. Thus, efforts at risk management, while still in their infancy, are clearly worth encouraging.

Further, largely through no fault of the insurers, only about half of the premium dollar goes to claimants.[9] The malpractice insurance industry would greatly improve its social utility if it were able to move more of its talents from managing claims and litigation to managing injuries and rehabilitation, possibly along the lines two of us (Bovbjerg and Sloan) have recently suggested elsewhere (Blumstein et al. 1991). Such changes will require legislation, as well as a willingness on the part of insurers to accept such broadened responsibilities.

NOTES

1. There are occasional reports of particular physicians surprised at their need to have tail coverage or caught unawares when a claims-made insurer left a state (Trepman 1989; Crane 1990). On the other hand, one insurer told us that it is not necessary to purchase tail coverage if the insured remains in-state.
2. As noted in Chapter 1, it is problematic whether a "crisis" has existed at any particular time. Here, too, we spare our readers any further use of the quotation marks.
3. One actuarial consultant, using reasonable assumptions, has calculated that a company needs to collect over half again more in premiums each year than it pays out in claims. Personal communication from James O. Wood, of Tillinghast, a Towers-Perrin company.
4. Quasi-populist complaints about profiteering seldom have empirical content. It is plausible that popular misunderstanding about the extent of profits is conditioned by the highly tangible image of insurers' office towers and by the tendency of the press to report on profits as a percentage change from a prior period rather than as a percentage of revenues or return on equity.
5. Some would disagree. Schwartz and Mendelson (1989b) estimated that physician-sponsored insurers each year drop 0.66 percent of their insureds for negligence-prone behavior, restrict the practices of 0.7 percent of active policyholders, and surcharge (or subject to deductibles) an additional 1.8 percent of policyholders—thus in some fashion sanctioning 3.2 percent of insured physicians, those found somehow substandard. This glass can be seen as 3 percent full or a much larger percentage empty, depending on one's perspective.
6. The data bank is required by the federal Health Quality Improvement Act of 1986, P.L. 99–660, codified as 42 U.S.C. sections 11,101 and 11,111–11,152, with subsequent technical modifications detailed by Bovbjerg (1989, 537–38). This enterprise actually started in late 1990.
7. Two of us have argued elsewhere in favor of certain reforms (Bovbjerg et al. 1989; Blumstein et al. 1991).
8. In Colorado, the physician-sponsored insurer changed from a trust to a mutual. It started as a trust for lack of initial capital. When Hartford Insurance Company left the state, the trust was reactivated to provide insurance for those policyholders formerly with Hartford to avoid straining the mutual's surplus.
9. There is no direct evidence on this for medical malpractice. The statement is for personal injuries more generally (see Kakalik and Pace 1986).

REFERENCES

Abraham, Kenneth S., *Distributing Risk: Insurance, Legal Theory, and Public Policy*. New Haven, CT: Yale University Press, 1986.

Aiuppa, Thomas A., and James S. Trieschmann, "An Empirical Analysis of the Magnitude and Accuracy of Incurred-But-Not-Reported Reserves," *The Journal of Risk and Insurance*, Vol. 54, No. 1, March 1987, pp. 110–18.

Alliance of American Insurers, *1986 Financial Condition of Medical Malpractice JUAs*. Schaumburg, IL: 1988.

A.M. Best, *Best's Aggregates and Averages*. Oldwich, NJ: A.M. Best Company, 1987.

A.M. Best, *Best's Reproduction of Convention Statements*. Oldwich, NJ: A.M Best Company, 1979–87.

A.M. Best, *Best's Insurance Reports—Property/Casualty*. Oldwich, NJ: A.M. Best Company, 1979–87.

A.M. Best, *Best's Casualty Loss Reserve Development*. Oldwich, NJ: A.M. Best Company, 1978–87.

American Medical Association, *A Proposed Alternative to the Civil Justice System for Resolving Medical Liability Disputes: A Fault-Based, Administrative System*. Chicago: AMA, Specialty Society Medical Liability Project, January 1988.

American Medical Association, *Trends in Health Care*. Chicago: AMA, 1987.

American Medical Association, *Physician Characteristics and Distribution in the U.S*. Chicago: AMA, 1986.

American Medical Association, *Professional Liability in the '80s, Report 3*. Chicago: AMA, March 1985.

American Medical Association, *Professional Liability in the '80s, Report 1*. Chicago: AMA, October, 1984a.

American Medical Association, *Professional Liability in the '80s, Report 2*. Chicago: AMA, November, 1984b.

American Medical Association, *Socioeconomic Characteristics of Medical Practice, 1984*. Chicago: AMA, 1984c.

American Medical Association, "Opinion Survey on Medical Malpractice," *Journal of the American Medical Association*, Vol. 164, No. 14, 1957, pp. 1583–94.

Anderson, Dan R., "Effects of Under- and Overvaluations in Loss Reserves," *The Journal of Risk and Insurance*, Vol. XXXVIII, No. 4, December 1971, pp. 585–600.

Ansley, Craig F., "Automobile Liability Insurance Reserve Adequacy and the Effect on Inflation," *CPCU Journal*, Vol. 31, June 1979, pp. 105–12.

Auerbach, Alan J., *The Taxation of Capital Income*. Cambridge, MA: Harvard University Press, 1983.

Aug, James S., and Tsong-Yue Lai, "Insurance Premium Pricing and Ratemaking in Competitive Insurance and Capital Asset Markets," *The Journal of Risk and Insurance*, Vol. LIV, No. 4, December 1987, pp. 767–79.

Bachman, James E., *Capitalization Requirements for Multiple Line Property-Liability Insurance Companies*. Philadelphia: University of Pennsylvania, The Wharton School, Huebner Foundation Monograph 6, 1978.

Balcarek, Rafal J., "Loss Reserve Deficiencies and Underwriting Results," *Best's Review* (*Property/Casualty Edition*), Vol. 76, July 1975, pp. 21–22, 88.

Bawcutt, Paul A., *Captive Insurance Companies: Establishment, Operation, and Management.* Homewood, IL: Dow Jones-Irwin, 1982.

Bernstein, Marver H., *Regulating Business by Independent Commission.* Princeton, NJ: Princeton University Press, 1955.

Biger, Nahum, and Yehuda Kahane, "Risk Considerations in Insurance Ratemaking," *The Journal of Risk and Insurance,* Vol. XLV, No. 1, March 1978, pp. 121–32.

Blumstein, James F., Randall R. Bovbjerg, and Frank A. Sloan, "Developing Better Tools for Assessing Damages for Personal Injuries," *Yale Journal on Regulation*, Vol. 8, No. 1, Winter 1991, pp. 149–86.

Borch, Karl, *The Mathematical Theory of Insurance.* Lexington, MA: D.C. Heath and Co., 1974.

Bovbjerg, Randall R., "Reforming a Proposed Tort Reform: Improving on the American Medical Association's Proposed Administrative Tribunal for Medical Malpractice," *Courts, Health Science and the Law*, Vol. 1, No. 1, July 1990, pp. 19–28.

Bovbjerg, Randall R., "Legislation on Medical Malpractice: Further Developments and a Preliminary Report Card," *U.C. Davis Law Review*, Vol. 22, No. 2, Winter 1989, pp. 499–556.

Bovbjerg, Randall R., "Medical Malpractice on Trial: Quality of Care Is the Most Important Standard," *Journal of Law and Contemporary Problems*, Vol. 49, No. 2, Spring 1986, pp. 321–48.

Bovbjerg, Randall R., and Clark C. Havighurst (eds.), "Medical Malpractice: Can the Private Sector Find Relief?" *Law and Contemporary Problems*, Vol. 49, No. 2, Spring 1986, pp. 1–348.

Bovbjerg, Randall R., Frank A. Sloan, and James F. Blumstein, "Valuing Life and Limb in Tort: Scheduling 'Pain and Suffering'," *Northwestern University Law Review*, Vol. 83, No. 4, Summer 1989, pp. 908–76.

Bovbjerg, Randall R., Frank A. Sloan, Avi Dor, and Chee Ruey Hsieh, "Juries and Justice: Are Malpractice and Other Personal Injuries Created Equal?", *Law and Contemporary Problems* (forthcoming) Vol. 53, No. 4, Fall 1990 no page #s yet.

Brainard, Calvin H., and Joel B. Dirlam, "Antitrust, Regulation, and the Insurance Industry: A Study in Polarity," *The Antitrust Bulletin*, Vol. 11, Nos. 1 and 2, January–April 1966, pp. 235–316.

Brand, Max, *Young Doctor Kildare*. New York: Grosset, 1941.

Brook, Robert H., Rudolf L. Brutoco, and Kathleen N. Williams, "The Relationship between Medical Malpractice and Quality of Care," *Duke Law Journal*, Vol. 6, 1975, pp. 1197–1232.

Calabresi, Guido, *The Cost of Accidents*. New Haven, CT: Yale University Press, 1970.

Carter, R. L., *Reinsurance*, 2nd edition. London: Kluwer Publishing Limited, 1983.

Commerce Clearing House, *State Tax Handbook*. Chicago: Commerce Clearing House, October 1, 1987.

Cooil, Bruce, "Using Medical Malpractice Data to Model the Frequency of Claims," unpublished manuscript, 1989.

Cooper, Robert W., *Investment Return and Property-Liability Insurance Ratemaking*. Homewood, IL: Richard D. Irwin, Inc., 1974.

Copeland, Thomas E., and J. Fred Weston, *Financial Theory and Corporate Policy*. Reading, MA: Addison-Wesley Pub. Co., 1983.

Corcoran, James P., *A Balanced Prescription for Change*, Report of the New York State Insurance Department, State of New York Insurance Department, 1988.

Cox, Larry A., and Gary L. Griepentrog, "Systematic Risk, Unsystematic Risk, and Property-

Liability Rate Regulation," *The Journal of Risk and Insurance*, Vol. LV, No. 4, December 1988, pp. 606–27.

Crane, Mark, "When Their Malpractice Insurer Lied, These Doctors Struck Back," *Medical Economics*, Vol. 66, No. 6, March 19, 1990, pp. 72–89.

Crane, Mark, "Risk Retention Insurance Is Cheap, But Is It Any Good?," *Medical Economics*, Vol. 66, No. 19, October 2, 1989a, pp. 23–32.

Crane, Mark, "How Much of a Gamble Is This Malpractice Coverage?", *Medical Economics*, Vol. 66, No. 24, December 4, 1989b, pp. 56–61.

Crane, Mark, "Nobody's Laughing at "Bedpan Mutuals" Now," *Medical Economics*, April 18, 1988, pp. 121–43.

Crenshaw, Albert B., "Insurance Industry Sees Curbs; House Panel Votes to Trim Exemption," *Washington Post*, June 21, 1990, Sect. C., p. 1, Col. 6.

Cummins, J. David, and Scott E. Harrington, "The Relationship Between Risk and Return: Evidence for Property-Liability Insurance Stocks," *The Journal of Risk and Insurance*, Vol. LV, No. 1, March 1988, pp. 15–31.

Cummins, J. David, and Scott E. Harrington, "Property-Liability Insurance Regulation: Estimation of Underwriting Betas Using Quarterly Profit Data," *The Journal of Risk and Insurance*, Vol. LII, No. 1, March 1985, pp. 16–43.

Cummins, J. David, Scott Harrington, and B. Smith, "An Analysis of the Impact of Alternative Rate Regulatory Systems on Underwriting Profitability in Property-Liability Insurance." Paper presented at the meetings of the American Risk and Insurance Association, Chicago, 1980.

Cummins, J. David, and J. Francois Outreville, "An International Analysis of Underwriting Cycles in Property-Liability Insurance," *The Journal of Risk and Insurance*, Vol. LIV, No. 2, June 1987, pp. 246–62.

D'Arcy, Stephen P., and Neil A. Doherty, *The Financial Theory of Pricing Property-Liability Insurance Contracts*. Homewood, IL: Richard D. Irwin, 1987.

Danzon, Patricia M., "Trends in Malpractice and Its Effects on Physician Practice," unpublished manuscript, 1989.

Danzon, Patricia M., "The Frequency and Severity of Medical Malpractice Claims: New Evidence," *Law and Contemporary Problems*, Vol. 49, No. 2, 1986, pp. 57–84.

Danzon, Patricia M., *Medical Malpractice: Theory, Evidence, and Public Policy*. Cambridge, MA: Harvard University Press, 1985.

Danzon, Patricia M., *The Medical Malpractice Insurance Crisis Revisited: Causes and Solutions*. Stanford, CA: The Hoover Institution. Duplicated, no. E-83-11, 1983a.

Danzon, Patricia M., "Rating Bureaus in U.S. Property Liability Insurance Markets: Anti- or Pro-Competitive?," *The Geneva Papers on Risk and Insurance*, Vol. 8, No. 29, October 1983b, pp. 371–402.

Danzon, Patricia M., *The Frequency and Severity of Medical Malpractice Claims*. No. R-2870-ICJ/HCFA DHEW. Santa Monica, CA: The Rand Corporation, 1982.

Davis, Kenneth Culp, *Administrative Law*. St. Paul, MN: West Publishing Co., 1951.

Dobbyn, J. F., *Dobbyn's Insurance Law in a Nutshell*. St. Paul, MN: West Publishing Co., 1981.

Doherty, Neil A., and S. M. Tinic, "Reinsurance Under Conditions of Capital Market Equilibrium: A Note," *The Journal of Finance*, Vol. XXXVI, No. 4, September 1981, pp. 949–53.

Drimmer, Jack, "My Malpractice Ordeal Is Over—After Only 26 Years," *Medical Economics*, Vol. 66, No. 19, October 2, 1989, pp. 50–53.

Dunningham, Anthony W., and Robin Lane, "Malpractice—The Illusory Crisis," *Florida Bar Journal*, Vol. 54, No. 2, February 1980, pp. 114–21.

Ellis, Randall P., Cynthia L. Gallup, and Thomas G. McGuire, "Should Medical Professional

Liability Insurance Be Experience Rated?", *The Journal of Risk and Insurance*, Vol. 57, No. 1, March 1990, pp. 66–78.

Fairley, William B., "Investment Income and Profit Margin in Property-Liability Insurance: Theory and Empirical Results," *The Bell Journal of Economics*, Vol. 10, No. 1, Spring 1979, pp. 192–210.

Fama, Eugene F., and Michael C. Jensen, "Separation of Ownership and Control," *Journal of Law and Economics*, Vol. XXVI, June 1983a, pp. 301–25.

Fama, Eugene F., and Michael C. Jensen, "Agency Problems and Residual Claims," *Journal of Law and Economics*, Vol. XXVI, June 1983b, pp. 327–49.

Fama, Eugene F., and James D. MacBeth, "Risk, Return, and Equilibrium: Some Empirical Tests," *Journal of Political Economy*, Vol. 81, No. 3, May-June 1973, pp. 607–36.

Feagles, Prentiss E., Betsy I. Carter, James A. Davids, Neal E. Tackabery, and Clay B. Tousey, Jr., "An Analysis of State Legislative Responses to the Medical Malpractice Crisis," *Duke Law Journal*, Vol. 6, January 1975, pp. 1417–68.

Finsinger, Jörg, and Mark V. Pauly, *The Economics of Insurance Regulation: A Cross National Study*. New York: St. Martin's Press, 1986, p. 2.

Fischer, Gerald C., *American Banking Structure*. New York: Columbia University Press, 1968.

Foster, George F., "Valuation Parameters of Property-Liability Companies," *Journal of Finance*, Vol. 32, No. 3, June 1977, pp. 823–35.

Freedman, Marian, "When Reinsurers Renege," *Best's Review*, Vol. 87, No. 12, April 1987, pp. 30–36, 108.

Friendly, Henry J., *The Federal Administrative Agencies: The Need for Newer Definitions of Standards*. Cambridge, MA: Harvard University Press, 1962.

German Alliance Insurance Company v. *Lewis*, 233 U.S. 389 (1914).

Goddard, Thomas, *The American Medical Association Is Wrong—There Is No Medical Malpractice Insurance Crisis*. Washington, DC: Association of Trial Lawyers of America, unpublished policy paper, 1985.

Goovaerts, M. J., F. De Vylder, and J. Haezendonck, *Insurance Premiums Theory and Applications*. Amsterdam: North Holland Publishing Co., 1984.

Grace, Elizabeth V., "Property-Liability Insurer Reserve Errors: A Theoretical and Empirical Analysis," *The Journal of Risk and Insurance*, Vol. LVIII, No. 1, March 1990, pp. 28–46.

Greenspan, Nancy T., "A Descriptive Analysis of Medical Malpractice Insurance Premiums, 1974–77," *Health Care Financing Review*, Vol. 1, No. 2, Fall 1979, pp. 65–71.

Group Life and Health Insurance Company v. *Royal Drug Company*, 440 U.S. 205 (U.S. Supreme Court decision), 1979.

Hafling, David N., "Incurred But Not Reported Expenses," *CPCU Journal*, Vol. 34, No. 1, March 1981, pp. 54–57.

Hamilton, James D., "Uncovering Financial Market Expectations of Inflation," *Journal of Political Economy*, Vol. 93, No. 6, December 1985, pp. 1224–41.

Hansmann, Henry, "The Organization of Insurance Companies: Mutual versus Stock," *Journal of Law, Economics, and Organization*, Vol. 1, No. 1, Fall 1985, pp. 125–53.

Harrington, Scott, "The Impact of Rate Regulation on Prices and Underwriting Results in the Property-Liability Insurance Industry: A Survey," *The Journal of Risk and Insurance*, Vol. 11, No. 4, December 1984, pp. 577–623.

Harrington, Scott, and Robert E. Litan, "Causes of the Liability Insurance Crisis," *Science*, Vol. 239, No. 4841, February 12, 1988, pp. 737–41.

Harvard Medical Practice Study, *Patients, Doctors, and Lawyers: Medical Injury, Malpractice Litigation, and Patient Compensation in New York*, Report of the Harvard Medical Malpractice Study. Boston: Harvard University, March 1990.

Hensler, Deborah R., and Mary E. Vaiana, James S. Kakalik, and Mark A. Peterson, *Trends in*

Tort Litigation: The Story Behind the Statistics. No. R-3583-ICJ. Santa Monica, CA: The Rand Corporation, 1987.

Hiebert, L. Dean, "Regulation and Price Rigidity in the Property-Liability Insurance Industry," *The Journal of Risk and Insurance*, Vol. XLIII, No. 1, 1976, pp. 129–38.

Hill, Raymond D., "Profit Regulation in Property Liability Insurance," *Bell Journal of Economics*, Vol. 10, No. 1, 1979, pp. 172–91.

Hill, Raymond D., and Franco Modigliani, "The Massachusetts Model of Profit Regulation in Nonlife Insurance: An Appraisal and Extensions," in J. David Cummins and Scott A. Harrington (eds.), *Fair Rate of Return in Property-Liability Insurance*. Boston: Kluwer-Nijhoff Publishing, 1987, pp. 27–53.

Hoerger, Thomas J., Frank A. Sloan, and Mahmud Hassan, "Loss Volatility, Bankruptcy, and Insurer Demand for Reinsurance," *Journal of Risk and Uncertainty*, Vol. 3, No. 3, 1990, pp. 221–45.

Holoweiko, Mark, "Is This the World Record for Malpractice Claims?", *Medical Economics*, Vol. 65, No. 8, April 17, 1989, pp. 192–211.

Holoweiko, Mark, "Which Practice Expenses Are Biting Deepest into Earnings?", *Medical Economics*, Vol. 65, No. 22, November 7, 1988, pp. 162–84.

Hossack, I. B., J. H. Pollard, and B. Zehnwirth, *Introductory Statistics with Applications in General Insurance*. Cambridge: Cambridge University Press, 1983.

Huber, Peter W., *Liability: The Legal Revolution and Its Consequences*. New York: Basic Books, 1988.

Institute of Medicine, *Medical Professional Liability and the Delivery of Obstetrical Care*, Volume 1. Washington, DC: National Academy Press, 1989a.

Institute of Medicine, *Medical Professional Liability and the Delivery of Obstetrical Care*, Volume 2. Washington, DC: National Academy Press, 1989b.

Insurance Information Institute, *1986–87 Property/Casualty Fact Book*. New York: Insurance Information Institute, 1987.

Ippolito, Richard A., "The Effects of Price Regulation in the Automobile Insurance Industry," *Journal of Law and Economics*, Vol. 22, No. 1, April 1979, pp. 55–89.

Jensen, Michael C., and William H. Meckling, "Theory of the Firm: Managerial Behavior, Agency Costs and Ownership Structure," *Journal of Financial Economics*, Vol. 3, October 1976, pp. 305–60.

Johnson, Richard E., "Reinsurance: Theory, the New Applications, and the Future," *The Journal of Risk and Insurance*, Vol. XLIV, No. 1, March 1977, pp. 55–66.

Joskow, Paul L., "Cartels, Competition and Regulation in the Property-Liability Insurance Industry," *Bell Journal of Economics*, Vol. 4, No. 2, Autumn 1973, pp. 375–427.

Kakalik, James S., and Nicholas M. Pace, *Costs and Compensation Paid in Tort Litigation*. Santa Monica, CA: The Rand Corporation, 1986.

Keeton, Robert E., *Keeton's Basic Text on Insurance Law*. St. Paul, MN: West Publishing Co., 1971.

Keeton, W. Page, Dan B. Dobbs, Robert E. Keeton, and David G. Owen, *Prosser and Keeton on the Law of Torts*, 5th edition. St. Paul, MN: West Publishing Co., 1984.

Kendall, Mark, and John Haldi, "The Medical Malpractice Insurance Market," in U.S. Department of Health, Education, and Welfare, *Report of the Secretary's Commission on Medical Malpractice* and *Appendix*. Pub. No. (OS) 73-88. Washington, DC: DHEW, 1973, pp. 494–608.

Kenney, Roger K., *1986 Financial Condition of Medical Malpractice JUAs*. Schaumburg, IL: Alliance of American Insurers, 1988.

Kimball, Spencer L., "The Purposes of Insurance Regulation: A Preliminary Inquiry Into the Theory of Insurance Law," *Minnesota Law Review*, Vol. 45, No. 4, March 1961, pp. 471–524.

Kimball, Spencer L., and Herbert S. Denenberg, *Insurance, Government, and Social Policy*. Homewood, IL: Richard D. Irwin, Inc., 1969.

Klerman, Lorraine V., and Sarah H. Scholle, "The Actual and Potential Impact of Medical Liability Issues on Access to Maternity Care," unpublished manuscript prepared for the Institute of Medicine, Washington, DC, 1988.

Kolbe, A. Lawrence, James A. Read, and George R. Hall, *The Cost of Capital: Estimating the Rate of Return for Public Utilities*. Cambridge, MA: MIT Press, 1984.

Landes, William M., and Richard A. Posner, "Market Power in Antitrust Cases," *Harvard Law Review*, Vol. 94, No. 5, March 1981, pp. 937–96.

Larson, Arthur, *The Law of Workmen's Compensation*, 1988 Cumulative Supplement. New York: Matthew Bender, 1988.

Law, Sylvia, and Steven Polan, *Pain and Profit: The Politics of Malpractice*. New York: Harper & Row, 1978.

Lemaire, Jean, "A Comparative Analysis of Most European and Japanese Bonus-Malus Systems," *The Journal of Risk and Insurance*, Vol. 55, No. 4, December 1988, pp. 660–81.

Lemaire, Jean, *Automobile Insurance: Actuarial Models*. Boston: Kluwer-Nijhoff Publishing, 1985.

Levy, Haim, "The CAPM and Beta in an Imperfect Market," *Journal of Portfolio Management*, Vol. 6, No. 2, Winter 1980, pp. 5–11.

Levy, Haim, "Equilibrium in an Imperfect Market: A Constraint on the Number of Securities in the Portfolio," *American Economic Review*, Vol. 68, No. 4, September 1978, pp. 643–58.

Litan, Robert E., and Clifford Winston (eds.), *Liability: Perspectives and Policy*. Washington, DC: The Brookings Institution, 1988, pp. 223–41.

Loomis, Carol J., "An Accident Report on Geico," *Fortune*, Vol. 43, June 1976, pp. 126–31, 192–96.

Manne, Henry G. *Medical Malpractice Policy Guidebook*. Unpublished report for the Florida Medical Association, 1985.

Mayers, David, and Clifford W. Smith, Jr., *Ownership Structure Across Lines of Property-Casualty Insurance*. Working Paper Series WPS 87-11. Columbus: Ohio State University, College of Business, January 1987.

Mayers, David, and Clifford W. Smith, Jr., "Contractual Provisions, Organizational Structure, and Conflict Control in Insurance Markets," *Journal of Business*, Vol. 54, No. 3, July 1981, pp. 407–34.

McCarran-Ferguson Act, 1945. Public Law No. CH.20, 59 Stat. 33, 15 U.S. Code sects. 1011–15.

Medical Malpractice Joint Underwriting Association of Massachusetts, "The Medical Malpractice Joint Underwriting Association of Massachusetts Experience Review Plan," unpublished document dated May 18, 1990.

Mehr, Robert I., and Emerson Cammack, *Principles of Insurance*. Homewood IL: Richard D. Irwin, Inc., 1980.

Miles, Robert H., and Arvind Bhambri, *The Regulatory Executives*. Beverly Hills, CA: Sage Publications, 1983.

Mills, Don Harper, and Orley Lindgren, *Physician Malpractice Profiles as Indicators of Quality*. Washington, DC: Office of Technology Assessment, duplicated draft, November 16, 1987.

Moore, W. Henson, and John S. Hoff, "H.R. 3084: A More Rational Compensation System for Medical Malpractice," *Law and Contemporary Problems*, Vol. 49, No. 2, Spring 1986, pp. 118–24.

Munch, Patricia, and Dennis E. Smallwood, "Solvency Regulation in the Property-Liability Insurance Industry: Empirical Evidence," *The Bell Journal of Economics*, Vol. 11, No. 1, Spring 1980, pp. 261–79.

Myers, Stewart C., "The Capital Structure Puzzle," *Journal of Finance*, Vol. 39, July, No. 3, 1984, pp. 575–92.

Myers, Stewart C., and Richard A. Cohn, "A Discounted Cash Flow Approach to Property-Liability Insurance Rate Regulation," in J. David Cummins and Scott A. Harrington (eds.), *Fair Rate of Return in Property-Liability Insurance*. Boston: Kluwer-Nijhoff Publishing, 1987, pp. 55–78.

National Association of Insurance Commissioners, *Report of the Advisory Committee to the NAIC Task Force on Profitability and Investment Income*. Milwaukee, WI: NAIC, 1987.

National Association of Insurance Commissioners, *Market Share Report—Medical Malpractice, 1986*. Milwaukee, WI: NAIC, 1986.

National Association of Insurance Commissioners, *Model Act*. Milwaukee, WI: NAIC, 1985.

National Association of Insurance Commissioners, *Report of the Advisory Committee to the NAIC Task Force on Profitability and Investment Income*. Milwaukee, WI: NAIC, January 1983.

National Association of Insurance Commissioners, *Malpractice Claims, 1975–1978*. Milwaukee, WI: NAIC, 1980.

National Association of Insurance Commissioners, *Monitoring Competition: A Means of Regulating the Property and Liability Insurance Business*. Milwaukee, WI: NAIC, unpublished staff study, 1974.

New York State Department of Health, *Monitoring Health Care Quality: Malpractice, Misconduct, Quality Assurance*. New York: March 1988.

Nye, Blaine F., and Alfred E. Hofflander, "Experience Rating in Medical Professional Liability Insurance," *The Journal of Risk and Insurance*, Vol. LV, No. 1, March 1988, pp. 150–57.

Nye, Blaine F., and Alfred E. Hofflander, "Economics of Oligopoly: Medical Malpractice Insurance as a Classic Illustration," *The Journal of Risk and Insurance*, Vol. LIV, No. 3, September 1987, pp. 502–19.

O'Connell, Jeffrey, "Neo-No-Fault Remedies for Medical Injuries: Coordinated Statutory and Contractual Alternatives," *Law and Contemporary Problems*, Vol. 49, No. 2, Spring 1986, pp. 125–42.

Opinion Research Corporation, *Professional Liability and Its Effects: Report of a 1987 Survey of ACOG's Membership*. Prepared for the American College of Obstetricians and Gynecologists. Washington, DC: ORC, March 1988.

Owens, Arthur, "Doctor-Owned Malpractice Insurers: Growing Pains or Death Throes?", *Medical Economics*, Vol. 58, No. 17, August 24, 1981, pp. 27–36.

Palfrey, Thomas R., and Chester S. Spatt, *The Rand Journal of Economics*, Vol. 16, No. 3, Autumn 1985, pp. 356–67.

Patterson, Edwin W., *The Insurance Commissioner in the United States: Study in Law and Practice*. Cambridge, MA: Harvard University Press, 1927.

Paul v. *Virginia*, 1868. 8 Wall 168, 75 U.S. 168.

Pauly, Mark V., Howard Kunreuther, and Paul Kleindorfer, "Regulation and Quality Competition in the U.S. Insurance Industry," in Jörg Finsinger and Mark V. Pauly (eds.), *The Economics of Insurance Regulation: A Cross National Study*. New York: St. Martin's Press, 1986, pp. 65–112.

Petersen, W., *Economic Determinants of Legislation. Regulatory Behavior and Market Performance in the Automobile Insurance Industry*. Ph.D. Dissertation, Harvard University, 1981.

Philbrick, Stephen W., "An Examination of Credibility Concepts," paper presented at meetings of the Casualty Actuarial Society, November 1981.

Phillips, Almarin (ed.), *Promoting Competition in Regulated Markets*. Washington, DC: The Brookings Institution, 1975.

Physician Insurers Association of America, *A Comprehensive Review of Alternatives to the Present System of Resolving Medical Liability Claims*. Lawrenceville, NJ: PIAA, 1989.

Physician Insurers Association of America, *1987 Membership Directory*. Lawrenceville, NJ: PIAA, 1987.

Posner, James R., "Trends in Medical Malpractice Insurance, 1970–1985," *Law and Contemporary Problems*, Vol. 49, No. 2, Spring 1986, pp. 37–56.

Posner, Richard A., and Frank H. Easterbrook, *Antitrust: Cases, Economic Notes, and Other Materials*, 2nd edition. St. Paul, MN: West Publishing Co., 1981.

Priest, George, "The Current Insurance Crisis and Modern Tort Law," *Yale Law Journal*, Vol. 96, No. 7, June 1987, pp. 1521–90.

Public Law 97-45. 1981. The Product Liability Risk Retention Act codified at 42 U.S.C. sect. 3901 et seq. (1982).

Public Law 99-563, 100 Stat. 3170. 1986. The Risk Retention Amendments of 1986, codified at 15 U.S.C. sect. 3901 et seq. (Supp. 1986).

Public Law 99-660, T. IV, 100 Stat. 3784. 1986. The Health Care Quality Improvement Act of 1986, codified at 42 U.S.C. sects. 11,101, 11,111–11,152 (1988).

Purdy, Roger J., "A Survey of Professional Liability Coverage in 1982," *Socioeconomic Report*, Vol. 22, No. 5, 1982, pp. 1–12 (California Medical Society, July-August).

Reynolds, Roger A., John A. Rizzo, and Martin L. Gonzalez, "The Cost of Medical Professional Liability," *Journal of the American Medical Association*, Vol. 257, No. 20, May 22–29, 1987, pp. 2776–81.

Robinson, Glen O., "The Medical Malpractice Crisis of the 1970's: A Retrospective," *Law and Contemporary Problems*, Vol. 49, No. 2, Spring 1986, pp. 5–36.

Roddis, Richard S. L., and Richard E. Stewart, "The Insurance of Medical Losses," *Duke Law Journal*, Vol. 1975, No. 6, January 1975, pp. 1282–1303.

Rolph, John E., "Some Statistical Evidence on Merit Rating in Medical Malpractice Insurance," *The Journal of Risk and Insurance*, Vol. XLVIII, No. 2, June 1981, pp. 247–60.

Rosenberg, Charlotte L., "Doctor-Owned Malpractice Carriers: Who's Winning, Who's Losing," *Medical Economics*, Vol. 61, No. 20, October 1, 1984, pp. 62–71.

Rothschild, Michael, and Joseph Stiglitz, "Equilibrium in Competitive Insurance Markets: An Essay on the Economics of Imperfect Information," *Quarterly Journal of Economics*, Vol. 90, No. 4, November 1976, pp. 629–49.

Samprone, Joseph Carl, Jr., *State Regulation of the Property-Liability Insurance Industry*. Unpublished Ph.D. dissertation. Santa Barbara, CA: University of California, Santa Barbara, 1975.

Sargent, Thomas, *Dynamic Macroeconomic Analysis* Cambridge, MA: Harvard University Press, 1987.

Scherer, F. M., *Industrial Market Structure and Economic Performance*. Chicago: Rand McNally, 1980.

Schiffman, J. R., "Medical Malpractice Insurance Rates Fall," *The Wall Street Journal*, April 28, 1989, p. B1.

Schlesinger, Harris, and Emilio Venezian, "Insurance Markets with Loss-Prevention Activity: Profits, Market Structure, and Consumer Welfare," *Rand Journal of Economics*, Vol. 17, No. 2, Summer 1986, pp. 227–38.

Schwartz, William B., and Daniel N. Mendelson, "Physicians Who Have Lost Their Malpractice Insurance: Their Demographic Characteristics and the Surplus-Lines Companies That Insure Them," *Journal of the American Medical Association*, Vol. 262, No. 10, 1989a, pp. 1335–41.

Schwartz, William B., and Daniel N. Mendelson, "The Role of Physician-Owned Insurance Companies in the Detection and Deterrence of Negligence," *Journal of the American Medical Association*, Vol. 262, No. 10, 1989b, pp. 1342–46.

Shanley, Michael G., and Mark A. Peterson, *Comparative Justice: Civil Jury Verdicts in San Francisco and Cook Counties, 1959–1980*. No. R-3006-ICJ. Santa Monica, CA: The Rand Corporation, 1983.

Shavell, Steven, *Economic Analysis of Accident Law*. Cambridge, MA: Harvard University Press, 1987.

Shayer, Natalie, "Driver Classification in Automobile Insurance," in Massachusetts Division of Insurance, *Automobile Insurance Risk Classification: Equity and Accuracy*. Boston: Division of Insurance, Commonwealth of Massachusetts, 1978, pp. 1–24.

Simon, LeRoy J., "The Excess of Loss Treaty in Casualty Insurance," in Robert W. Strain (ed.), *Reinsurance*. New York: College of Insurance, 1980, pp. 214–51.

Sloan, Frank A., "Experience Rating: Does It Make Sense for Medical Malpractice Insurance?" *American Economic Review*, Vol. 80, No. 2, May 1990, pp. 128–33.

Sloan, Frank A., "State Responses to the Medical Malpractice Insurance 'Crisis' of the 1970s: An Empirical Assessment," *Journal of Health Politics, Policy, and Law*, Vol. 9, No. 4, 1985, pp. 629–46.

Sloan, Frank A., "Physicians and Hospitals: Implications of an Expanding Physician Supply," in Eli Ginzberg and Miriam Ostow (eds.), *The Coming Physician Surplus*. Totowa, NJ: Rowman and Allanheld, 1984, pp. 99–116.

Sloan, Frank A., "Effects of Health Insurance on Physicians' Fees," *Journal of Human Resources*, Vol. 17, No. 4, Fall 1982, pp. 533–57.

Sloan, Frank A., and Judith K. Bentkover, *Access to Physicians and the U.S. Economy*. Lexington, MA: D.C. Heath, 1979.

Sloan, Frank A., and Randall R. Bovbjerg, *Medical Malpractice: Crises, Response and Effects*. Research Bulletin. Washington, DC: Health Insurance Association of America, May 1989.

Sloan, Frank A., and Mahmud Hassan, "Equity and Accuracy in Medical Malpractice Insurance Pricing," *Journal of Health Economics*, Vol. 9, No. 3, November 1990, pp. 289–319.

Sloan, Frank A., and Chee Ruey Hsieh, "Variability in Medical Malpractice Payments: Is the Compensation Fair?", *Law and Society Review*, Vol. 24, No. 4, 1990, pp. 601–650.

Sloan, Frank A., Paula M. Mergenhagen, and Randall R. Bovbjerg, "Effects of Tort Reform on the Value of Closed Medical Malpractice Claims: A Microanalysis," *Journal of Health Politics, Policy, and Law*, Vol. 14, No. 4, Winter 1989a, pp. 663–89.

Sloan, Frank A., Paula M. Mergenhagen, W. Bradley Burfield, Randall R. Bovbjerg, and Mahmud Hassan, "Medical Malpractice Experience of Physicians: Predictable or Haphazard?" *Journal of the American Medical Association*, Vol. 262, No. 23, December 15, 1989b, pp. 3291–97.

Smith, Barry, "An Analysis of Auto Liability Loss Reserves and Underwriting Results," *The Journal of Risk and Insurance*, Vol. XLVII, No. 2, June 1980, pp. 305–20.

Smith, Clifford W., Jr., "On the Convergence of Insurance and Finance Research," *The Journal of Risk and Insurance*, Vol. LIII, No. 4, December 1986, pp. 693–717.

Southeast Underwriters Association v. *United States*, 1944. 322 U.S. 533.

Stevenson, Richard, "California Insurers in Turmoil," *New York Times*, November 11, 1988, p. A1, Col. 6.

Steves, Myron F., Jr., "A Proposal to Improve the Cost to Benefit Relationships in the Medical Professional Liability Insurance System," *Duke Law Journal*, Vol. 1975, No. 6, January 1975, pp. 1305–34.

Stigler, George J., "The Theory of Economic Regulation," *Bell Journal of Economics and Management Science*, Vol. 2, No. 1, Spring 1971, pp. 3–21.

Strain, Robert W. (ed.), *Reinsurance*. New York: College of Insurance, 1980.

Tancredi, Laurence R., "Designing a No-Fault Alternative," *Law and Contemporary Problems*, Vol. 49, No. 2, Spring 1986, pp. 277–86.

Tancredi, Laurence R., and Jeremiah A. Barondess, "The Problem of Defensive Medicine," *Science*, Vol. 200, No. 4344, May 26, 1978, pp. 879–82.

The Economist, "Insurance: Voters' Revenge," November 19, 1988, p. 33.

The Economist, "Remember Me: A Survey of Insurance," June 6, 1987, pp. 3–22.

Tillinghast, *1990 Captive Insurance Company Directory*. Stanford, CT: Tillinghast Publications, 1990.

Tillinghast, *1987 Captive Insurance Company Directory*. Stanford, CT: Tillinghast Publications, 1987.

Trebilcock, Michael J., "The Insurance-Deterrence Dilemma of Modern Tort Law," *San Diego Law Review*, Vol. 24, No. 4, 1987, pp. 929–1041.

Trepman, E., "Malpractice Insurance: Caught by the Tail," *New England Journal of Medicine*, Vol. 320, No. 5, February 2, 1989, pp. 321–22.

Troxel, Terri E., and Cormick L. Breslin, *Property-Liability Insurance Accounting and Finance*, 2nd edition. Malvern, PA: American Institute for Property and Liability Underwriters, 1983.

United States v. *E.I. duPont deNemours and Company*, 351 U.S. 377 (1956) (Cellophane).

U.S. Department of Health and Human Services, Task Force on Medical Liability and Malpractice, *Report of the Task Force on Medical Liability and Malpractice*. Washington, DC: DHHS, August 1987.

U.S. Department of Health, Education, and Welfare, *Report of the Secretary's Commission on Medical Malpractice*. Pub. No. (OS) 73-88. Washington, DC: DHEW, 1973a.

U.S. Department of Health, Education, and Welfare, *Appendix, Report of the Secretary's Commission on Medical Malpractice*. Pub. No. (OS) 73–89. Washington, DC: DHEW, 1973b.

U.S. Department of Justice, *Report of the Tort Policy Working Group on the Causes, Extent and Policy Implications of the Current Crisis in Insurance Availability and Affordability*. Washington, DC: DOJ, February 1986.

U.S. Department of Justice, *Merger Guidelines*. Washington, DC: DOJ, June 14, 1984.

U.S. Department of Justice, *The Pricing and Marketing of Insurance*. Report to the Task Group on Antitrust Immunities. Washington, DC: DOJ, January, 1977.

U.S. General Accounting Office, *Medical Malpractice: Characteristics of Claims Closed in 1984*. No. GAO/HRD-87-55. Washington, DC: GAO, 1987a.

U.S. General Accounting Office, *Profitability of the Medical Malpractice and General Liability Lines*. Report to Congressional Requesters. Washington, DC: GAO, July 1987b.

U.S. General Accounting Office, *Medical Malpractice: Insurance Costs Increased But Varied Among Physicians and Hospitals*. No. GAO/HRD-86-112. Washington, DC: GAO, September 1986a.

U.S. General Accounting Office, *Medical Malpractice: No Agreement on the Problems or Solutions*. No. GAO/HRD-86-50. Washington, DC: GAO, February 1986b.

U.S. General Accounting Office, *Issues and Needed Improvements in State Regulation of the Insurance Business*. Report to Congress, No. PAD-79-72. Washington, DC: GAO, October 9, 1979.

U.S. Senate, *Medical Malpractice, Patient versus the Physician*. Washington, DC: Committee Print, 91st Congress, 1st Session, November 20, 1969.

Venezian, Emilio C., "Ratemaking Methods and Profit Cycles in Property and Liability Insurance," *The Journal of Risk and Insurance*, Vol. LII, No. 3, September 1985, pp. 477–500.

Wall Street Journal, "Small Firms Face Sharp Cost Hikes for Insurance—If They Can Get It," *The Wall Street Journal*, August 5, 1985, p. 23.

Wandel, William H., *The Control of Competition in Fire Insurance*. Lancaster, PA: Art Printing Co., 1935.

Warren, David G., and Richard Merritt (eds.), *A Legislator's Guide to the Medical Malpractice Issue*. Washington, DC: Georgetown University Health Policy Center, 1976.

Webb, Bernard, J. J. Launie, Willis P. Rokes, and Norman A. Baglini, *Insurance Company Operations*, Volume I, 3rd edition. Malvern, PA: American Institute for Property and Liability Underwriters, 1984a.

Webb, Bernard, J. J. Launie, Willis P. Rokes, and Norman A. Baglini, *Insurance Company Operations*, Volume II, 3rd edition. Malvern, PA: American Institute for Property and Liability Underwriters, 1984b.

Wedig, Gerard A., Mahmud Hassan, and Frank A. Sloan, "Hospital Investment Decisions and the Cost of Capital," *The Journal of Business*, Vol. 62, No. 4, October 1989, pp. 517–37.

Weiss, Mary, "A Multivariate Analysis of Loss Reserving Estimates in Property-Liability Insurers," *The Journal of Risk and Insurance*, Vol. LII, No. 2, June 1985, pp. 199–221.

Winslow, Ron, "Malpractice Study Finds Many Deaths Due to Negligence," *New York Times*, March 1, 1990, p. B4, Col. 6.

Winter, Ralph A., "The Dynamics of Competitive Insurance Markets," unpublished manuscript, July 1989.

Winter, Ralph A., "The Liability Crisis of 1984–86 and the Economics of Competitive Insurance Markets," unpublished manuscript, August 1988a.

Winter, Ralph A., "The Liability Crisis and the Dynamics of Competitive Insurance Markets," *Yale Journal on Regulation*, Vol. 5, No. 2, Summer 1988b, pp. 455–500.

Winter, Ralph A., "Solvency Regulation and the Property-Liability 'Insurance Cycle'," unpublished manuscript, August 1988c.

Wish, Paul E., "Review and Preview: 1989 and 1990," *Best's Review*, *Property-Casualty Insurance Edition*, Vol. 89, No. 9, January 1990, pp. 18–24, 107–12.

Zuckerman, Stephen, "Medical Malpractice Claims, Legal Costs, and the Practice of Defensive Medicine," *Health Affairs*, Vol. 3, No. 3, Fall 1984, pp. 128–34.

Zuckerman, Stephen, Randall R. Bovbjerg, and Frank A. Sloan, "Effects of Tort Reforms and Other Factors on Medical Malpractice Insurance Premiums," *Inquiry*, Vol. 27, Summer 1990, pp. 167–82.

Index